Advances in Theory and Practice of Emerging Markets

Series Editor

Yogesh K. Dwivedi
EMaRC, School of Management
Swansea University Bay Campus
Swansea, UK

CW01499216

Series Regional Editors

David Brown, Lancaster University, UK
Regions: China and UK

Lemuria Carter, Virginia Commonwealth University, USA
Region: North America

Marijn Janssen, TU Delft, The Netherlands
Region: Europe

Samuel Fosso Wamba, Toulouse Business School, France
Region: Africa

More information about this series at http://www.springer.com/series/15802

James Baba Abugre
Ellis L. C. Osabutey • Simon P. Sigué

Editors

Business in Africa in the Era of Digital Technology

Essays in Honour of
Professor William K. Darley

 Springer

Editors
James Baba Abugre
University of Ghana Business School
Accra, Ghana

Ellis L. C. Osabutey
Business School
University of Roehampton
London, UK

Simon P. Sigué
Faculty of Business
Athabasca University
Edmonton, AB, Canada

Series Editor
Yogesh K. Dwivedi

ISSN 2522-5006   ISSN 2522-5014   (electronic)
Advances in Theory and Practice of Emerging Markets
ISBN 978-3-030-70540-4   ISBN 978-3-030-70538-1   (eBook)
https://doi.org/10.1007/978-3-030-70538-1

This Springer imprint is published by the registered company Springer Nature Switzerland AG
The registered company address is: Gewerbestrasse 11, 6330 Cham, Switzerland

Preface: Tribute to Professor William K. Darley

This book, sponsored by the African Academy of Business and Development (AABD), is the first of its kind. It pays tribute to Professor William K. Darley's many academic achievements and his extraordinary dedication and contributions to building Africa-related business research capacity and advancing business knowledge worldwide.

William K. Darley is a Professor Emeritus at the University of Toledo and taught at several others, namely the American University of Lebanon, the Ghana Institute of Management and Public Administration, King Abdulaziz University, and Millersville University of Pennsylvania where he also served as the Dean of Research.

William K. Darley is one of the eight "founding fathers" of the AABD in 1999, including Joseph Aiyeku, Jerry Kolo, Franklyn Manu, Sonny Nwankwo, Alphonso Ogbuehi, O. Ben Oumlil, and Robert Rugimbana. Like the other founding fathers, his dream was to build an organization committed to advancing functional education, research-based knowledge, and finding solutions to business and economic development challenges with the goal of making Africa a better continent to live in and do business. From the first day of the creation of this organization until today that he has retired, he spared no effort for the triumph of this ideal.

William K. Darley has attended almost all AABD annual conferences since its inception. Better, he has been involved in all strategic initiatives and major projects of this organization and informally serves as an adviser to the successive executive committees. For instance, due to his honor and credibility, he has served as committee chair for all elections for the past decade and contributed to the last constitutional revision of 2019. With the latest reorganization of the governance of the Academy, he now chairs the Professional Development Committee that he inspired with the organization of pre-conference workshops for doctoral students and young researchers for several years. We owe him the establishment of the first mentoring program between the University of Dar Es Salaam, Tanzania, and AABD, which offers an opportunity to established scholars over the world to connect with emerging scholars in this institution and support their professional development. He is working with AABD to duplicate this very successful first experience to reach other emerging scholars in other institutions and countries in Africa. As a result of his dedication and commitment, William K. Darley received two of this academy's most prestigious awards: the "Outstanding Service Award" in 2010 and the "Distinguished Service AABD Award" in 2019.

William K. Darley is one of the best published marketing scholars who identifies with Africa and is proud to share his expertise with other Africans. His research has been published in the main and internationally recognized top journals in the field such as *Journal of Consumer Research*, *Journal of Marketing*, *Journal of Marketing Research*, *Journal of the Academy of Marketing Science*, and *Marketing Science*. As of November 22, 2000, his Google Scholar profile shows 3264 citations, with an h-index of 23. He served as an associate editor for the *Journal of Business Research* and a guest editor for *Psychology & Marketing*. A complete list of his publications is included in this volume.

If with these personal academic achievements William K. Darley is already an incontestable model for the AABD community, it must be said that what earns him our collective admiration is above all his proximity to young African business scholars and his unequaled dedication to supporting their development in Africa as in other parts of the world. He has mentored and guided many of us, not only in our research but also in all other aspects of our academic careers such as navigating internal politics in our respective institutions, with a special touch of humility, respect, generosity, and friendship.

As a gifted son of Africa, William K. Darley has generously given back to the mother Continent, which is grateful to him through this book.

Accra, Ghana   James Baba Abugre
London, UK   Ellis L. C. Osabutey
Edmonton, AB, Canada   Simon P. Sigué

Contributions by William K. Darley

Papers in Refereed Journals

Darley, W.K, & Blankson, C. (2020). Sub-Saharan African belief system and entrepreneurial activities: A Ghanaian perspective. *Africa Journal of Management, 6*(2), 67–84.

Moswete, N., Thapa, B., & Darley, W.K. (2020). Local communities attitudes and support of Kgalagadi Transfrontier Park in Southwest Bostwana. *Sustainability, 12*(4), 1524.

Darley, W.K., & Luethge, D.J. (2019). Service value and retention: Does gender matter. *Journal of Retailing and Consumer Services, 48*(March), 178–185.

Darley, W.K., & Luethge, D.J. (2019). Management and business education in Africa: A post-colonial perspective of international accreditation. *Academy of Management Learning & Education, 18*(1), 99–111.

Darley, W.K., & Lim, J.-S. (2018). Mavenism and e-maven propensity: Antecedents, mediators and transferability. *Journal of Research in Interactive Marketing, 12*(3), 293–308.

Blankson, C., Cowan,K., & Darley, W.K. (2018). Marketing practices of rural macro and small businesses in Ghana: The role of policy. *Journal Macro-marketing, 38*(1), 29–56.

Lim, J.-S., Darley, W.K., & Marion, D. (2017). Market orientation, innovation commercialization capability and firm performance relationships: The moderating role of supply chain Influence. *Journal of Business and Industrial Marketing, 32*(7), 913–924.

Khizindar, T.M., & Darley, W.K. (2017). A study of female middle Eastern entrepreneurs: A resource-based view. *Journal of Research in Marketing and Entrepreneurship, 19*(1), 42–58.

Darley, W.K., & Luethge, D.J. (2016). The role of faculty research in the development of a management research and knowledge culture in African educational institutions. *Academy of Management Learning & Education, 15*(2), 325–344.

Darley, W.K., & Khizindar, T.M. (2015). Effect of early-late stage entrepreneurial activity on perceived challenges and the ability to predict consumer needs: A Saudi Perspective. *Journal of Transnational Management, 20*(1), 67–84.

Darley, W.K., Luethge,D.J., & Blankson, C. (2013). Culture and international marketing: A Sub-Saharan African context. *Journal of Global Marketing, 30*(1), 188–202.

Coker-Kolo, D. & Darley, W.K. (2013). The role for African universities in a changing world. *Journal of Third World Studies, 30*(1), 11–38.

Darley, W.K. (2012). Increasing Sub-Saharan Africa's share of foreign direct investment: Public policy challenges, strategies, and implications. *Journal of African Business, 13*(1), 62–69.

Moswete, N., & Darley, W.K. (2011). Tourism survey research in Sub-Saharan Africa: Problems and challenges. *Current Issues in Tourism, 15*(4), 363–383.

Darley, W.K., Blankson, C., & Luethge, D.J. (2010). Toward an integrated framework for online consumer behavior and decision-making process: A review. *Psychology & Marketing, 27*(2), 94–116.

Darley, W.K. (2010). The interaction of online technology on consumer shopping experience. *Psychology & Marketing, 27*(2), 91–93.

Lim, j.-S., & Darley, W.K. (2009). Evaluations of foreign-made products in a limited choice environment: A replication and extension of the direct mediation model. *Marketing Management Journal, 19*(1), 96–112.

Darley, W.K., & Blankson, C. (2008). African culture and business markets: Implications for marketing practices. *Journal of Business and Industrial Marketing, 23*(6), 374–383.

Darley, W.K., Luethge, D.J., & Tatte, A. (2008). Exploring the relationship of perceived automotive salesperson attributes, customer satisfaction and intentions to automotive service department patronage: The moderating role of gender. *Journal of Retailing and Consumer Services, 15*(6), 469–479.

Smith, R, Mackenzie, S.B., Yang, X., Buchholz, L., & Darley, W.K. (2007). Modeling the determinants and effects of creativity in advertising. *Marketing Science, 26*(November–December), 819–833.

Holiday-Goodman, M., Darley, W.K., Lively, B.T., Siganga, W., & Deshukh-Estoll, H.C. (2007). An exploratory investigation of consumer choice of community, mail order or Internet pharmacies. *Journal of Pharmacy Technology, 23*(1), 16–22.

Darley, W.K. (2003). Public policy challenges and implications of the Internet and the emerging E-commerce for Sub-Saharan Africa: A business perspective. *Information Technology for Development, 10*(1), 1–12.

Darley W.K. (2002). Advertising regulations in Sub-Saharan Africa: Trends and outlook. *Journal of African Business, 3*(3), 53–68.

Darley, W.K. (2002). Enhancing Sub-Saharan Africa's export performance: Challenges, opportunities, and implications. *Journal of African Business, 3*(2), 7–32.

Darley, W.K. (2002). Advertising in Sub-Saharan Africa: A Look at the environment and practice. *Journal of African Business, 3*(1), 31–48.

Darley, W.K. (2001). The Internet and emerging E-Commerce: Challenges and implications for management in Sub-Saharan Africa. *Journal of Global Information Technology Management, 4*(4), 4–18.

Darley, W.K. (2000). Status of replication studies in marketing: A validation and extension. *Marketing Management Journal, 10*(Fall/Winter), 121–132.

Darley, W.K. (1999). The relationship of antecedents of search and self-esteem to adolescent search effort and perceived product knowledge. *Psychology & Marketing, 16*(August), 409–427.

Darley, W.K. (1999). The moderating influence of style of information processing on media perceptions and information exposure. *Journal of Marketing Communications, 5*(4), 181–193.

Darley, W.K., & Lim, J.-S. (1999). Effects of shopping frequency and distance traveled on store image and attitude toward secondhand stores. *International Journal of Retail & Distribution Management, 27*(8), 311–318.

Lim, J.-S., & Darley, W.K. (1997). An assessment of demand artifacts in country of origin studies using three alternative approaches. *International Marketing Review, 14*(4), 201–217.

Darley, W.K., & Smith, R.E. (1995). Gender differences in information processing strategies: An empirical test of the selectivity model in advertising response. *Journal of Advertising, 24*(Spring), 41–56.

Lim, J.-S., Darley, W.K., & Summers, J.O. (1994). An assessment of country of origin effects under alternative presentation formats. *Journal of the Academy of Marketing Science, 22*(Summer), 274–282.

Darley, W.K., & Johnson, D.M. (1994). The dimensions of beliefs toward advertising in developing countries: A comparative analysis. *Journal of International Consumer Marketing, 7*(1), 5–21.

Darley, W.K., & Johnson, D.M. (1993). A cross-national comparison of attitudes toward consumerism in multiple developing country environments. *Journal of Consumer Affairs, 27* (Summer), 37–54.

Darley, W.K., & Lim, J.-S. (1993). Assessing demand artifacts in consumer research: An alternative perspective. *Journal of Consumer Research, 20*(December), 489–495.

Darley, W.K, & Smith, R.E. (1993). Advertising claim objectivity: Antecedents and effects. *Journal of Marketing*, *57*(October), 100–113.

Darley, W.K., & Lim, J.-S. (1993). Store-choice behavior for pre-owned merchandise. *Journal of Business Research*, *27*(May), 17–31.

William K. Darley and Denise M. Johnson (1993), "Effects of Adolescent Locus of Control on Shopping Behavior, Fashion Orientation, and Information Search," The International Review of Retail, Distribution and Consumer Research, *3*(April), 149–165.

Darley, W.K., & Lim, J.-S. (1992). The effects of consumers' emotional reactions on behavior intention: The moderating role of personal relevance and self-monitoring. *Psychology & Marketing*, *9*(July/August), 329–346.

Darley, W.K. (1992). The role of need for cognition in media evaluation and usage. *Journal of Promotion Management*, *1*(3), 21–37.

Book Chapters

Darley, W.K. (2016). Brand building via integrated marketing communications. In F. Dall'Olmo, J. Singh, & C. Blankson (eds.), *Companion to Brand Management*, Routledge.

Darley, W.K, & Williams, J.D. (2006). Methodological issues in ethnic marketing research: Changing consumer demographics and implications. In C. P. Rao, (ed.), *Marketing and Multicultural Diversity* (pp. 93–118), London: Ashgate Publishing Company.

Darley, W.K, & Luethge, D.J. (2003). Cross-cultural communications and promotion. In R. Rugimbana & S. Nwankwo (eds.), *Cross-cultural Marketing* (pp. 141–160), London: Thomson Learning.

Conference Proceedings

Darley, W.K. (2005). Using focus group research methodology in Africa: The moderating role of culture," *In Proceedings of the 2005 International Academy of African Business and Development*, Dar Es Salaam, Tanzania, April 6–9 (pp. 200–206).

Darley, W.K., & Lim, J.-S. (1991). Personal relevance as a moderator of the effect of public service advertising on behavior. In R.H. Holman & M. R. Solomon (eds.), *Advances in Consumer Research*, Association for Consumer Research, Vol. 18 (pp. 303–309).

Darley, W.K., & Lim, J._S. (1986). Family decision making in leisure-time activities: An exploratory investigation of the impact of locus of control and parental type on perceived child influence. In R.J. Lutz (ed.), *Advances in Consumer Research*, Association for Consumer Research, Vol. 13 (pp. 370–374).

Darley, W.K. (1985). Cognitive and interaction effects of modality, product type, and message content: A cognitive response perspective. In *American Institute for Decision Sciences Third Annual Doctoral Consortium Proceedings* (Competitive Student Papers), Las Vegas, Nevada, November (pp. 210–211).

Darley, W.K., & Johnson, D. (1985). A contemporary analysis of the low-income consumer: An international perspective. In *Historical Perspective in Consumer Research: National and International Perspectives*, Association of Consumer Research International Meeting, Singapore, July (pp. 206–210).

Darley, W.K., & Johnson, D. (1983). Advertising in selected developing countries: Implications and strategies for multi-national enterprises. In *Proceedings of the 1983 World Marketing Congress*, Halifax, Canada (pp. 142–151).

Wilson, M.M., & Darley, W.K. (1982). The undergraduate marketing core, marketing issues, and other education related topics of the 1980's: Views of educators and Practitioners. *In 1982 American Marketing Association Educator's Conference Proceedings* (pp. 152–156).

Acknowledgments

We thank the contributors and reviewers of the chapters published in this volume for their commitment and collaboration at the different stages of this project, despite the many challenges created by COVID-19.

We are grateful to the Executive Committee of the Academy of African Business and Development (AABD) for subscribing to the idea of starting to honor its members who stand out for their contribution to the advancement of its mission in this way and for sponsoring this book, which is the first in a series.

Finally, our thanks also go to a few individuals who have provided assistance in various ways throughout this project. We would like to single out the generosity of Professor William K. Darley who provided us with his CV without questioning us about its intended use, thus allowing us to keep this project secret until the end. Kirthika Selvaraju and Faith Su who coordinated the production of this book at Springer were very understanding in giving us successive extensions to allow its completion in the difficult context of COVID-19. Charles Blankson read and provided valuable comments on the early versions of the preface.

Contents

About the Editors and Contributors

About the Editors

James Baba Abugre is an Associate Professor of Human Resource Management at the University of Ghana Business School and a Senior Consultant with the Corporate Support Group, Ghana. He is the Executive Secretary of the Academy of African Business and Development (AABD) and holds a PhD in International Human Resource Management from Swansea University in the United Kingdom, MPhil in Human Resource Management, and MA in Communication Studies from the University of Ghana. He teaches and researches in human resource management and development in both multinational and local organizations, cross-cultural and comparative management, organizational and interpersonal communication.

Ellis L. C. Osabutey is a Reader in International Business & Strategy at Roehampton Business School, University of Roehampton. His research focuses on foreign direct investment, technology and knowledge transfer, SME innovation strategies, mobile technology and financial inclusion, etc. His empirical work generally covers developing countries and is focused on, but not limited to, sub-Saharan Africa. Ellis is Associate Editor of the *Journal of African Business* and an Editorial Board Member for *Technological Forecasting and Social Change*.

Simon P. Sigué is a Full Professor of Marketing at Athabasca University, the President of the Academy of African Business and Development (AABD), and a former Editor of the *Journal of African Business*. His research covers such topics as entrepreneurial marketing, franchising, marketing channels, customer relationship management, game theory, and international marketing and is published in leading marketing, management science, and economics journals.

Contributors

James Baba Abugre University of Ghana Business School, Accra, Ghana

Kweku Adams Department of Management, Huddersfield Business School, University of Huddersfield, Queensgate, UK

Bamidele Adekunle SEDRD, University of Guelph, Guelph, ON, Canada

Ted Rogers School of Management, Ryerson University, Toronto, ON, Canada

Anthony Ayakwah Koforidua Technical University, Koforidua, Ghana

Altante Désirée Biboum ESSEC of Douala, CERAME, University of Douala, Douala, Cameroon

Charles Blankson Department of Marketing, Logistics and Operations Management, The G. Brint Ryan College of BusinessUniversity of North Texas, Denton, TX, USA

Rhoda Boachie-Ansah University of Ghana Business School, Accra, Ghana

Isaac S. Damoah Bournemouth University, Bournemouth, UK

Mesia Ilomo University of Dar es Salaam Business School, Dar es Salaam, Tanzania

Christine Kajumba Independent Consultant, Ottawa, Ontario, Canada

Ken Kamoche Nottingham University Business School, Nottingham University, Nottingham, UK

Linley Chiwona-Karltun Swedish University of Agricultural Sciences, Uppsala, Sweden

Serge Koukpaki York Business School, York St John University, York, UK

Aminu Mamman Global Development Institute, University of Manchester, Manchester, UK

Ellis L. C. Osabutey Business School, University of Roehampton, London, UK

Ade Oyedijo Department of Logistics and Management Systems, Hull University Business School, University of Hull, Hull, UK

Christopher J. Rees Global Development Institute, University of Manchester, Manchester, UK

Peter Renner New York Life Insurance Company, New York, NY, USA

Lettice Kinunda Rutashobya University of Dar es Salaam Business School, Dar es Salaam, Tanzania

Mohamed Semkunde University of Dar es Salaam Business School, Dar es Salaam, Tanzania

Simon P. Sigué Faculty of Business, Athabasca University, Edmonton, AB, Canada

Merezia Wilson University of Dar es Salaam Business School, Dar es Salaam, Tanzania

Introduction

James Baba Abugre, Ellis L. C. Osabutey, and Simon P. Sigué

The growing importance of business in Africa has increased the continent's attractiveness to business and management practitioners and academics. This has led to several calls for much more critical exploration of issues that would improve understanding of the business environment. Such literature is expected to benefit policymakers and local and foreign investors as well as accelerate economic growth and development. The digital era has been characterized by new and emerging information and communications technology (ICT) platforms that shape individual and institutional behavior. In the private sector, digitization is believed to facilitate the creation of new value, generate additional income streams, streamline business operations, and reduce operational costs. In the public sector, African governments are mainstreaming digitization into their policy frameworks to improve the quality of their services, accountability, and transparency and to support and accelerate business development. As companies and governments embrace digitization in Africa, the literature on this transformation is limited. Consequently, some applications and innovations in digital technologies and their impacts on business in Africa are not well known. Also, knowledge about the stakes and challenges of digitalization in Africa remains very scarce.

J. B. Abugre
University of Ghana Business School, Accra, Ghana
e-mail: jbabugre@ug.edu.gh

E. L. C. Osabutey
Business School, University of Roehampton, London, UK
e-mail: ellis.osabutey@roehampton.ac.uk

S. P. Sigué (✉)
Faculty of Business, Athabasca University, Edmonton, AB, Canada
e-mail: simons@athabascau.ca

There is, therefore, a need for an academic literature that studies business policies and practices in this rapidly changing technological environment. This book showcases contemporary realities of business and highlights the transformational role of digital technologies in both the public and private sectors in Africa. It encapsulates the potential vision of how digital technologies can transform economies and gives insights on potential opportunities and challenges while providing theoretical, managerial, and policy implications. Essentially, it gives insights on businesses in the digital era and encourages the exploitation of digital technologies to improve transparency, efficiency, and productivity in Africa.

The book includes nine additional chapters, with one thing in common. All contributors are either management scholars in reputable universities spread around the globe or experienced business practitioners with proven experience. It is organized into two parts. The first part focuses on digitalization and public and private sector transformation. The second part deals with other aspects of business in Africa in the digital era.

1   Digitalization and Public and Private Sector Transformation in Africa

Part 1 of the book sheds light on digitalization in the public and private sectors in Africa. In Chapter 2, "Digitalization in Africa: The Case of Public Programs in Ghana", A. Ayakwah, I. S. Damoah, and E. L. C. Osabutey focus on the government digitalization programs and related challenges in Ghana. They use secondary sources to examine digitalization programs in ports and harbors, national health insurance services, utility bill payments, financial services, and digital addressing systems. Their findings support the view that digitalization increases innovation, efficiency, transparency, etc. in both public and private sectors. This chapter draws attention to the challenges created by weak infrastructure, inadequate human capital, insufficient stakeholder engagement, and user education and training and highlights the need for cyber security expertise. In Chapter 3, "Maximizing Human Resource Development in Sub-Saharan Africa in the Digital Era", J. B. Abugre outlines the importance of digitalization to maximize human resource development in sub-Saharan Africa. A survey of employees from public and private organizations in Ghana confirmed that human resource development/management (HRM/D) can be maximized through digitalization. In addition, digitalizing HRM practices enhances flexible work systems and employee loyalty and commitment. The chapter concludes that digitalizing HRM/D in Africa could improve human capital development for global competitiveness. In Chapter 4, "Digitizing Recruitment and Selection of Employees in Ghana: A Social Media Network Perspective" J. B. Abugre and R. Boachie-Ansah draw on how social media networking sites support recruitment and selection processes of multinational enterprises (MNEs) in Ghana. A qualitative study revealed the impact of extensive social media networking sites for recruitment and selection. Their findings highlight the merits and demerits of digitally mediated social media recruitment and selection and conclude that social media networking sites create the dynamics of multiple channels of dialog and platforms of communication between employers and prospective employees. In Chapter 5, "Gender and Rural Entrepreneurship in Digitizing Sub-Saharan Africa", L. K. Rutashobya, L. C. Karltun, M. Wilson, M. Ilomo, and M. Semkunde explore how digitalization addresses issues related to gender constraints to enhance rural entrepreneurship in Africa. Supported by data from Tanzania the chapter explored how digitalization enhances rural women's entrepreneurial engagements. Their findings revealed that digitalization enhances women engagement in rural entrepreneurship through diminishing socio-spatial challenges (gendered social and physical mobility). The chapter recommends investments in digital technology in rural areas to address gender disparities. In Chapter 6, "Social Media and Economic Development: The Role of Instagram in Developing Countries" B. Adekunle and C. Kajumba explore Instagram's role in promoting digital entrepreneurship in Africa. They throw light on how Instagram has been used to promote agriculture, tourism, art, health, political economy, etc. The chapter also presents a conceptual framework to exemplify Instagram's importance in the production and marketing of spices in Zanzibar and proffer related recommendations on the promotion of appropriate use of Instagram in Africa.

2   Business and Management in Africa in the Digital Era

Part 2 captures business and management issues not specific to digital technology but affected by it. In particular, it draws tangents to how digital technologies could enhance such business and management operations. In Chapter 7, "Franchising in the Gasoline Retail Industry in Cameroon: A Strategic Perspective" , S. P. Sigué and A. D. Biboum propose a strategic perspective to understand the use of franchising in the gasoline retail industry in Cameroon. They postulate that the choice among organizational forms such as company-owned and company-operated, company-owned and dealer-operated, and dealer-owned and dealer-operated for an outlet in this industry depends essentially on relevant organizational and environmental factors, including the local digital infrastructure, which reduces operational costs and makes some forms more attractive than others in some contexts. In Chapter 8, "Supply Chain Management Systems in Africa: Insights from Nigeria", A. Oyedijo, K. Adams, and S. Koukpaki examine supply chain management systems in Africa with empirical insights from Nigeria. A qualitative study revealed the fragmented nature of supply chain management systems. Among others, they support the view that digital technologies can enhance the management of supply chain systems in Africa. In Chapter 9, "Understanding Rural Micro and Small Business Marketing Practices in Ghana" C. Blankson and P. Renner sought to enhance our understanding of rural micro and small business marketing practices in the digital era context using Ghana as the empirical focus. Their findings reveal that indigenous and informal market orientation strategies contribute to livelihood development, poverty reduction, and rural economic development. These businesses cultivate customer loyalty through friendship. In Chapter 10, "Attitudes to Globalization in the Public, Private and NGO Sectors", A. Mamman, K. Kamoche, and C. J. Rees, who consider digital technology as an enabler of globalization, examine the attitudes of globalization in the public, private, and nongovernmental organization (NGO) sectors in Africa. They use a sample of managers and professionals in the private and public and NGO sectors in Kenya to explore the proposition that beliefs and attitudes to globalization can influence attitudes to the role of government in the economy. A takeaway from this work is that there are strong relationships between specific attitudes to globalization and preferences for roles of government in the economy.

Overall, this book provides new perspectives of business in Africa in the digital era. It emphasizes how African businesses and policy makers are taking advantage or can further take advantage of digitalization to enhance their competitiveness. The book also depicts business and public transformation potential and highlights how government policies and programs could enhance the benefits that can be derived from digitalization. It emphasizes the need for more focus on policies that anticipate and address the related stakes and challenges.

Part I
Digitalization and Public and Private Sector Transformation in Africa

Digitalization in Africa: The Case of Public Programs in Ghana

Anthony Ayakwah, Isaac S. Damoah, and Ellis L. C. Osabutey

1 Introduction

The emergence of technological platforms of information and communications technology (ICT) has catalysed the digital era. ICT is having significant and unprecedented influences in many aspects of our social and economic lives (Nicoletta and Andrea 2002: Gukurume and Mahiya 2020). These ICT-induced technological developments served as early advances of digitalization, thereby contributing to the emergence of whole new industries that employ millions of workers performing tasks that did not exist a couple of decades ago (Gupta and Bose 2019). Digitalization is often described as an integral component of the modern global economy which contributes to a more rational resource management (Bouwman et al. 2017; Ohemeng and Ofosu-Darkwah 2014), ensures full utilization of business management models (Asamoah 2019; Rachinger et al. 2019) and transforms business structures (Heavin and Power 2018). It also enhances technological processes, accelerates innovation cycles (Latos et al. 2018; Bekoe et al. 2016), facilitates the operations of supply chain management systems (Vendrell-Herrero et al. 2017), promotes business start-ups and internationalization (Neubert 2018) and enhances service delivery (Vendrell-Herrero et al. 2017). Subsequently, we describe digitalization as the private and public sector transformation in processes, capabilities and offerings and

A. Ayakwah
Koforidua Technical University, Koforidua, Ghana
e-mail: ayakwah.anthony@ktu.edu.gh

I. S. Damoah
Bournemouth University, Bournemouth, UK

E. L. C. Osabutey (✉)
Business School, University of Roehampton, London, UK
e-mail: ellis.osabutey@roehampton.ac.uk

© The Author(s), under exclusive license to Springer Nature Switzerland AG 2021   7
J. B. Abugre et al. (eds.), *Business in Africa in the Era of Digital Technology*,
Advances in Theory and Practice of Emerging Markets,
https://doi.org/10.1007/978-3-030-70538-1_2

their associated ecosystems to progressively create, deliver and capture increased service value enabled by a broad range of digital technologies.

Digitalization is facilitating new value creation and generating new revenue streams for organizations (Bekoe et al. 2016; Kumar et al. 2013) and typically, goes "hand in hand with embracing a digital technology strategy" (Parida et al. 2015: 41). The emerging literature on digital technology captures these trends (Rachinger et al. 2019; Vendrell-Herrero et al. 2017). Digitalization is both a driver and an enabler of effective revenue mobilization (Senyo et al. 2020a; Vendrell-Herrero et al. 2017) and may enable new forms of innovation and business models in public sector firms (Sjödin et al. 2016; Darley 2003). For example, digitalization is currently enabling companies to migrate from product-centric models to digital service-oriented offerings with higher value-generating potential (Ardolino et al. 2018; Adrodegari and Saccani 2017). Digitalization changes customers' value propositions and alters how (i.e. through processes and capabilities) a company creates and captures value through co-creation with customers to meet their evolving needs (Iansiti and Lakhani 2014; Lenka et al. 2017).

Digitalization is often used as a strategic tool to differentiate products within the marketplace—which provides competitive advantage for the providers (Osei-Kojo 2017; Opresnik and Taisch 2015). This helps such market players to explore new revenue streams (Parida et al. 2019). Thus, digitalization offers the opportunities for firms to expand revenue streams by synchronizing their products, services, connectivity and data analytics into product-services (Kohtamäki et al. 2019; Luz Martín-Peña et al. 2018). Digital technologies, therefore, enable radical changes in products, services, innovation processes, business models and the very nature of business activities in industrial ecosystems that follow the logic of digital servitization (Sklyar et al. 2019; Sjödin et al. 2020).

These gains from digitalization has made it attractive for not only businesses but also for governments interested in maximizing the opportunities that the digitalized economy brings. Many governments are therefore incorporating digitalization into the policy framework and developing countries such as those in Africa are no exception. African nations such as Ghana are adopting digital platformization to improve efficiency and development (Senyo et al. 2020a). While research on digitalization is growing, the literature appears to be limited in the treatment of the adoption into public policy and programs in Africa. In addition, the challenges associated with digitalization in developing country setting deserves attention. This chapter addresses these gaps by reviewing theoretical and empirical literature on the role of digital technology adoption in public policies and programs and the related challenges in Ghana. The chapter seeks to address the following key research questions: To what extent is digitalization being used in public sector policies and programs and what are the related challenges?

The remainder of the chapter is presented as follows. The next section reviews extant literature on digitalization in emerging and developing economies with particular emphasis on Africa. We subsequently explain the method used to gather evidence and literature for the review. We then present and discuss the empirical evidence before finally drawing conclusions.

2 Literature and Theoretical Background

2.1 Digitalization in Developing Economies and Africa

In recent years, most emerging and developing economies like Argentina, India, Brazil, South Africa, Nigeria, Kenya and Ghana are beginning to see the relevance of using digital technology in making payments (Patil et al. 2017; Winn 2015). For instance, in 2015, the Organization for Economic Co-operation and Development (OECD) recommended strategies which will leverage digital technologies to emerging and developing countries (OECD 2018). For instance, India used e-participation as a means of informing, engaging and convincing the public and other stakeholders in the use of digital technologies (Prasad 2012; Miklian and Hoelscher 2017). Such initiatives demonstrate that the use of ICT and digitalization at the grassroots level for the delivery of public services can facilitate greater public input into decision making as well as increase revenue mobilization (Kumar et al. 2013; Prasad 2012). Thus, digitalization in developing countries can provide channels for feedback on the services of local government authorities on revenue mobilization, transparency and accountability.

In most respects, Africa lags in terms of technology adoption and utilization (Osabutey et al. 2014). Kanyengo (2009) points out that Africa is lagging among most parts of the world in the adoption of use of digital technologies. Hence, there is now a growing quest for digitalization to succeed in Africa (Sigauke and Nengomasha 2011). African governments are mostly burdened with huge resource constraints which hinder their capacity to embark on developmental projects (Misuraca 2007; Amagoh 2015). They also lack the institutions and innovation systems to facilitate rapid acquisition and deployment of new technologies for development (Osabutey and Croucher 2018). Despite these constraints, most African countries have seen the need to pursue digitalization. For example, since 2017 the government of Ghana has embarked on pursuing the benefits of digitalization to reduce corruption and increase revenue mobilization (Senyo et al. 2020a).

2.2 Benefit of Digitalization

Digital technologies have gained worldwide relevance and significance than earlier waves of innovations in technology and has led to disruptive modification of business models and industry (Nohumba et al. 2020; Choi et al. 2020). Subsequently, there is a burgeoning global digital economy, defined by Bukht and Heeks (2018) as the element of economic output derived solely or primarily from digital technologies with a business model based on digital goods or services. Indeed, the digital economy firms have disrupted incumbents across a wide range of sectors, with platform-centred business models that have proven highly successful (Mkalama and Ndemo 2020; Bukht and Heeks 2018; Darley 2003). Digitalization is facilitating revenue mobilization, transforming tangible data and information and generating networks across different regions to ensure cross-border data and information transfer (Owusu Kwateng et al. 2019; OECD 2018; Bukht and Heeks 2018).

Further, digitalization has revolutionized the banking sector across the world. In Africa, for example, digital technology has become a strategic resource in the achievement of higher levels of efficiency, operational controls, interconnectivity and overall productivity and profitability (Nohumba et al. 2020; Choi et al. 2020). Therefore, banking transactions have become more flexible and streamlined, thereby reducing transaction costs. There is emerging evidence that digital technologies are reducing corruption by public sector revenue collectors in African countries such as Ghana (Senyo et al. 2020a; Ewusi-Mensah 2012). The deployment of digital technologies at the public sector was found to expedite administrative functions like monitoring and control, which seeks to result in increased transparency and accountability (Senyo et al. 2020a; Tsvetkova 2018). One of the prime aims of digitalization is to make the frontiers of decision-making in the governance process more visible to citizens and to make bureaucrats accountable to the people (Myovella et al. 2020; OECD 2018).

2.3   Digitalization Challenges in Africa

Digitalization in Africa has been on an upsurge because of the increasing availability and affordability of electronic gadgets such as mobile phones and computers. Subsequently, the youth have taken advantage of these to improve capacity and usage of these gadgets (Bellucci and Otenyo 2019). Despite the growing penetration of digital technologies in different sectors in Africa, progress has been inadequate due to several institutional constraints (Bellucci and Otenyo 2019; Senyo et al. 2020a). Digital infrastructure in Africa continues to fall behind the pace of growing demand for digital services, mainly due to accessibility and connectivity issues (Darley 2001; Fuchs and Horak 2008; Arakpogun et al. 2020). Indeed, these infrastructural weaknesses, symptomatic of developing economies, show the digital disparity between developing and developed economies. The growing urbanization in developing economies and the increasing need for data and accessibility for cloud computing for economic activities are putting additional pressure on the existing infrastructure (Bukht and Heeks 2018).

The infrastructural constraints for operationalizing a digital economy in Africa is compounded by affordability and inconsistent supply of electricity (Mommoh and Abubakar 2019). For instance, only 10% of Nigeria's daily energy needs are met by its current production with over 60% not connected to the national grid (GSMA 2011). In countries that have a wide coverage, the supply of electricity is unreliable and fluctuates very frequently, hindering connectivity and data storage (Greengard 2010). Several companies, especially those in the mobile telecommunication industry, are compelled to generate their own energy through installation of generators with its attendant cost of operation which is passed onto consumers (Mommoh and

Abubakar 2019). In addition, there are issues of access as most rural communities in Africa are still confronted with mobile signal availability (Darley 2001; Okeleke and Stryjak 2015). There are also high prohibitive costs associated with shifting from 3G to 4G connectivity, and providers do not find it cost-effective to implement or expand particularly within the areas of low population density, unreliable electricity supply and inadequate security (Manyika et al. 2016). Senyo et al. (2020a) argue that these constraints suppress expansion and building of new networks which has implication for expanding the digital economy in Africa. There is also significant unevenness in Internet penetration in Africa. For example, while Chad, Democratic Republic of Congo, Madagascar and Burundi have Internet penetration of only 10%, Kenya, Libya and Seychelles have over 70% (Statista 2020; Internetworldstats.com 2020).

The issue of affordability remains central to increasing Internet penetration and a digitalized economy in Africa. As a result of higher bandwidth costs, average monthly broadband prices are significantly higher in developing economies (ITU 2015; OECD 2018). This situation is worsened by relatively higher tariffs and tax regimes on digital technology, which is intended to augment government revenue sources, a situation that deviates from those in developed economies (Meltzer 2014). This influences the cost of operation which has significant implication on the level of Internet diffusion not only at the individual and digital entrepreneur levels but also on the growth of the African digital economy.

Another key issue that hampers the utilization of the benefits of digitalization is the digital content and the limited use of indigenous African languages. The top ten languages out of the approximately 6000 languages in the world reflect 77% of the users with only 2.8% meant for Africa using indigenous African language (UNESCO 2011; Nyirenda-Jere and Biru 2015). Hussain and Mohan (2008) argued that though emphasis has been given to English and French in the usage, less than 10% of the population even speak these official languages. The situation has implications for the development of digital content for Africa. The absence of appropriate digital content and services has the tendency to discourage individuals from being part of the digital world (Dutta et al. 2015).

3 Method

Based on a systematic review of literature that identifies the role of digital technology adoption in public policies and programs in Ghana, the study draws from secondary sources (Tranfield et al. 2003). This approach is in conformity with the procedure prescribed by Khan et al. (2003), Ke et al. (2009) and Lu and Liu (2014) which begins with framing the research question. We adopt their procedure in the framing of the following research questions: To what extent is digitalization being used in public sector policies and programs and what are the related challenges? Ke et al. (2009) propose to the use of plural forms of keyword searches. This will ensure that the search range will be wide to capture the necessary literature (Lu and

Liu 2014). We began the search with the following keywords: developing econo-mies and digitalization, digitalization in Ghana, digitalization strategy, digitaliza-tion challenges, etc.

The data selection sources are the second stage of the procedure. To ensure that the literature is reliable, Khan et al. (2003) state that a comprehensive and extensive search must be carried out from relevant and reputable database and journals. Lu and Liu (2014) consequently suggest that there is a need to identify and select for review, journals in the relevant field of study, to obtain citations that are most rele-vant and appropriate. We employed the database source of *ScienceDirect* as the primary and first search engine because it contains most journals on digitalization strategy and programs and policies in emerging and developing economies.

Ke et al. (2009) and Lu and Liu (2014) explained that the third step in the sys-tematic literature review involves the performing of preliminary search that uses keywords that are defined within specific domains such as Abstract, Titles and Keywords. By following this prescription, we searched, in relation to Ghana, for digitalization, digital technology, digital economy and digital infrastructure. Inserting and entering the keyword searches is done via the identified databases or journals (Ke et al. 2009; Lu et al. 2014). The search included phrases such as digi-talization in Ghana; telecommunication and digital infrastructure in Ghana; digital technology in Ghana; digitalization drive in Ghana; challenges faced in the process of digitalization. To ensure consistency, searches at this phase should be restricted to the parameters of search criteria (Lu et al. 2014; Ke et al. 2009). We capture the emerging literature on digitalization programs and policies in Ghana and in other developing economies (see Table 1).

In the fourth stage of the review, the emphasis is on assessing quality of the stud-ies to ensure academic rigour (Khan et al. 2003). The search words and phrases were however narrowed down to the exact focus of the study. They include digitaliz-ing Ghana's ports and harbours, health sector digitalization, digitalized utility pay-ments, digital addressing systems, digital banking and constraint or challenges in digitalization. The data collected is summarized at the fifth stage. This involves the identification of a detailed review through analysis and synthesis of appropriate lit-erature (Lu and Liu 2014). We then identified themes (main) and sub-themes, and therefore in line with recommendations from Khan et al. (2003) and Lu and Liu (2014), we evaluated similarities identified in the literature. This is evident in Table 1. Khan et al. (2003) prescribed the last step as the interpretation of findings. The procedure involved in this last phase includes synthesizing data, discussions and drawing conclusions.

Table 1 Summary of key literature on digitalization in Ghana

Area of digitalization in Ghana	Author(s)	Key theme
Digitalization in the port and harbour systems in Ghana	Senyo et al. (2020a)	Digital platformization as public sector transformation strategy
	Trujillo et al. (2013)	Reform process of African ports
	Addo and Senyo (2020)	Process reengineering and digitalization and corruption
	Amankwah-Sarfo et al. (2018)	Import clearance digitalization and socioeconomic development
	Atehnjia et al. (2020)	Factors affecting the implementation of a paperless port system
	Amegboe (2019)	Paperless system and its impact on employee performance
Digital payment for National Health Insurance	Boaheng et al. (2019)	Paying national health insurance premium with mobile phone
	Renner-Micah et al. (2020)	Institutionalization of health insurance digital claims platform
Payment of utility bills in Ghana	Boakye and Nyieku (2010)	Cost recovery analysis GWCL
	Sualihu and Rahman (2014)	Payment behaviour of electricity consumers
	Amankwaa et al. (2020)	Diffusion of electronic water payment innovations
Digital financial sector and mobile money interoperability (MMI)	Aboagye and Anong (2020)	Mobile money and microfinance integrations
	Agyekum et al. (2016)	Financial inclusion and digital financial services
	Adaba et al. (2019)	Contribution of mobile money to Well-being
	Adaba and Ayoung (2017)	Development of a mobile money service
	Narteh et al. (2017)	Customer behavioural intentions towards mobile money service adoption
	Amoah et al. (2020)	Mobile money as a financial inclusion instrument
	Senyo et al. (2020b)	Improving financial inclusion through mobile money
Digital addressing in Ghana	Abebrese (2019)	Street addressing system in an evolving urban Centre
	Okae (2018)	Smartphone usage patterns

4 Discussion of Findings

4.1 Adopting Digitalization in Ghana

Ghana has witnessed recent significant government policy initiatives primarily aimed at improving revenue mobilization, minimizing corruption, increasing productivity and efficiency to facilitate economic growth (Adu et al. 2020; Ghanaweb. com 2019; Osei-Kojo 2017). This chapter examines government programs in ports and harbours, national health insurance services, utility bill payments, financial services and digital addressing systems.

4.1.1 Digitalization in Port and Harbour Systems in Ghana

The digitalization of port operations in Ghana since September 2017 was aimed at reducing revenue leakages, promoting faster customer turnaround as well as generating higher returns (GNA 2017; Senyo et al. 2020a). Empirical research reveals that digitalization resulted in improved efficiency in clearance and revenue collection and also supressed corrupt activities. (Amankwah-Sarfo et al. 2018; Senyo et al. 2020a). An earlier study by Trujillo et al. (2013) showed that the Takoradi and Tema ports in Ghana recorded a corruption index of 3.50 each. Corruption, underdeveloped institutions, constraints on business competition, weak governance and inefficient port in Africa make international trade and investment more costly and highlight the urgency for port sector reforms (Trujillo et al. 2013; Amankwah-Sarfo et al. 2018; Amegboe 2019). In addition, bureaucracy at the Ghana port before digitalization provided opportunities for corruption (Trujillo et al. 2013; Senyo et al. 2020a). This is because the port clearing processes prior to digitalization involved navigating several intermediaries of logistic service providers and government bodies by making several cash payments before completing clearance (Amegboe 2019; Addo and Senyo 2020). The eventual digitalization at the Tema port, for example, led to the conversion of traditional, bureaucratic and paper-based processes onto digital platforms which increased efficiency and reduced corruption (Senyo et al. 2020a).

In developing countries, import clearance digitalization is seen as a crucial tool for achieving socioeconomic development (UNCTAD 2019). From the stakeholder perspective, Amankwah-Sarfo et al. (2019) examine the successes and failures that digital infrastructure poses to the goals of stakeholders. Digital port administration has been found out to drastically minimize the associated cost of doing business at Ghana's ports. A situation that has meant that freight forwarders are able to make significant savings on rents and demurrages (Atehnjia et al. 2020). Ports worldwide, including Tema port in Ghana, have used various forms of digital infrastructure technologies to meet the current requirements, reduce cost and increase efficiency (Trujillo et al. 2013; Senyo et al. 2020a), support scheduling and equipment control process and provide real-time accurate data for operations within container terminals, thereby improving the operational performance of ports and quality of container handling processes (Citifmonline.com 2017; Addo and Senyo 2020).

Additionally, many countries including Ghana have used the opportunity to enable digital technologies to improve connectivity and communication between people, companies, public agencies and non-governmental organizations (Amegboe 2019; Amankwah-Sarfo et al. 2018). Substantively, the benefits brought by the digitalization of administrative procedures at Ghana's ports include reducing documentation transfer and processing time costs while minimizing errors and improving information exchange and accuracy (Amegboe 2019; Senyo et al. 2020a).

However, some challenges are associated with the port's digitalization in Ghana. These include technical constraints on the GCNet portal (Atehnjia et al. 2020). Indeed, Internet and network issues as well as acquiring the tactics and skills to effectively harness digitalization opportunities have come with constraints. For instance, Amegboe (2019) identified that network and Internet issues, support/training for staff and clients, security issues, and complicated processes and procedures and document requirements are the challenges of the paperless ports system that constrain employee performance. Cyber security issues in particular do not seem to be receiving attention in the port's digitalization program in Ghana. In addition, inadequate stakeholder engagement also emerged during the implementation of the paperless port system. There were stakeholder agitations prior to the implementation of the paperless system. These were compounded by general uncertainty in the paperless processes at the take-off because of an initial lack of understanding and appreciation of the process mainly due to inadequate engagement with key stakeholders (Graphiconline.com 2017a). Indeed, Amegboe (2019) noticed that stakeholders' understanding of the paperless processing, coordination between customs, revenue collectors, banks, etc. was insufficient.

4.1.2 Digital Payment for National Health Insurance Scheme in Ghana

In December 2018, the National Health Insurance Scheme (NHIS) in Ghana introduced digitalization into the enrolment and renewal of health insurance to also enable customers receive renewal alerts (NHIS 2019). The new system uses the digital banking system to allow members to renew their membership on any of the mobile money platforms (Boaheng et al. 2019). The digital enrolment and renewal system came at the backdrop of relatively inflexible payment schedules that provided no alert or reminder to the customer on renewal dates. Prior to the implementation of the digital payment system, there were long waiting queues at the various registration and renewal centres (NHIS 2019). The adoption of the mobile money payment platforms also increased enrolment for customers in the informal sector (Renner-Micah et al. 2020; Boaheng et al. 2019).

The use of mobile phone for enrolment, renewal and payment increased efficiency and participation (Boaheng et al. 2019). Indeed, the NHIS (2019) reports that "With the introduction of the NHIS Mobile Renewal Service, over 5 million people took advantage to renew their membership at the comfort of their homes, workplace, market, etc. without having to physically visit the Scheme offices" (NHIS 2019: 1). As a result, the earlier challenges associated with costs of renewals and enrolment were addressed. Therefore, "there are no more long queues at the NHIS district offices thereby creating enough space for staff to attend to pregnant and indigent customers also promote the scheme in the communities" (NHIS 2019: 1). Subsequently, previous customers who were hitherto constrained have re-joined, beefing up the overall enrolment because of digitalization (NHIS 2019). The offline verification platform also allows NHIS service providers to confirm membership, so that only verified claims would be processed to reduce false claims and avoid rejections. Consequently, the NHIS is able to anticipate in real time the volume of claims on the platform and provide essential data for policy and planning in both private and public sector institutions (NHIS 2019). Some notable challenges include the heterogeneity in the environment within which these healthcare providers operate, the legal and institutional technological environment and the institutional capacity to manage the innovation process as well as address related security issues (Renner-Micah et al. 2020). There is the need to developing requisite cyber security expertise to improve the confidence of stakeholders.

4.1.3 Payment of Utility Bills in Ghana

One of the conspicuous muddles that warranted the need for digitalization in public payment systems is that the traditional payment systems were replete with inefficiencies. For instance, improper billing, non-payment of water bills and constraints associated with monitoring the corrupt activities of meter readers worsened the cost burden of the utility provider—Ghana Water Company Limited (GWCL) (Boakye and Nyieku 2010). The Electricity Company of Ghana (ECG), prior to the introduction of prepaid meters, also experienced significant losses and leakages in the supply of electricity. For instance, Sualihu and Rahman (2014) explain that timely payment of post-paid electricity bills on the part of customers was generally poor in Ghana, necessitating the introduction of smart meters.

Subsequently, measures to ensure convenience in utility payments, revenue collection and cost recovery were adopted through the use of mobile money platforms, mobile banking, utility provider app and other e-payment services (GWCL 2018; Amankwaa et al. 2020). The decision to adopt digitalized payments into GWCL was hinged on the level of mobile phone penetration and the use of mobile phone in the financial sector of Ghana (NCA 2017; GSMA 2017). This was to ensure that consumers are satisfied through the use of top-ups at their convenience so as to reduce operating cost in terms of time utilized by meter readers on the field (Safewaternetwork.org 2018; Amankwaa et al. 2020). Recently, the vice president of Ghana launched "ECG power", a mobile application, designed by staff of the ECG, to bring convenience to customers in terms of the purchase of ECG cards and payment of electricity bills (Graphiconline.com 2020). This is to ensure that over 73% of their customers can make purchases of power and enjoy the various services provided by the ECG. As a result, there is a drive to introduce smart meters across

Ghana to enable the wider operationalization of the payment platform (Graphiconline. com 2020).

There are currently some teething challenges. Although the estimated value of 72% baseline survey shows that consumers were on the mobile money platform, it does not translate into higher payments of utilities (Amankwaa et al. 2020). In fact, in the case of water bill payment, a pilot study carried out shows that mobile money accounted for 10% of revenue during the period of the study (Safewaternetwork.org 2018). Report from Safewaternetwork.org (2018) shows that mobile payment expanded in the month immediately after sensitization programme but dwindled with time. This indicates that despite the growing mobile money usage in Ghana, the level of awareness remains a challenge and may affect the operationalization of this digitalized payment platform. It is also possible that customers require more confidence in the system, thereby making cyber security an important issue that needs to be addressed.

4.1.4 Digital Financial Sector and Mobile Money Interoperability (MMI) in Ghana

Digitalization has greatly impacted the financial sector in Ghana. A World Bank Group (2019) report indicated that Ghana's financial sector expanded due to the fast-growing mobile money market. The "4th Ghana Economic Update", which focuses on financial sector development and financial inclusion, further highlighted how digital financial services will enhance financial inclusion (World Bank Group 2019). The launch of the first interoperability mobile money switch in Africa expanded the existing Ghlink switch to allow interoperability across several instruments, thereby expanding financial inclusion (Amoah et al. 2020; World Bank Group 2019). Moreover, the mobile phone penetration, complemented by the launch of Mobile Money Interoperability (MMI), created opportunities for the expansion of financial services and increased the role of non-financial institutions as much as e-money issuers, positioning Ghana as the fastest growing mobile money market in Africa (Senyo et al. 2020b; World Bank Group 2019). The huge jump in the MMI volume could be attributed to increased awareness that funds can now be transferred across wallets of different telecommunication networks. Mobile subscription indicators reveal increasing financial inclusion, suggesting that the widespread adoption of mobile network services will impact favourably on the financial sub-sector. The drive towards inclusion made possible by the mobile phone platform does not discriminate along income, class or age group lines (Agyekum et al. 2016; Adaba et al. 2019). The use of a mobile phone in financial transactions increases the likelihood of being financially included as mobile technology allows the previously unbanked to perform financial transactions via mobile phones. With such a unique platform as a mobile money facility, payments for utility bills, fees, fund transfers (domestic and cross-border) and other financial services can be carried out (Agyekum et al. 2016; Senyo et al. 2020b).

Digital payments have both facilitated or enhanced the receipt of payments as well as strengthened and expanded informal insurance networks among poor households (Amoah et al. 2020). It has become evident that non-bank-based digital financial services are cost-effective financial services for the unbanked population. This milestone has been achieved through growing mobile cellular penetration and expanding Internet usage (Agyekum et al. 2016). The growth in MMI has been phenomenal with thebftonline.com (2020) reporting that the half year performance of MMI in the Ghana Interbank Payment and Settlement System (GhIPSS)—January to June 2020—stood over 400% compared to the same period last year.

Businesses that adopt mobile payments will not just lower transaction cost, but also decrease cash management, which in turn will improve processing speeds to promote customer satisfaction and inclusion (Amoah et al. 2020; Baffour et al. 2020). Subsequently, the flexibilities in the usage of mobile money across several networks have made the platform preferable to traditional financial services (Narteh et al. 2017; Amoah et al. 2020). The use of mobile payment empowers the citizenry to participate in financial system and generate well-being outcomes in education, health and employment. According to Adaba et al. (2019), these benefits help to sustain livelihoods and improve family and social networks with significant human development potential.

However, erratic power supply and weak network signals remain key challenges in realizing the full benefits of such digital platforms. More so, when these challenges are a common feature in predominantly poor rural communities. Subsequently, citizenry in these communities is unable to fully utilize the advantages of mobile technology and financial inclusion (Adaba et al. 2019; Adaba and Ayoung 2017). Other challenges include fraud and security concerns particularly among uneducated and older customers in the Ghanaian society (Akomea-Frimpong et al. 2019; Aboagye and Anong 2020). Indeed, the integrity of the mobile money services is often questioned given prevalent error failures in the network systems and the rise in fraudulent activities due to issues of poor consumer education and sensitization (Aboagye and Anong 2020). This further emphasizes the importance of cyber security particularly within the financial sector and urgent need for expertise.

4.1.5 Digital Address System in Ghana

The Ghana property address system (GhanaPostGPS) software was launched in October 2017 to help locate of lands and buildings (Citifmonline.com 2017; Okae 2018). Digital addressing is a new technology-driven approach to assigning unique address identifiers to streets and individuals including properties and organizations within a given space. Ghana's town and city dwellers have an opportunity to be uniquely identified and located for improved service delivery (Abebrese 2019). With digital addresses, every property, individual or organization stands to be identified uniquely and located. The importance of digital address system is its capacity to enhance governmental and non-governmental organizations to deliver efficient services such as emergency responses, tax mobilization efforts, etc. (Okae 2018;

Ghanaweb.com 2019). The digital address system assists in projecting areas of informal settlement or slums that are often overlooked in the urban areas and provide a platform essential for census information needed for infrastructure planning in Ghana. For instance, it could assist emergency service delivery, support financial service delivery and provide security (Ghanaweb.com 2019; Abebrese 2019). Property address navigation technology has been reported to assist opening financial accounts to obtain business loans, etc. It has also led to the emergence and operation of delivery businesses and has formalized aspects of the informal sectors of the Ghanaian economy to expand the tax bracket (Amarinfotech.com 2018).

Despite the numerous benefits espoused both in research works and newspaper publications on digital addressing system in Ghana, there remains several constraints that may impede the actualization of this innovative venture. It is not evident how the changes in business and home locations of individuals and the potential use of multiple addresses could be monitored and controlled to reduce impersonation. In this area too some related cybersecurity expertise is required. There are also issues with respect to slums in urban centres which have not been properly demarcated with roads, streets or street names to facilitate the addressing process (Graphiconline.com 2017b; Abebrese 2019). This is largely due to poor planning and supervision from the institutions and agencies responsible for organizing physical structures in the urban centres. The presence of temporary structures, not properly demarcated, with no location or house number is a common feature in the urban centres not to talk non-urban communities (Graphiconline.com 2017b). Such deficiencies can introduce further security concerns.

5 Conclusion

This chapter sought to review the use of digital technologies in an African context focusing on the public programs in Ghana as an exemplar. The chapter sought to evaluate the burgeoning digitalization policies and programs and their related challenges. Digitalization has augmented public sector reforms in areas such as health insurance registration and renewal, utility payments, clearing at the ports, address systems, etc. Digitalization has inadvertently led to the gathering and management of information necessary for public policy and planning. This review confirms that digitalization increases innovation, efficiency, transparency, etc. in both public and private sectors. While it is evident that digital technologies improve the collection of revenue by enhancing efficiency as well as reducing corruption, the limited stakeholder engagement and sensitization require some attention.

Specifically, the chapter highlights poor stakeholder engagement, sensitization and awareness creation as inhibiting the potential gains from digitalization. Erratic power supplies and weak network signals are pertinent infrastructure development challenges. Indeed, the problem of development being ahead of planning in developing countries such as Ghana can limit the wider utilization of digital technologies. For example, network signals in some remote urban and rural areas reduce the mobile money interoperability. The digital address systems are also hampered by the fact that some urban and rural areas have been poorly demarcated with roads and streets. There are also evident skill gaps and capacity building issues. It is evident that these laudable digitalization programs are also open to cyber security issues. It is therefore surprising that cyber security does not seem to be an area where there is a national programme in Ghana? Cyber security and fraud in the digital space needs a lot of attention. Despite these challenges, digitalization has become inevitable and can be instrumental in economic growth and social interventions. African countries should seek to develop excellence in the application of digital platforms to solve economic and social problems. Given the immense opportunities that digital platforms provide for public sector transformation, there is the need for an all-encompassing and focused policy review of digitalization. It is imperative that countries in Africa develop specific policies that will encourage and support digitalization in both the public and private sectors. In addition to improved related infrastructure development, government policies can support education and training in digital technologies across the educational system. There should also be adult education programs on the use of digital technologies. Indeed, social interventions that involve financial payments and receipts need to adopt digital technologies. All programs should incorporate a critical evaluation of the related cybersecurity issues. Meanwhile, it is important that public and private sector organizations begin to build capabilities to combat the potential related cyber security and fraud issues. Governments in Africa need to develop a policy framework which will encourage the adoption of digital platforms by corporates and government agencies.

References

Abebrese, K. (2019). 'Implementing street addressing system in an evolving urban center. A case study of the Kumasi metropolitan area in Ghana' Graduate Theses and Dissertations. 16949. Retrieved from https://lib.dr.iastate.edu/etd/16949

Aboagye, J., & Anong, S. (2020). Provider and consumer perceptions on mobile money and microfinance integrations in Ghana: A financial inclusion approach. *International Journal of Business and Economics Research. Special Issue: Microfinance and Local Development, 9*(4), 276–297.

Adaba, G. B., & Ayoung, D. A. (2017). The development of a mobile money service: An exploratory actor-network study. *Information Technology for Development, 23*(4), 668–686.

Adaba, G. B., Ayoung, D. A., & Abbott, P. (2019). Exploring the contribution of mobile money to Well-being from a capability perspective. *The Electronic Journal of Information Systems in Developing Countries, 85*(4), e12079.

Addo, A., & Senyo, P. K. (2020). *Does process reengineering and digitalization eliminate corruption? Exploring 'paperless' vehicle clearance at Ghana's port.* Research papers 107. Retrieved from https://aisel.aisnet.org/ecis2020_rp/107

Adrodegari, F., & Saccani, N. (2017). Business models for the service transformation of industrial firms. *The Service Industries Journal, 37*(1), 57–83.

Adu, E. P., Buabeng, T., Asamoah, K., & Damoah, C. M. (2020). Digitization of local revenue collection in Ghana: An evaluation of Accra metropolitan assembly (AMA). *The Electronic Journal of Information Systems in Developing Countries, 86*(1), e12112.

Agyekum, F., Locke, S., & Hewa-Wellalage, N. (2016). *Financial inclusion and digital financial services: Empirical evidence from Ghana.*

Akomea-Frimpong, I., Andoh, C., Akomea-Frimpong, A., & Dwomoh-Okudzeto, Y. (2019). Control of fraud on mobile money services in Ghana: An exploratory study. *Journal of Money Laundering Control., 22*(2), 300–317.

Amagoh, F. (2015). An assessment of e-government in a west African country: The case of Nigeria. *International Journal of Public Administration in the Digital Age (IJPADA), 2*(3), 80–99.

Amankwaa, G., Asaaga, F. A., Fischer, C., & Awotwe, P. (2020). Diffusion of electronic water payment innovations in urban Ghana. Evidence from Tema Metropolis. *Water, 12*(4), 1011.

Amankwah-Sarfo, F., Effah, J., & Boateng, R. (2018). *Import clearance digitalization and socio-economic development: The case of Ghana.*

Amankwah-Sarfo, F. K., Effah, J., & Boateng, R. (2019). Digital infrastructure for port container handling and success or failure of stakeholders' goals: A case study of Ghana.

Amarinfotech.com. (2018). *Why digital address system Ghana Post GPS become popular?* Retrieved August 8, 2020, from https://www.amarinfotech.com/why-digital-address-system-ghana-post-gps-become-popular.html

Amegboe, W. N. (2019). The introduction of the paperless system and its impact on employee performance: A study of Tema port (Doctoral dissertation, University of Ghana).

Amoah, A., Korley, K., & Asiama, R. K. (2020). Mobile money as a financial inclusion instrument: What are the determinants? *International Journal of Social Economics, 47*(10), 1283–1297.

Arakpogun, E. O., Elsahn, Z., Nyuur, R. B., & Olan, F. (2020). Threading the needle of the digital divide in Africa: The barriers and mitigations of infrastructure sharing. *Technological Forecasting and Social Change, 161*, 120263.

Ardolino, M., Rapaccini, M., Saccani, N., Gaiardelli, P., Crespi, G., & Ruggeri, C. (2018). The role of digital technologies for the service transformation of industrial companies. *International Journal of Production Research, 56*(6), 2116–2132.

Asamoah, K. (2019). Digitalization in Africa's local governments: Public services in Ghana optimize the use of websites and social media?

Atehnjia, D., Nsoh, C., & Obeng, F. (2020, 2020). Examining the factors affecting the implementation of a paperless port system. *International Journal of Engineering Research and Advanced Technology (IJERAT), 6*(7). https://doi.org/10.31695/IJERAT.2020.3626.

Baffour, P. T., Rahaman, W. A., & Mohammed, I. (2020). Impact of mobile money access on internal remittances, consumption expenditure and household welfare in Ghana. *Journal of Economic and Administrative Sciences.*

Bekoe, W., Danquah, M., & Senahey, S. K. (2016). Tax reforms and revenue mobilization in Ghana. *Journal of Economic Studies, 43*(4), 522–534. https://doi.org/10.1108/JES-01-2015-0007.

Bellucci, S., & Otenyo, E. E. (2019). Digitisation and the disappearing job theory: A role for the Ilo in Africa? In *The ILO@ 100* (pp. 203–222). Leiden: Brill Nijhoff.

Boaheng, J. M., Amporfu, E., Ansong, D., & Osei-Fosu, A. K. (2019). Determinants of paying national health insurance premium with mobile phone in Ghana: A cross-sectional prospective study. *International Journal for Equity in Health, 18*(1), 1–9.

Boakye, E., & Nyieku, I. E. (2010). Cost recovery analysis of Ghana water company limited (Gwcl): A case study of Sekondi-Takoradi Metropolis. *European Journal of Scientific Research, 46*(1), 119–125.

Bouwman, H., de Reuver, M. & Shahrokh, N. (2017). The impact of digitalization on business models: How IT artefacts, social media, and big data force firms to innovate their business model. In *14th International Telecommunications Society (ITS) Asia-Pacific regional conference*, Kyoto, June 24–27.

Bukht, R. & Heeks, R. (2018). Digital economy policy in developing countries. Paper no. 6. DIODE. Retrieved from www.diode.network/publications/

Choi, J., Dutz, M. A., & Usman, Z. (2020). *The Future of Work in Africa: Harnessing the Potential of Digital Technologies for all.* Washington: World Bank. Retrieved April 2020, from https://www.caasitechacademy.com/media/Future%20of%20Work%20-%20Africa.pdf.

Citifmonline.com. (2017). Single window system will ease congestion at port – GPHA [WWW DOC]. Retrieved June 10, 2020, from http://citifmonline.com/2015/01/single-window-system-will-ease-congestion-at-ports-gpha/

Darley, W. K. (2001). The internet and emerging E-commerce: Challenges and implications for management in sub-Saharan Africa. *Journal of Global Information Technology Management, 4*(4), 4–18.

Darley, W. K. (2003). Public policy challenges and implications of the internet and the emerging E-commerce for sub-Saharan Africa: A business perspective. *Information Technology for Development, 10*(1), 1–12.

Dutta, S., Geiger, T., & Lanvin, B. (2015). *The global information technology report 2015: ICTs for inclusive growth.* Gevena: World Economic Forum.

Ewusi-Mensah, K. (2012). Problems of information technology diffusion in sub-Saharan Africa: The case of Ghana. *Information Technology for Development, 18*(3), 247–269.

Fuchs, C., & Horak, E. (2008). Africa and the digital divide. *Telematics and Informatics, 25*(2), 99–116.

Ghanaweb.com. (2019). Government to issue number plate to every house in Ghana. Retrieved August 8, 2020, from https://www.ghanaweb.com/GhanaHomePage/NewsArchive/Government-to-issue-number-plates-to-every-house-in-Ghana-763093

GNA. (2017). Digitization of Ghana's Economy Top Priority Of Government. Ghana News Agency (24th December 2017) https://www.modernghana.com/news/824832/digitization-of-ghanas-economy-top-priority-of.html (assessed on 12th July 2020)

Graphiconline.com. (2017a). Paperless operations takes-off with challenges. Retrieved June 10, 2020, from https://www.graphic.com.gh/news/general-news/paperless-operation-takes-off-with-challenges.html

Graphiconline.com. (2017b). Thinking aloud on digital addressing system. Retrieved October 24, 2020, from https://www.graphic.com.gh/features/civic-realities/thinking-aloud-on-digital-addressing-system.html

Graphiconline.com. (2020). Ghana to become the hub of digitisation in West Africa. Retrieved October 23, 2020, from https://www.graphic.com.gh/news/politics/ghana-news-ghana-to-become-hub-of-digitization-in-west-africa-bawumia.html

Greengard, S. (2010). Cloud computing and developing nations. *Communications of the ACM, 53*(5), 18. Retrieved from http://portal.acm.org/citation.cfm?doid=1735223.1735232.

GSMA. (2011). *African Mobile Observatory 2011: Driving economic and social development through mobile services.* London: GSMA. Retrieved from http://www.gsma.com/spectrum/wpcontent/uploads/2011/12/Africa-Mobile-Observatory-2011.pdf.

GSMA. (2017). Country overview, Ghana: Driving Mobile-enabled digital transformation; GSMA: London, UK, 2017. Retrieved June 20, 2020, from https://www.gsma.com/mobilefordevelopment/wp-content/uploads/2020/05/Ghana-Country-Overview.pdf

Gukurume, S., & Mahiya, I. T. (2020). Mobile money and the (un) making of social relations in Chivi, Zimbabwe. *Journal of Southern African Studies, 1*–15.

Gupta, G., & Bose, I. (2019). Strategic learning for digital market pioneering: Examining the transformation of Wishberry's crowdfunding model. *Technological Forecasting and Social Change, 146*, 865–876. https://doi.org/10.1016/j.techfore.2018.06.020.

GWCL. (2018). *GWCL e-Billing Project: Progress Report; number 21.12.07.18.* Accra, Ghana: Ghana Water Company Limited.

Heavin, C., & Power, D. J. (2018). Challenges for digital transformation–towards a conceptual decision support guide for managers. *Journal of Decision Systems, 27*(sup1), 38–45.

Hussain, S., & Mohan, R. (2008). Localization in Asia Pacific. In F. Librero & P. B. Arinto (Eds.), *Digital review of Asia Pacific 2007/2008, 43*–58. Ottawa: International Development Research Centre. Retrieved from https://www.idrc.ca/en/book/digital-review-asia-pacific-2007-2008.

Iansiti, M., & Lakhani, K. R. (2014). Digital ubiquity: How connections, sensors, and data are revolutionizing business. *Harvard Business Review, 92*(11), 19.

Internetworldstats.com. (2020). Internet users statistics for Africa; Africa Internet Usage, 2020 Population Stats and Facebook Subscribers. Retrieved November 29, 2020, from https://www.internetworldstats.com/stats1.htm

ITU. (2015). *ICT facts & figures: The world in 2015*. Geneva: International Telecommunication Union. Retrieved from http://www.itu.int/en/ITUD/Statistics/Documents/facts/ICTFactsFigures2015.pdf.

Kanyengo, C. W. (2009). Managing digital information resources in Africa: Preserving the integrity of scholarship. *The International Information & Library Review, 41*(1), 34–43.

Ke, Y., Wang, S., Chan, A. P., & Cheung, E. (2009). Research trend of public-private partnership in construction journals. *Journal of Construction Engineering and Management, 135*(10), 1076–1086.

Khan, K. S., Kunz, R., Kleijnen, J., & Antes, G. (2003). Five steps to conducting a systematic review. *Journal of the Royal Society of Medicine, 96*(3), 118–121.

Kohtamäki, M., Parida, V., Oghazi, P., Gebauer, H., & Baines, T. (2019). Digital servitization business models in ecosystems: A theory of the firm. *Journal of Business Research, 104*, 380–392.

Kumar, T., Misra, H., & Mishra, D. P. (2013). Decentralisation and e-governance in Indian context: A case-based study. In *Research paper funded by Sir Ratan Tata Trust; presented at 5th International Conference on E-governance (ICEG)*, 28–30 December, Hyderabad.

Latos, B. A., Harlacher, M., Burgert, F., Nitsch, V., Przybysz, P., & Niewohner, S. M. (2018). Complexity drivers in digitalized work systems: Implications for cooperative forms of work. *Advances in Science, Technology and Engineering Systems Journal, 3*(5), 171–185.

Lenka, S., Parida, V., & Wincent, J. (2017). Digitalization capabilities as enablers of value co-creation in servitizing firms. *Psychology & Marketing, 34*(1), 92–100.

Lu, W., & Liu, J. (2014). Research into the moderating effects of progress and quality performance in project dispute negotiation. *International Journal of Project Management, 32*(4), 654–662.

Luz Martín-Peña, M., Díaz-Garrido, E., & Sánchez-López, J. M. (2018). The digitalization and servitization of manufacturing: A review on digital business models. *Strategic Change, 27*(2), 91–99.

Manyika, J., Lund, S., Singer, M., White, O., & Berry, C. (2016). *Digital finance for all: Powering inclusive growth in emerging economies*. San Francisco, CA: McKinsey Global Institute. Retrieved August 2020, from https://www.mckinsey.com/global-themes/employment-andgrowth/how-digital-finance-could-boost-growth-in-emerging-economies.

Meltzer, J. (2014). Supporting the internet as a platform for international trade opportunities for small and medium-sized enterprises and developing countries. *Global Economy & Development*, (February), 69. Retrieved from https://www.brookings.edu/wp-content/uploads/2016/07/02-internet-internationaltrade-meltzer.pdf.

Miklian, J., & Hoelscher, K. (2017). Smart cities, Mobile technologies and social cohesion in India. *Indian Journal of Human Development, 11*(1), 1–16.

Misuraca, G. (2007). *E-governance in Africa, from theory to action: A handbook on ICTs for local governance*. IDRC.

Mkalama B. & Ndemo B. (2020). *Orchestrating Smart cities, new disruptive business models and informal enterprises [online first]*. IntechOpen. Retrieved December 3, 2020, from https://www.intechopen.com/online-first/orchestrating-smart-cities-new-disruptive-business-models-and-informal-enterprises. https://doi.org/10.5772/intechopen.94075

Mommoh, R. L., & Abubakar, S. K. (2019). Digitization of library materials in special libraries in Abuja, Nigeria. *Information Impact: Journal of Information and Knowledge Management, 10*(1), 14–23.

Myovella, G., Karacuka, M., & Haucap, J. (2020). Digitalization and economic growth: A comparative analysis of sub-Saharan Africa and OECD economies. *Telecommunications Policy, 44*(2), 101856.

Narteh, B., Mahmoud, M. A., & Amoh, S. (2017). Customer behavioural intentions towards mobile money services adoption in Ghana. *The Service Industries Journal, 37*(7–8), 426–447.

NCA. (2017). *Quarterly Statistical Bulletin on Communications in Ghana*. July–September 2017. Retrieved January 28, 2018, from https://nca.org.gh/assets/Uploads/stats-bulletin-Q3-2018.pdf

Neubert, M. (2018). The impact of digitalization on the speed of internationalization of lean global startups. *Technology Innovation Management Review, 8*(5), 44–54.

NHIS. (2019). Mobile renewal service anniversary marked national. Health insurance scheme. Retrieved June 2020, from http://www.nhis.gov.gh/News/nhis-mobile-renewal-service-anniversary-marked-5274

Nicoletta, C., & Andrea, O. (2002). Measuring the digital divide: A framework for the analysis of cross-country differences. *Journal of Information Technology, 17*, 9–19.

Nohumba, I., Nyambuya, C., & Nyambuya, G. (2020). Integrating offline and online platforms for seamless banking experience. *Journal of Management & Administration, 2020*(1), 45–72.

Nyirenda-Jere, T., & Biru, T. (2015). *Internet development and internet governance in Africa*. Geneva: Internet Society. Retrieved from https://www.internetsociety.org/resources/doc/2015/internetdevelopment-and-internet-governance-in-africa/.

OECD. (2018). *Digital government review of Argentina - accelerating the digitalisation of the public OECD 2018*. Retrieved June 2020, from https://www.oecd.org/gov/digital-government/digital-government-review-argentina-key-findings-2018.pdf.

Ohemeng, F. L. K., & Ofosu-Darkwah, K. (2014). Overcoming the digital divide in developing countries. *Journal of Developing Societies, 30*(3), 297–322. https://doi.org/10.1177/0169796X14536970.

Okae, P. (2018). A qualitative study of smartphone usage patterns: The case of Ghana. *Science World Journal, 13*(2), 58–63.

Okeleke, K., & Stryjak, J. (2015). *Building digital societies in Asia*. London: GSMA. Retrieved from https://www.gsmaintelligence.com/research/?file=bd5b3cf1d0533f9c9641039ba6966864&download.

Opresnik, D., & Taisch, M. (2015). The manufacturer's value chain as a service-the case of remanufacturing. *Journal of Remanufacturing, 5*(1), 2.

Osabutey, E. L. C., & Croucher, R. (2018). Intermediate institutions and technology transfer in developing countries: The case of the construction industry in Ghana. *Technological Forecasting and Social Change, 128*, 154–163.

Osabutey, E. L. C., Williams, K., & Debrah, A. Y. (2014). The potential for technology and knowledge transfers between foreign and local firms: A study of the construction industry in Ghana. *Journal of World Business, 49*(4), 560–571.

Osei-Kojo, A. (2017). E-government and public service quality in Ghana. *Journal of Public Affairs, 17*(3), e1620.

Owusu Kwateng, K., Osei-Wusu, E. E., & Amanor, K. (2019). Exploring the effect of online banking on bank performance using data envelopment analysis. *Benchmarking: An International Journal, 27*(1), 137–165. https://doi.org/10.1108/BIJ-06-2018-0154.

Parida, V., Sjödin, D. R., Lenka, S., & Wincent, J. (2015). Developing global service innovation capabilities: How global manufacturers address the challenges of market heterogeneity. *Research-Technology Management, 58*(5), 35–44.

Parida, V., Sjödin, D., & Reim, W. (2019). Reviewing literature on digitalization, business model innovation, and sustainable industry: Past achievements and future promises. *Sustainability, 11*(2), 391.

Patil, P. P., Dwivedi, Y. K., & Rana, N. P. (2017). Digital payments adoption: An analysis of literature. In *Conference on e-business, e-services and e-society* (pp. 61–70). Cham: Springer.

Prasad, K. (2012). E-governance policy for modernizing government through digital democracy in India. *Journal of Information Policy, 2*, 183–203.

Rachinger, M., Rauter, R., Müller, C., Vorraber, W., & Schirgi, E. (2019). Digitalization and its influence on business model innovation. *Journal of Manufacturing Technology Management, 30*(8), 1143–1160.

Renner-Micah, A., Effah, J., & Boateng, R. (2020). Institutionalisation of Health Insurance Digital Claims Platform (2020). AMCIS 2020 Proceedings. Retrieved November 12, 2020, from https://aisel.aisnet.org/amcis2020/global_dev/global_dev/13

Safewaternetwork.org. (2018). Digitising payment for household water connections in Ghana: Quantifying the impact of digital finance for household connections in Ghana. Retrieved from https://www.safewaternetwork.org/sites/default/files/SWN_Field_Insight_Digitizing_Payments_Ghana_Aug2018.pdf

Senyo, P. K., Effah, J. & Osabutey, E. L. C. (2020a). Digital platformisation as public sector transformation strategy: A Case of Ghana's Paperless Port. *Technological Forecasting and Social Change*. https://doi.org/10.1016/j.techfore.2020.120387.

Senyo, P. K., Osabutey, E. L., & Seny Kan, K. (2020b). Pathways to improving financial inclusion through mobile money: A fuzzy set qualitative comparative analysis. *Information Technology & People*.

Sigauke, D. & Nengomasha, C. (2011). Challanges and prospects facing digitization of historical records for their preservation. In *Paper presented at the 2nd international conference on African digital libraries and archives. South Africa*.

Sjödin, D. R., Parida, V., & Kohtamäki, M. (2016). Capability configurations for advanced service offerings in manufacturing firms: Using fuzzy set qualitative comparative analysis. *Journal of Business Research, 69*(11), 5330–5335.

Sjödin, D., Parida, V., Jovanovic, M., & Visnjic, I. (2020). Value creation and value capture alignment in business model innovation: A process view on outcome-based business models. *Journal of Product Innovation Management, 37*(2), 158–183.

Sklyar, A., Kowalkowski, C., Tronvoll, B., & Sörhammar, D. (2019). Organizing for digital servitization: A service ecosystem perspective. *Journal of Business Research, 104*, 450–460.

Statista. (2020). Internet penetration in Africa, by country. Retrieved November 18, 2020, from https://www.statista.com/statistics/1124283/internet-penetration-in-africa-by-country/

Sualihu, M. A., & Rahman, M. A. (2014). Payment behaviour of electricity consumers: Evidence from the greater Accra region of Ghana. *Global Business Review, 15*(3), 477–492.

Thebftonline.com. (2020) IMM volume jumps over 400% in first half of 2020. Retrieved September 8, 2020, from https://thebftonline.com/23/07/2020/mmi-volume-jumps-by-over-400-in-first-half-of-2020/#:~:text=The%20huge%20jump%20in%20MMI,partner%20institutions%20have%20been%20running

Tranfield, D., Denyer, D., & Smart, P. (2003). Towards a methodology for developing evidence-informed management knowledge by means of systematic review. *British Journal of Management, 14*(3), 207–222.

Trujillo, L., González, M. M., & Jiménez, J. L. (2013). An overview on the reform process of African ports. *Utilities Policy, 25*, 12–22.

Tsvetkova, N. (2018). Digital technologies and Asian and African countries. *Asia and Africa Today, 9*, 25–32. https://doi.org/10.31857/S032150750000688-8.

UNCTAD. (2019). Digital economy report 2019; Value creation and capture: implications for developing countries. United Nations. Retrieved August 2020, from https://unctad.org/system/files/official-document/der2019_en.pdf

UNESCO. (2011). *Broadband: A platform for Progress: A report by the broadband Commission for Digital Development*. Paris: International Telecommunication Union and UNESCO. Retrieved from http://unesdoc.unesco.org/images/0021/002198/219825e.pdf.

Vendrell-Herrero, F., Bustinza, O. F., Parry, G., & Georgantzis, N. (2017). Servitization, digitization and supply chain interdependency. *Industrial Marketing Management, 60*, 69–81.

Winn, J. K. (2015). Mobile payments and financial inclusion: Kenya, Brazil and India as case studies. University of Washington School of law research paper. 2015.

World Bank Group. (2019). Ghana Digital Economy Diagnostic. Retrieved September 7, 2020, from http://documents1.worldbank.org/curated/en/395721560318628665/pdf/Fourth-Ghana-Economic-Update-Enhancing-Financial-Inclusion-Africa-Region.pdf

Maximizing Human Resource Development in Sub-Saharan Africa in the Digital Era

James Baba Abugre

> *Bringing advanced information technologies to sub-Saharan Africa will enable the region to leapfrog over traditional stages of development at a surprisingly low cost. In a world where information and information technology has become the engine of economic growth, failure to be fully "engaged" at the government level in the Internet and emerging e-commerce puts sub-Saharan African businesses at a serious disadvantage.*
>
> William K. Darley (2003: 11)

1 Introduction

The development of human resource management (HRM) in sub-Saharan Africa (SSA) has become a vibrant area of interest for understanding how human resource (HR) concepts and designs which are often attributed to Western management concepts are used in developing countries (Budhwar and Debrah 2009; Cooke 2017). This vibrant and burgeoning interest in investigating the development of HR is born out of many decades of neglect of African management system. Consequently, the complexities and diversity including the challenges of HRM in Africa are not explained to the maximization of human capital management of multinational companies (MNCs) working across Africa, including domestic Africa companies (Kamoche et al. 2003). Accordingly, recent academic investigation in Africa management systems has shown how the conceptualization and practice of HRM have evolved in organizations due to institutional changes in the African context. For example, Kamoche (2002) argues that managing HR development in Africa is burdened with problems such as governmental interference, social-cultural factors

J. B. Abugre (✉)
University of Ghana Business School, Accra, Ghana
e-mail: jbabugre@ug.edu.gh

© The Author(s), under exclusive license to Springer Nature Switzerland AG 2021
J. B. Abugre et al. (eds.), *Business in Africa in the Era of Digital Technology*,
Advances in Theory and Practice of Emerging Markets,
https://doi.org/10.1007/978-3-030-70538-1_3

which may be at odds with contemporary HR management imperatives, inappropriate leadership styles, confrontational labor relations, and others. The author therefore recommends more research in order to understand the definitive characteristics of HRM in Africa. Accordingly, Jackson (2002) proposes a cross-cultural model that integrates the value of people in organizations and therefore the building of cross-cultural synergies. On the other hand, Abugre and Nasere (2020) advise that effective development of HR in the African context requires innovative workplace practices that would engender both indirect and direct impetus to boost employee job satisfaction and productivity.

However, according to Darley (2003), in this age of digitization, African governments have an important responsibility to provide an enabling business environment with respect to information and Internet infrastructure that takes on an added value to human development. Darley's assertion has been supported by current writers on HR development that digitization has taken up the center stage of human lives and businesses, in which technological advancement is continuously growing with a considerable increase in data and the speed of processing information (Angrave et al. 2016). In fact, the current trend of digitization is indeed changing the face of people management in organizations with unparalleled potential in analytics and forecasting in the development of HR management. For example, according to Corral and Rodríguez-Lluesma (2018), digitalization also known as the process of adopting digital environments as an alternative to analogical ones impacts on work processes and business services including HR models. As a result, the competitive context of the market economy is being redefined, and traditional models are undergoing disruption with the application of technologies such as cloud computing, the Internet of things, artificial intelligence (AI), virtual reality and/or augmented reality, big data, additive manufacturing and 3D printing, machine learning and/or deep learning, and blockchain, among others. In addition to these technologies, digitalization also has effect on organization and the way people think, feel, and behave. For example, the use of information and communication technologies (ICT), computer-mediated communication (CMC), the Internet and the web, social media, computational decision making, and nanotechnologies are all defining and changing people's behavior and attitude to work patterns. All these can transform the current state of HR development in SSA and facilitate organizational inertia.

Thus, according to Ball (2000), the current trend in human resource development which emphasizes strategic objectives and a focus on shareholder value has significantly affected jobs and expectations of HR practitioners. The initiation of Internet/intranet and information technology influence daily activities at work. The change in wave to HR development is now directed toward incorporating technological advancement to assist human resource managers in performing their responsibilities. HRM-focused technologies and digital assistants are being deployed across MNCs' subsidiaries with businesses having a clear focus on outcomes and return on investment of the newly created digital assets.

In the words of Corral and Rodríguez-Lluesma (2018), the way we communicate, plan and choose our activities, exchange experiences and opinions, complete business transactions, and work has been subjected to considerable modification as digitization and advanced technologies have been rapidly introduced into our society. These have gained an enormous number of users, as compared to the technological advances of previous industrial revolutions.

In this chapter, we take our inspiration from William K. Darley and his words *"information technology has become the engine of economic growth, failure to be fully "engaged" at the government level in the Internet and emerging e-commerce puts sub-Saharan African businesses at a serious disadvantage"* (Darley 2003: 11). Accordingly, we employ a quantitative survey of full-time employees in both public and private organizations in Ghana to assess the dearth and deficiency of application, cultural awareness, knowledge, and usefulness of digital and IS application of human resource management in organizations in SSA. For example, what is the level of knowledge of employees about digital HRM? How important is digitalization of HRM to the African business environment? This chapter unearths some answers to these questions and relate their discussion to Darley's (2003) words above on the application of information technology and digitalization of HRM in the sub-continent. Additionally, the chapter discusses the value and interface between HRM and new technology contextually destined, and the positive outcomes that e-enabled HRM is likely to be for people management in the SSA economic environment.

The next section reviews extant literature on human resource management and digitalization in Africa. Subsequently, the chapter looks at the challenges of digital HRM in Africa. We next explain the method and empirical approach used to gather data for the study. We then present the study results and discussion of the findings with the chapter conclusion.

2   Human Resource Management (HRM) in the Digital Era

The competitive business environment has created a condition whereby organizations are introducing innovations into their activities to enable them to explore the opportunities and to overcome their challenges (Toshani et al. 2011). According to Bouwman et al. (2018), organizations have over the years invested a lot in information systems (IS) to ensure that their businesses function effectively and efficiently. The point is that organizations are expected to use technology on people management to achieve and sustain competitive edge leading to organizational performance (David 2011). That is because technology adoption and HRM are highly significant for high performance work systems. Thus, digital technology has reinforced the internal and external competition within the global market (Şahin and Topal 2018). Consequently, organizations are fast adopting new and innovative technologies in doing business to stay relevant in today's competitive business environment (Khera and Gulati 2012). Since digitalization and technology adoptions impact on human capital development, its adoptions by businesses are meant to enhance organizational workforce with the required knowledge, skills, and abilities so as to function effectively on the job (Meijerink and Habraken 2018). Earlier writers had argued for the necessity to apply digitalization and advanced technology on HRM practices as a critical strategy for firm performance, since human resource is the most valuable among all resources within organizations (Armstrong and Taylor 2014; Chugh 2014). Hence, the adoption and application of digitalization in HRM have been identified with different terminologies such as "Computerized Human Resource Information Systems (CHRIS), Electronic Human Resource Management (E-HRM), Human Resource Management Information System (HRMIS), digital HRM, web-based HRM, virtual HRM, online HRM and Human Resource Information Technology (HRIT)" (Bondarouk and Ruël 2013: 101). With all these technologies, the most popular and researched ones are the HRMIS, e-HRM, and CHRIS. E-HRM has been defined as "the planning, implementation and application of information technology for networking and supporting at least two individuals or collective actors in their shared performance of HR activities" (Strohmeier 2007: 20). Computerized Human Resource Information Systems (CHRIS) has been explained as "a fully integrated, organization-wide networks of HR related data, information, services, databases, tools and transactions" (Sugata and Bhattacharjee 2019). HRIS has also been defined by Hendrickson (2003: 2) as "an integrated system used to gather, store and analyze information regarding an organization's human resource."

It is clear from the above descriptions that integration is key as far as adoption of IS in HRM is concerned. Accordingly, van Kruining (2017) remarks that the basic function of digitization of HRM is the integration of HR practices, policies, and procedures. Besides, the integration of HR activities is a critical factor for ensuring successful management of human resources in work organizations. This assertion is supported by Meijerink et al. (2018) who argue that the adoption of technology in HRM has brought about a situation where Internet is facilitating HR activities such as recruitment and selection, training and development, payroll management, and many others. Moreover, more contemporary studies have expanded the e-HRM definition with a network structure as a central focus. For example, Strohmeier (2007) sees digital HRM as the advantage accrued to an organization based on the application of IS network to support the collective and hard performance of HR activities. Lepak and Snell (1998), on the other hand, refer digital HRM as "virtual HR" to describe a "network-based structure that mediates IS technology to support firms acquire, develop, and deploy intellectual capital.

According to Amarakoon et al. (2018), adopting technology into HR is increasing at a faster pace since it helps organization's workforce to take responsibility of information that is deemed personal to them. Apparently, human resource management in organizations is responsible for making sure employees take ownership of their own information, and this is mostly achieved by e-HRM. Most empirical studies have found a positive relationship between digitization of HRM and improved quality service delivery. For instance, according to Dery et al. (2009), high performance is achieved by HR using HRMIS in carrying out HR activities which consequently affects other departments such as finance and accounting, operations and logistics, marketing, and administration. This assertion is in consonance with Kim and Choi's (2018) research which also acknowledged that customers have become discerning and that organizations could leverage on technology in its functional units to achieve customer satisfaction culminating into profitability. Due to the increasing benefits of technology to organizations, it is evident from empirical studies that several organizations are adopting digitization of HRM in their organizations to realize their goals (Sugata and Bhattacharjee 2019). Poisat and Mey (2017) state that the adoption ICT in HR by most organizations is because of its positive impact on line managers. They further indicated that HR could use e-HRM to ensure improved and effective communication between line managers and their subordinates. In addition, e-HRM can be used to design and improve gathering and analysis of data system that can assist line managers in managerial decisions. To this extent, managers could constantly be informed of the happenings in the organization, and this can lead to increased organizational performance. Accordingly, Kupper et al. (2019) believe that the developments of digitization have heavily impacted on the activities of HRM since, it (digitization) is changing the nature of work in organization. This means that as HRM activities are shifting to online platforms, HR practitioners could constantly be in touch with their employees and customers. This new phenomenon means that employees should prepare themselves in terms of developing their career to meet the new trend of digitization. Thus, Pagani and Pardo (2017) assert that automation of different functional units of organization requires a complete new set of skills to survive in their organizations. Moreover, Meijerink et al. (2018) argue that digitization in the form of automation of jobs is an indication that the activities of HRM have become important and complex to employees if they want to stay relevant in today's competitive organizations.

3 Digitizing Human Resource Development in Africa: An Imperative for Change

Organizations and businesses in sub-Saharan Africa must develop a strategic understanding of how their human capital can contribute effectively to the success of these businesses and organizations. The call for innovative management systems in spite of the presence of heavy human capital in most SSA businesses and public institutions implies job dissatisfaction and the lack of supportive and co-operant tools to aid employees in work organizations (Abugre 2014).

If digitizing HRM is meant to create and leverage value for human capital development, then the adoption and application of digitization and advanced technology by SSA institutions are now. Therefore, Sparrow et al. (2015) affirm strongly that if a strategy is to create, capture, leverage, and protect value for HR, then it is unique and must be adopted. Accordingly, Angrave et al. (2016) agree that this kind of strategic insight is essential for organizational leadership to develop digital HR and analytics capabilities to meet the current global competition of people management in organizations.

Thus, in this era of increasing global technological transformation, digitalization has created a platform of linkages to engage businesses and their competitors. As a result, the survival and growth in a rapidly changing business management requires SSA organizations to associate themselves with digitization of human capital management in order to embrace internal innovation that adds value to human resource development in the continent. Hence, Darley (2003) advocates for digital and Internet infrastructure which not only will boost local businesses to compete in the global marketplace but will gain access to new markets. This assertion suggests understanding the mechanisms of human resource digitalization. HRM digitization comprise of Human Resource Information System (HRIS) as technology and the use of software designed to carry out different HR processes; HR analytics as the use of data and software to drive HR development that will add value to HR planning and strategy. Thus, with the right metrics, HR can make a strong case for being an important part of strategy development and implementation in SSA business environment.

L'Ecuyer and Raymond (2017) in their study found that there is a significant relationship between e-HRM and performance of organizations. Their finding was corroborated by McDonald et al. (2017) who also identified in their study that there is a positive correlation between e-HRM and profitability. They further claimed that e-HRM leads to increased organizational performance in that it reduces the cumbersome processes that used to characterize the activities of HRM. Heikkilä et al. (2017) agree with this assertion in which they posited that e-HRM has the capacity to get things at a faster rate compared to the manual system of processing HR activities. Their findings also alluded to the fact that e-HRM plays a very important role in reducing cost to organizations. The findings of Bos-Nehles and Bondarouk (2018) indicated that e-HRM not only decreases cost but also minimizes a lot of information errors that used to characterize paperwork in organizations. According to Holm and Haahr (2018), owing to the fact that there are so many advantages associated with the adoption of technology, digital HRM helps to attract well-qualified candidates with the needed competences during recruitment and selection. Shahibi et al. (2016) also came out with similar findings by revealing in their study that human resource information system (HRMIS) has made recruitment and selection easier as compared to the old practices. Additionally, Liboni et al. (2019) contend that digitized HRM is critical for organizations to maintain quality relationship with their workers in order to motivate, develop, and retain them.

Based on this, Ziebell et al. (2019) believe that HR in the past decade has seen much improvement and this is because of how it has been impacted by technology. It can be inferred from the above discussion that digitizing HRM in organizations is the way to go for African businesses, especially as organizations in SSA seek to achieve competitive advantage in the global market. Digitizing HR in SSA would take them out of the current serious disadvantage of global business they find themselves in (Darley 2003).

4   Challenges of Digital HRM in Africa

According to Adewoye and Olugbenga (2018), though digital or e-HRM is important for Africa to enhance the skills, knowledge, and competencies of the workforce
to achieve high performance and productivity, digitization of HRM is fraught with
many difficulties. Rahman et al. (2018) agree with the above assertion by stating
that digitization and its adoption into HRM in Africa can be challenging. In fact,
they state that e-HRM application comes in different forms, and adoption of a specific application should take into consideration the size and the uniqueness of the
organization, so that a competitive advantage can be achieved. However, the challenge in Africa is that organizations sometimes adopt e-HRM without considering
these factors (Shiferaw et al. 2015). As a consequence, the application of digitized
HRM is facing a lot of challenges which could lead to the product becoming unde-
rutilized. Similarly, Poisat and Mey (2017) indicated that in some cases African
organizations failed to link e-HRM to performance and productivity. They lament
that although e-HRM is supposed to reduce costs and ensure increased productivity
and profit but in most cases, organizations in Africa fail to have a valid measure to
ensure that there is a link between digitization of HR and productivity. Additionally,
Mbuyisa and Leonard (2015) argue that a key reason of ICT adoption into a business is to reduce cost because the cost of ICT infrastructure is very high. However,
they indicate that the high cost of ICT infrastructure poses a challenge to most businesses in Africa since the infrastructure is often not effectively utilized to ensure
overall cost reduction. Besides, as pertain in other regions, the political and socio-
cultural systems are different across regions and countries and therefore adopting a
new system must take the local context into consideration (Amant 2016).
Unfortunately, some of the applications designed for Africa fail to consider whether
they fit African context, therefore rendering the infrastructure "culturally unfit"
(Horwitz 2012).

According to Lippert and Michael Swiercz (2005), one of the major challenges
of adopting e-HRM in organizations is lack of top management support and commitment. They observed that in most organizations, top management does not consider the HR department as critical as they consider other departments such as
operations and marketing. They therefore give more priority by digitizing these
departments leaving the HR departments. For instance, Nagendra and Deshpande
(2014) acknowledge that some organizations do not find e-HRM too important as
they do not see the direct link between HRM department and the organization's
profitability. Some organizations also fail to digitize HRM because of inadequate
capital and know-how (Sugata and Bhattacharjee 2019) to install the new technology. While Toshani et al. (2011) admit that HR personnel sometimes find technology adoption as something difficult for them to operate. These personnel perceive
new technology to be complex and therefore find it difficult to accept. Lack of
knowledge of new technology is sometimes coupled with an existing organizational
culture where activities were done manually by personnel. Some of the personnel

also have the fear that the adoption of technology in HRM could render them redundant and therefore find possible means to oppose its adoption.

5 Study Context and Empirical Approach of Digitization of People Management

To ground this project work in the context of practicality, the study gathered empirical data from divers and full-time employees from both public and private sector organizations in Ghana—a sub-Saharan African context. A quantitative design approach to survey employees from multiple organizations in Ghana was considered most appropriate to unearth knowledge in their evaluation process of digitization of HRM and information systems adoption in their respective organizations. Accordingly, participants were randomly sampled from these multiple public and private sector organizations in Ghana. To be included in the study, participants must have been full-time employees in either a private organization or public organization within the Accra metropolis—the capital city of Ghana. Hence, 150 survey questionnaires were personally distributed to individuals working in these organizations. However, 147 questionnaires were effectively retrieved from the participants.

The instrument used to collect the data comprised of a myriad of questions soliciting their knowledge on the significance of digital HRM and information systems (IS) in the various organizations, and knowledge and participation IS and digital training of participants in their respective organizations. Table 1 presents the demographics of participants in the study.

Table 1 Demographic characteristics of respondents ($N = 147$)

Characteristic	Frequency	Percentage
Gender		38.8
Female	57	61.2
Male	90	
Age (years)		
25–35	84	57.2
36–45	45	30.6
46–55	15	10.2
56–65	3	2.0
Academic qualification		
HND	41	27.9
First degree	81	55.1
Master's	14	9.5
Professional	6	4.1
PhD	5	3.4

Fig. 1 Frequency of
training of employees on
IS and digital services

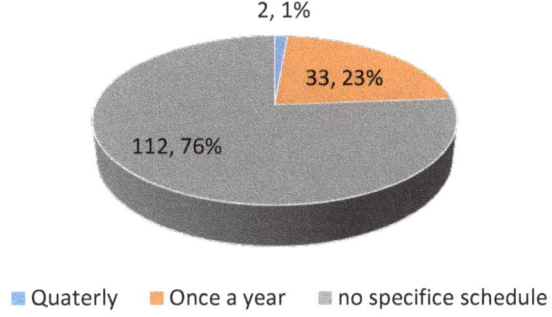

Fig. 1 Frequency of
training of employees on
IS and digital services

How often do your organisation train employees
in IS and advanced technology?

Fig. 2 Adequacy of
training on IS and digital
services to improve
employee performance

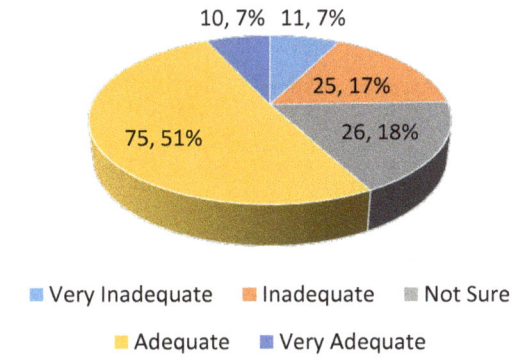

Fig. 2 Adequacy of
training on IS and digital
services to improve
employee performance

Do you consider the current training you receive
in IS and tecnology to be adequate to improve
your performance?

Figure 1 solicited responses of the respondents on how often they are trained on information systems (IS) and advanced technology in their organization in this era of digitalization. The results showed that 112 respondents representing 76% indicated that there is no specific schedule for training in IS and advanced technology in their organization, 33 respondents representing 23% indicated that they receive training once a year on digital services, and 2 respondents representing 1% indicated quarterly.

Figure 2 sought the views of respondents as to whether they consider the current training they receive in IS and digital technology on human resources to be adequate to improve their performance. The results indicated that 10 respondents representing 7% revealed that the training they receive currently is very adequate, 75 respondents representing 51% revealed that the training is adequate, 25 respondents representing 17% were of the view that the training is inadequate, 11 respondents representing 7% indicated that the training is very inadequate and 26 respondents representing 18% were not sure.

From Fig. 3, respondents' views were sought on the relevance of digitization of HRM in Africa. The results showed that 125 respondents representing 85% of the total sampled size indicated that digitization of HRM is very relevant, while 11 respondents representing 8% indicated that digitization in HRM in Africa is relevant however, 3 respondents representing 2% indicated that it is not relevant, 2 respondents representing 1% indicated that digitization of HRM is not relevant at all, and 6 respondents representing 4% were not sure what to say.

Table 2 shows the frequencies and percentages of employee responses about digitization in their organizations. On the importance of digitization of HRM in today's competitive global world, all respondents 147 (100%) affirmed the answer. On whether respondents are aware of their organization's policy on digitization and ICT, the results indicated that 90 respondents representing 61.2% answered yes while 51 respondents representing 38.8% said no. Additionally, on whether respondents are aware of organizational policies on digitization of HRM in their respective organizations, 98 respondents representing 66.7% said yes and 49 respondents representing 33.3% said no. Furthermore, 34 respondents representing 23.1% said they have had some training in IS and technology related to their work while 113 respondents representing 76.9% said they have not had some training in IS and technology related to their work. With regard to respondents' opinion on whether they think digitizing the entire HR activities will improve their performance, 135 respondents representing 91.8% said yes, while 12 respondents representing 8.2% said no.

From Table 3, on the issues of HRM maximization through digitization, respondents were asked whether digitization of HRM will enhance their personal development, and the results indicated that 78.8% (12.9% + 65.3%) of the respondents agreed, 8.2% (1.4% + 6.8%) disagreed while 13.6% respondents remained neutral. Second, respondents were asked whether training and development in information systems (IS) programs and advanced digitization will help them network with other employees in and outside their organization and the results indicated that 72.2%

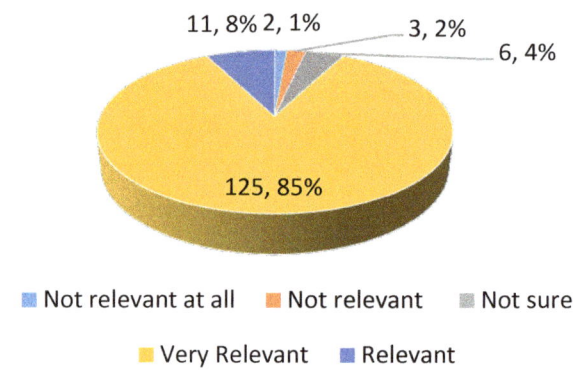

Fig. 3 Relevance of digitization of HRM in the African business environment

Table 2 Digitization of HRM in organization

Frequency/percentage responses ($N = 147$)		
Statements	Yes	No
Do you consider digitization of HRM important in today's competitive world?	147 (100)	–
Are you aware of your organization's policy on digitization and ICT?	90 (61.2)	57 (38.8)
Are you aware of your organization's policy on training and development in IS and technological application on work?	98 (66.7)	49 (33.3)
Have you had any form of training in IS and technological application of your work?	34 (23.1)	113 (76.9)
In your opinion, do you think digitizing the entire HR activities will improve your job performance?	135 (91.8)	12 (8.2)

Table 3 Maximizing HR development through digitization

	Frequency/percentage responses ($N = 147$)				
Statement	SA	A	N	D	SD
Digitization of HRM will enhance my personal development	96 (65.3)	19 (12.9)	20 (13.6)	2 (1.4)	10 (6.8)
Training and development in IS programs and advanced digitization will help me network with other employees in and outside my organization	91 (62)	15 (10.2)	29 (19.7)	4 (2.7)	8 (5.4)
Training and development in IS programs and advanced digitization will help me perform better in my job	107 (72.8)	30 (20.4)	3 (2.0)	2 (1.4)	5 (3.4)
Participating in training and development in IS programs will help me stay up to date on my new processes and procedures related to my job	84 (57.1)	24 (16.4)	32 (21.8)	4 (2.7)	3 (2.0)

Note: *SA strongly agree, A agree, N neutral, D disagree, SD strongly disagree*

(10.2% + 62%) agreed, 8.1% (2.7% + 5.4%) disagreed, and 19.7% remained neutral. Third, respondents were asked whether training and development in IS programs and advanced digitization will help employees perform their job better, and the results indicated that 93.2% (20.4% + 72.8%) agreed, 4.8% (1.4% + 3.4%) disagreed and 2% remained neutral. Fourth, respondents were asked whether participating in training and development in IS programs will help them stay up to date on their new processes and procedures related to their job, and the results indicated that 73.5% (16.4% + 57.1) agreed, 4.7% (2.7% + 2%) disagreed and 21.8% remained neutral.

Table 4 illustrates the various benefits digitized HRM would have on African business. Accordingly, majority of the participants 95.2% (81.6% + 13.6%) agreed that digitizing HRM would bring about innovation of business processes in the African business environment. Additionally, 78.2% (12.9% + 65.3%) agreed that digitization of HRM would bring about talent attraction, while 74% (10.2% + 62%) believe that digitization of HRM quickens technological speed and advancement of

Table 4 Benefits of digitization of HRM in African business

Statement	Frequency/percentage responses ($N = 147$)				
	SA	A	N	D	SD
Innovation of business processes	120 (81.6)	20 (13.6)	6 (4.0)	1 (0.7)	–
Talent enabler and attraction	19 (12.9)	96 (65.3)	20 (13.6)	2 (1.4)	10 (6.8)
Technological speed and advancement	15 (10.2)	91 (62)	29 (19.7)	4 (2.7)	8 (5.4)
Transparency and ease of workflow	30 (20.4)	107 (72.8)	3 (2.0)	2 (1.4)	5 (3.4)
Flexible work system and production	24 (16.4)	84 (57.1)	32 (21.8)	4 (2.7)	3 (2.0)

Note: *SA strongly agree, A agree, N neutral, D disagree, SD strongly disagree*

organizations. Furthermore, 93.2% (20.4% +72.8%) believe that digitizing HRM brings about transparency and ease of workflow in organizations. Also, 73.5% (16.4% + 57.1%) of the respondents agreed that digitized HRM enhances flexible work systems, thereby increasing employee productivity.

6 Discussion and Theoretical Implication

The astronomical growth in digital technology and its application in all spheres of business in today's global world cannot be overemphasized. Hence, in this chapter, we focused on Professor Bill Darley's statement (cited above) on the adoption of advanced technology on sub-Saharan African businesses in order to leapfrog their impact in the global business marketplace. Our reflection on his (Prof. Darley) assertion above is linked to our research question about digitization and the advancement of information technology in the sub-region. We are encouraged by his statement that advanced IT and digitization are the key to leapfrog African businesses to economic growth. Accordingly, through empirical research, this study has investigated digital human resource development within public and private organizations in Ghana. Analysis from the empirical results reveal the overwhelming support for digital HRM to maximize high-performance people management in the sub-Saharan Africa business environment. There are a number of theoretical contributions emanating from this study.

First, our results strongly confirmed the relevance of digitization of HRM in the African business environment and contributes to the technological adoption debate. The possibilities of digital HRM to speed up organizational decision-making and performance are not only growing but are also embracing a wider scope of activities and business functions in contemporary organizations. This is evident by our results of 96.8% of respondents who see the relevance of digital HRM as a link to employee performance and organizational productivity. Digitization of HRM implies high performance of employees to achieve and meet the objectives and targets set by an organization in a speedy manner. As the impact of digitization has become very visible globally, the implication of our work suggests that by integrating digitization and IS in HRM, there would indeed be an added value to people management and development in SSA organizations. This assertion is in consonance with Angrave et al. (2016) who argued that unless HR professionals embrace both the potential and drawbacks of digitization, it will be difficult for organizations to deliver transformational change.

Second, our work confirmed that HR development in SSA business environment can be maximized through digitization. Our findings demonstrate that digitization of HRM enhances personal development of staff and, therefore, maximizes the entire HR development of the organization. Besides, employee networking with each other is greater with digitization and facilitates work processes and procedures. This is better explained when staff undergo training in IS and advanced technologies within the organization. Accordingly, training employees in IS and digital services results in acquisition of high technological skills essential for organizational performance, since workers are able to develop capacity in information that can link both co-workers and customers, together with information processes, information storage, and information retrieval. Thus, when employees participate in IS and ICT training, they maximize their HR skills through the improved skills they acquired from the training. By this, both employees and the organization would benefit from the organized IS and ICT training. This finding validates the work of Corral and Rodríguez-Lluesma (2018) who confirmed that through digital or e-HRM, organizations become very efficient by simplifying routine tasks and by gaining a deeper understanding of their consumers.

Third, the results of this work provoke some essential benefits that would accrue to African business from digitization of HRM. Majority of respondents approved that digitized HRM would maximize innovation of business process and empower talent management and attraction in the Ghanaian organizations. The implication of this finding is that, by adopting IS and advanced technologies in HRM, business models of SSA organizations would change positively and radically as their HR departments adapt their skill sets to the digital world. This is possible through high data generation and storage that can help administrative systems of firms to optimize their information and communication systems.

Fourth, the findings in this chapter confirm the benefits of technological speed and advancement, and also, transparency and ease of workflow. The implication of this finding is that digitized HRM enables speed in the coordinating mechanisms of management. By this, HR departments are able to review and revise both management and employee actions quickly in response to grievances and normal communication between workers. This system also encourages transparency of actions and responsibilities of people. Besides, digitalization of organizational HR facilitates flexible work systems and ease of employee workflow. The use of telecommuting and tele networking emanate from digital and high information systems application, which can help employees to adapt to modern hustle.

Thus, there are certainly many and enormous benefits that would accrue to the African business environment by integrating technologies and digital capacity to human resource management and development. Undoubtedly, digitalization makes it easier to share information with employees to increase staff engagement levels in work organizations. Application of digital technology to HR development also enhances the participation of other physical and material resources within the organization, and thus facilitating some flexibility in terms of time and place, and trainee evaluation during staff training programs.

7 Conclusion

The aim of this chapter has been to contribute to the current calls for the use of technologies in human resource development to improve organizational efficiency. The work specifically anchors its drive on Professor William K. Darley's call to embrace digital technology on sub-Saharan African business to advance their business operations globally. Accordingly, digital HRM enables the prompt data analysis for people management that can predict a host of HR practices like turnover and forecasting of demand and supply of organizational HR.

In conclusion, this chapter has demonstrated a myriad of benefits that would help maximize human resource development in sub-Saharan Africa. Digital HRM otherwise known as e-HRM or human resource information system (HRIS) can speedily generate synergies and bring market knowledge among organizations and states within SSA. Additionally, e-HRM enables increase in brand awareness of both small and large firms, and thereby help them to achieve economies of scale. In spite these advantages there are few limitations that come along with digitalization. Among the major limitations of digitalization of HRM are: capital intensive requirements for organizations to be fully automated, potential clash of cultures as digitalization may intrude negatively into the African values systems, and lastly, the benefits of both partners need to be clearly demarcated and this can cause rift among businesses.

References

Abugre, J. B. (2014). Job satisfaction of public sector employees in sub-Saharan Africa: Testing the Minnesota satisfaction questionnaire in Ghana. *International Journal of Public Administration, 37*(10), 655–665.

Abugre, J. B., & Nasere, D. (2020). Do high-performance work systems mediate the relationship between HR practices and employee performance in multinational corporations (MNCs) in developing economies? *African Journal of Economic and Management Studies, 11*(4), 541–557.

Adewoye, J. O., & Olugbenga, O. B. (2018). Evaluation of the effects of E-HRM on customer deposits in selected deposit money banks in Nigeria. *Noble International Journal of Economics and Financial Research, 3*(9), 95–105.

Amant, K. (2016). Introduction to the special issue: Cultural considerations for communication design: Integrating ideas of culture, communication, and context into user experience design. *Communication Design Quarterly Review, 4*(1), 6–22.

Amarakoon, U., Weerawardena, J., & Verreynne, M. L. (2018). Learning capabilities, human resource management innovation and competitive advantage. *The International Journal of Human Resource Management, 29*(10), 1736–1766.

Angrave, D., Charlwood, A., Kirkpatrick, I., Lawrence, M., & Stuart, M. (2016). HR and analytics: Why HR is set to fail the big data challenge. *Human Resource Management Journal, 26*(1), 1–11.

Armstrong, M., & Taylor, S. (2014). *Armstrong's handbook of human resource management practice*. London: Kogan Page Publishers.

Bondarouk, T., & Ruël, H. (2013). The strategic value of e-HRM: Results from an exploratory study in a governmental organization. *The International Journal of Human Resource Management, 24*(2), 391–414.

Bos-Nehles, A., & Bondarouk, T. (2018, November). A Sociomateriality perspective of sustainable E-HRM implementation. In *7th e-HRM conference "Humanity of e-HRM" 2018: HRM 4.0 for human-centered organizations*.

Budhwar, P., & Debrah, Y. A. (2009). Future research on human resource management systems in Asia. *Asia Pacific Journal of Management, 26*(2), 197.

Chugh, R. (2014). Role of human resource information Systems in an Educational Organization. *Journal of Advanced Management Science, 2*(2), 149–153.

Corral, J. and Rodríguez-Lluesma, C (2018), Digitalization and people management, IESE Business School-University of Navarra, DPON-146-E.

Darley, W. K. (2003). Public policy challenges and implications of the internet and the emerging e-commerce for sub-Saharan Africa: A business perspective. *Information Technology for Development, 10*(1), 1–12.

David, F. R. (2011). *Strategic Management: Concept and cases* (12th ed.). Florence, SC: Francis Marion University Press.

Dery, K., Grant, D., & Wiblen, S. (2009, August). Human resource information systems (HRIS): Replacing or enhancing HRM. In *Proceedings of the 15th World Congress of the International Industrial Relations Association IIRA* (pp. 24–27).

Heikkilä, J. P., Rentto, O., & Feng, Y. (2017). Aiming for strategic e-HRM: Motives and consequences of e-HRM implementation in an MNC. *Electronic HRM in the Smart Era*, 173–199.

Holm, A. B., & Haahr, L. (2018). E-recruitment and selection. In *e-HRM* (pp. 172–195). London: Routledge.

Horwitz, F. M. (2012). Evolving human resource management in southern African multinational firms: Towards an afro-Asian nexus. *The International Journal of Human Resource Management, 23*(14), 2938–2958.

Jackson, T. (2002). Reframing human resource management in Africa: A cross-cultural perspective. *International Journal of Human Resource Management, 13*(7), 998–1018.

Kamoche, K. (2002). Introduction: Human resource management in Africa. *International Journal of Human Resource Management, 13*(7), 993–997.

Kamoche, K., Debrah, Y., Horwitz, F., & Muuka, G. N. (Eds.). (2003). *Managing human resources in Africa* (Vol. 2). London: Routledge.

Khera, S. N., & Gulati, K. (2012). Human resource information system and its impact on human resource planning: A perceptual analysis of information technology companies. *IOSR Journal of Business and Management, 3*(6), 6–13.

Kim, D. G., & Choi, S. O. (2018). Impact of construction IT technology convergence innovation on business performance. *Sustainability, 10*(11), 3972.

Kupper, D. M., Klein, K., & Volckner, F. (2019). Gamifying employer branding: An integrating framework and research propositions for a new HRM approach in the digitized economy. *Human Resource Management Review, 31*, 100686.

L'Ecuyer, F., & Raymond, L. (2017). Aligning the e-HRM and strategic HRM capabilities of manufacturing SMEs: A "gestalts" perspective. In *Electronic HRM in the Smart Era (The Changing Context of Managing People, Volume)* (pp. 137–172).

Lepak, D., & Snell, S. A. (1998). Virtual HR: Strategic human resource management in the 21st century. *Human Resource Management Review, 8*(3), 215–234.

Liboni, L. B., Cezarino, L. O., Jabbour, C. J. C., Oliveira, B. G., & Stefanelli, N. O. (2019). Smart industry and the pathways to HRM 4.0: Implications for SCM. *Supply Chain Management: An International Journal, 24*(1), 124–146.

Lippert, S. K., & Michael Swiercz, P. (2005). Human resource information systems (HRIS) and technology trust. *Journal of Information Science, 31*(5), 340–353.

Mbuyisa, B., & Leonard, A. (2015). ICT adoption in SMEs for the alleviation of poverty. In *International Association for Management of Technology, IAMOT 2015 Conference Proceedings*.

McDonald, K., Fisher, S., & Connelly, C. E. (2017). E-HRM systems in support of "smart" workforce management: An exploratory case study of system success. In *Electronic HRM in the smart era* (pp. 87–108).

Meijerink, J., & Habraken, M. (2018). Human resource management and value creation in the digitized economy: Toward a taxonomy and conceptual framework. *Academy of Management Global Proceedings, 2018*, 2.

Meijerink, J., Boons, M., Keegan, A., & Marler, J. (2018). Special issue of the international journal of human resource management: Digitization and the transformation of human resource management. *The International Journal of Human Resource Management*, 1–6.

Nagendra, A., & Deshpande, M. (2014). Human resource information systems (HRIS) in HR planning and development in mid to large sized organizations. *Procedia-Social and Behavioral Sciences, 133*, 61–67.

Pagani, M., & Pardo, C. (2017). The impact of digital technology on relationships in a business network. *Industrial Marketing Management, 67*, 185–192.

Poisat, P., & Mey, M. R. (2017). Electronic human resource management: Enhancing or entrancing? *SA Journal of Human Resource Management, 15*(1), 1–9.

Rahman, M., Mordi, C., & Nwagbara, U. (2018). Factors influencing E-HRM implementation in government organisations. *Journal of Enterprise Information Management, 31*(2), 247–275.

Şahin, H., & Topal, B. (2018). Impact of information technology on business performance: Integrated structural equation modeling and artificial neural network approach. *Scientia Iranica, 25*(3), 1272–1280.

Shahibi, M. S., Saidin, A., & Izhar, T. A. T. (2016). A framework based on human resource management information system (HRMIS) for the evaluation of users satisfaction. *International Journal of Academic Research in Business and Social Sciences, 6*(10), 62–76.

Shiferaw, B., Kebede, T., Kassie, M., & Fisher, M. (2015). Market imperfections, access to information and technology adoption in Uganda: Challenges of overcoming multiple constraints. *Agricultural Economics, 46*(4), 475–488.

Sparrow, P., Hird, M., & Cooper, C. (2015). *Do We need HR? Repositioning people Management for Success*. Basingstoke: Palgrave Macmillan.

Strohmeier, S. (2007). Research in e-HRM: Review and implications. *Human Resource Management Review, 17*, 19–37.

Sugata, D., & Bhattacharjee, A. (2019). Uses and applications of computerized human resource information system (HRIS) in the central universities of north-East India. *Journal of the Gujarat Research Society, 21*(11), 517–526.

Toshani, I., Jerram, C., & Hill, S. (2011). Exploring the public sector adoption of HRIS. *Industrial Management & Data Systems, 111*(3), 470–488.

van Kruining, I. (2017). The disappearance of HRM: Impact of digitization on the HRM profession. *Electronic HRM in the Smart Era, 311*.

Ziebell, R. C., Albors-Garrigos, J., Schoeneberg, K. P., & Marin, M. R. P. (2019). Adoption and success of e-HRM in a cloud computing environment: A field study. *International Journal of Cloud Applications and Computing (IJCAC), 9*(2), 1–27.

Digitizing Recruitment and Selection of Employees in Ghana: A Social Media Network Perspective

James Baba Abugre and Rhoda Boachie-Ansah

1 Introduction

In human resource management, recruitment and selection refer to the acquisition and procurement of the desired personnel to work in an organization. They involve the practice of generating a pool of competent people to apply for available jobs in an organization (Bratton and Gold 2003). Acquiring and procuring quality human capital for organizational use have long been regarded as a critical function for organizational survival (Breaugh 2013; Acikgoz 2019).

Recruitment and selection are two separate HR practices, but they are generally and mostly used together because they are closely linked and cannot separately be accomplished without the other. While recruitment can be described as the process of generating a pool of qualified applicants for organizational jobs, selection is the process of choosing individuals from this generated pool who have relevant qualifications to fill existing or projected job openings (Bohlander and Snell 2013). Therefore, the selection of job candidates is achieved when the recruitment process has also begun and closed or accomplished. The recruitment and selection processes would usually consist of job analysis or assessing the availability of job vacancies in the organization, which involve job description and individual specification. This assertion is affirmed by many scholars on recruitment and selection of employees (Foot and Hook 2011) who identified key stages of a systematic approach to recruitment as being job analysis, job description, person specification, and attracting applicants through the various methods of recruitment.

The successful recruitment and selection of personnel for organizational work continue to be a crucial aspect of organizational performance (Breaugh 2013).

J. B. Abugre (✉) · R. Boachie-Ansah
University of Ghana Business School, Accra, Ghana
e-mail: jbabugre@ug.edu.gh

© The Author(s), under exclusive license to Springer Nature Switzerland AG 2021   43
J. B. Abugre et al. (eds.), *Business in Africa in the Era of Digital Technology*,
Advances in Theory and Practice of Emerging Markets,
https://doi.org/10.1007/978-3-030-70538-1_4

Consequently, management's aspiration for organizational success and survival has created a constant lookout for the best method of obtaining quality human resources among companies (Dutta 2014); and this motivation of finding and adopting new avenues to attract and recruit quality human resources has extended the traditional method of recruitment, and selection of candidates via digital and technological means to embrace online recruitment methods (Melanthiou et al. 2015; Jobvite 2016).

Therefore, online recruitment also known as e-recruitment or digital recruitment and selection process has become a recognized and a competitive organizational practice for procuring organizational human capital. Thus, organizations are currently making use of their corporate websites, online job boards, and lately social network websites for recruiting and selecting employees in addition to the traditional methods of recruitment (Doherty 2010; Acikgoz and Bergman 2016).

Social networking websites (known also as social networking sites), a recently adopted online recruitment tool, are among the most prevalent social media applications and platforms on the internet today (Nikolaou 2014). The popularity of social media is attributed to the internet revolution occurrence in the 1990s which has led to the rise of an actively connected world of people in present-day (Aguado et al. 2016). According to Boyd and Ellison (2008), social networking websites or social media are internet-based services that enable its users to create either a public or semi-public personal profile, build a connection and share information within one's connection on the social network. Social media websites also enable its users to create and share user-generated information with other users on the network (Kaplan and Haenlein 2010). Thus, with the rise and ever-increasing usage of social networking websites, people are able to share information about themselves, about businesses, and about companies over the internet at a speedy rate and reaching a larger audience. Employers, as well as HR managers, are therefore seizing the opportunities that are derived from the worldwide usage of social network sites to find, attract, and hire qualified and skillful candidates (Doherty 2010; Nikolaou 2014). There is therefore no better time in this era of increasing technological transformation, where global businesses are making use of social media platforms to create unique methods for human resource engagement, than for African businesses to effectively implement the digitalization of their human capital procurement through social networking sites.

The wave of change in HR management and development relatively to technological advancement should assist HR managers in performing their responsibilities in the recruitment and selection of candidates in organizations. Accordingly, the ManpowerGroup (Firm) (2013) argues that the most common strategies that organizations use to survive in this competitive business world are retention initiatives and improvement of recruitment and selection practices (ManpowerGroup (Firm) 2013). Consequently, HRM-focused technologies and digital assistants are being deployed across MNCs' subsidiaries to enhance recruitment and selection practices with a clear focus on outcomes and return on investment of these digital assets. Thus, improvement in digitalization of recruitment and selection practices has become a blazing issue and a way for companies or organizations to enhance their outcomes (Hunt 2014).

Despite all these positive outcomes generated through digitalization of recruitment and selection practices of firms, many sub-Saharan African companies are still hesitant to adopt to this relatively new practice of digitalized recruitment (Rahman et al. 2018). Moreover, with the current upsurge of digitization, and growth in social media, specifically the social networking websites, sub-Saharan African businesses have not leveraged on these strategic digital tools (LinkedIn, Facebook, Twitter, etc.) to identify, attract, and recruit both active and passive potential candidates (Caers and Castelyns 2011; Doherty 2010; Hunt 2014; Nikolaou 2014; Daniel 2018). Hence, the objective of this chapter is to investigate social media websites as source of recruitment for African businesses. The chapter further attempts to identify the usage and application of social networking websites in recruitment and selection of workforce in Ghanaian corporations. Additionally, the chapter looks at how and when social networking websites are employed in the recruitment process and the advantages of online recruitment and selection of employees for African business.

The chapter proceeds as follows. First is an overview of the theoretical explanation of social media networking in the digital era. Next, we discuss digital recruitment and selection of employees in sub-Saharan Africa and then the challenges of social networking and recruitment in Africa. We then present the methodological approach to data gathering for this study. Subsequently, the analysis and results of the chapter is presented. The chapter then discusses the results and presents some theoretical contributions with a conclusion.

2   Social Media in the Digital Era

Social media have become an integral part of the twenty-first century's workplace. These new media are highly interactive platforms that use mobile and web-based technologies (Kietzmann et al. 2011) and offer the possibility of reaching and involving large audiences (El Ouirdi et al. 2015).

It is not surprising therefore that, for close to a decade now, social media networking sites have been used as a persuasive communication window in the form of advertising for job openings, background window, and source of information about job applicants to avoid negligent hiring issues (Melanthiou et al. 2015). For instance, in many developed and developing countries, online social network sites such as Twitter, Facebook, and LinkedIn are employed by multinational companies not only to advertise their corporate culture and vision but also search for and attract qualified candidates to fill job vacancies (Mwasha 2013; Uzair et al. 2017; Masa'd 2015; Melanthiou et al. 2015). Similarly, in Ghana, MTN Ghana—a multinational telecommunication corporation—has a page on LinkedIn where advertisements are made about vacant positions (https://www.linkedin.com/company/mtn-ghana/). Also, there are many other multinational companies that post advertisements about job openings on LinkedIn to attract qualified candidates for vacant positions in their subsidiaries (http://www.linkedin.com/jobs). Hence, the wave of social media is blowing across global HR where organizations are taking advantage of the digitalization to improve their management practices.

Although the initial purpose and use of social networking websites as an e-recruitment channel was restricted to recruitment (to attraction qualified job applicants) as an HR practice, the current prevalent usage of social networking sites by HR managers and practitioners has become more of a strategy in which important assessments and inferences of users are relied on to make decision (Caers and Castelyns 2011; Aguado et al. 2016). Thus, the utilization of these online networking sites can support HR professionals to make assessments or inferences during employment selection process, through candidates' existing information on online social networks in order to arrive at a hiring decision (Brown and Vaughn 2011). Although some social network websites such as Facebook protect the display of personal data of its users as default from non-connected users, the profile pictures of users are often displayed (Boyd and Ellison 2008), and this gives a background information about the person. Profile pictures are more easy-to-read and offer additional signals of an individual's personality than the typical passport pictures attached to curriculum vitae (Kluemper and Rosen 2009). Thus, all information shared by users on these websites can be accessible to corporate bodies as source of information to rely on in making decision on employment issues (Caers and Castelyns 2011).

3 Digitization of Personnel Recruitment in Sub-Saharan Africa

According to Adeola and Adebiyi (2016), recruitment in sub-Saharan Africa is gradually moving away from the traditional form of recruitment to a modern and digitized form called e-recruitment. The traditional form of recruitment in which many organizations in Africa are still engaged as means of staffing their businesses involves, the advertisement of jobs to identify qualified applicants who are persuaded to apply through the advertised job positions in newspapers. In this form, applications are received and screened to determine shortlisted candidates (who are contacted and informed about the results through posting of letters) for the next step which is interviews. Other researchers (Zottoli and Wanous 2000; Breaugh 2008) have also described this traditional method of recruitment as procedures conducted using only methods and sources such as advertisements (on televisions, radio, and billboards), referrals from friends/relatives/employees, internal job posting, employment agencies, job fairs, campus visits, and walk-ins. However, these methods of recruitment have now been regarded as insufficient in attracting and acquiring talented employees because its focus seems to be on a narrow and small active pool of job seekers which may not provide businesses access to the highly desired talents in a global pool of job seekers (Dutta 2014). Accordingly, the traditional method of recruitment is gradually given way to a more sophisticated form of recruitment

(Kapp et al. 2013). They indicated that the use of technology in personnel recruitment is gaining importance, and many organizations are fast adopting this new trend of technological application of recruitment.

Technological application of recruitment encompasses the use of internet resources to fish for personnel to accomplish the human resource needs of the organization. Hence, the use of technology for recruitment of personnel has been termed by scholars as e-recruitment (Hada and Gairola 2015). E-recruitment has been defined by Kumar and Priyanka (2014) as "the process of using internet to identify and attract potential employees to the organisation." According to Curtis (2014), the internet has drastically changed the face of recruitment and has been considered as one of the important recruitment resources to the business world. Nonetheless, Pavon and Brown (2010) are of the view that even though digitization of personnel recruitment has been adopted by many organizations in developed countries for long, the new phenomenon is now emerging in sub-Saharan Africa. As the digitized form of recruitment is gaining grounds globally, many organizations in SSA are seeing the impact of digitized or e-recruitment on business performance (Daniel 2018). This assertion was earlier argued by Sanusi and Martadha (2011) who indicated that organizations in Africa must embrace digitization of recruitment because it can help solve the numerous challenges associated with the traditional recruitment approach. For instance, they revealed that recruitment of job candidates in most organizations in Africa is characterized by delays due to the slow nature of the process. They further claimed that these delays and bottlenecks of traditional recruitment process have the tendency to create vacuums in certain portfolios for longer period which could negatively affect the smooth operations of organization in Africa. For Pavon and Brown (2010), the use of internet can help solve most of the recruitment challenges like delays and other bottlenecks of recruitment in Africa, and this can go a long way to enhance the human capital procurement of organizations. Consequently, Madera (2012) revealed that online recruitment allows for swift information exchange between recruiters and potential employees, and it reduces cost of communication incurred by employers during the recruitment process. In support of this assertion, Mwasha (2013) argues that adopting online recruitment of personnel could benefit organizations in Africa in diverse ways. For instance, digitizing recruitment could help companies in Africa to reach out for many job candidates as possible. This can give African businesses the ability to widen their scope and range for many candidates, and the opportunity to attract more qualified candidate with the requisite knowledge, skills and abilities needed for the businesses. In a study conducted on public sector reforms and e-recruitment, Nigeria, Sanusi and Martadha (2011) argued that for public sector to function effectively in Africa, there is the need for governments to adopt online recruitment to ensure high performance. They concluded that digitization of the recruitment process could do away with the numerous inconveniences that characterized the traditional recruitment system. Accordingly, Mwasha (2013) emphasized that, the fact that African countries are lagging behind in development, there is the need to digitize recruitment in organizations, especially, in the public sector in order to capture a wide range of good skills for African businesses. The reason is that recruitment is pivotal to every organization and countries can make economic progress only when their organizations both private and public function effectively. However, in most African countries, HR processes including organizational recruitment policies are not considered important part of the business strategy development and implementation because of the lack of importance attached to human capital as strategic partner. This notion has impeded the mechanisms of HR digitalization to enable African businesses embrace the gains associated with digitalization across organizations.

4   Challenges of Social Networking and Recruitment Process in Africa

According to Kapp et al. (2013), many challenges are involved in using social networking websites for recruitment of personnel in organizations. A major challenge identified in literature is the lack of internet infrastructure to support the online recruitment activities. For instance, Daniel (2018) conducted a study on e-recruitment and its effect on organizational creativity and innovation in Nigeria. He found out that, it was very difficult to achieve success with online recruitment in most developing countries due to poor internet connection in most parts of these countries. Earlier investigation by Mwasha (2013) indicated that, unreliable internet coupled with low-speed internet services in most developing countries pose a big challenge to the use of social networking websites for recruitment. Thus, the phenomenon of low internet speed, and absence of internet in most parts of Africa has the tendency to deny qualified applicants with high knowledge and competencies. Accordingly, Jonathan et al. (2019) suggest that for developing countries to also enjoy the benefits of social networking recruitment, there is the need for governments of these countries to develop the ICT infrastructure as well as internet facilities to facilitate online recruitment activities. However, some researchers have argued that the building and provision of enhanced ICT infrastructure in Africa alone may not solve the numerous problems associated with digitization in Africa. For example, Mwasha (2013) contended that high rate of illiteracy in ICT education hinder the use of social networking platforms in most parts of Africa. Additionally, he argued that most students in Africa complete school with no basic knowledge in ICT and therefore engaging in online interaction with such individuals is difficult even if the online services are available. This is supported by Alabi et al. (2015) who indicated that low level of ICT knowledge in most parts of developing countries do not support online recruitment system, and thus renders the e-recruitment opportunities inactive. According to them, most people may need support of others with knowledge in ICT to guide them through the process which may create a lot of inconvenience. Hence, they recommend that developing countries should first make ICT education a priority, so that students who complete their education will be equipped with basic knowledge in information technology. Additionally, high poverty level in most part of the world has been identified as one of the major challenges to social networking recruitment. For instance, Fosu (2017) in his research on inequality and poverty reduction in developing countries indicated that most people in developing countries live below $1 per day. This implies that poverty levels are so high that acquiring ICT facilities and gadgets to access internet and information by some people will be very difficult. Owing to high poverty levels and the associated inability of people to acquire for themselves computers and smart phones, recruiters will find it difficult to adopt social networking recruitment. In relation to the high poverty levels in the sub-region, Mwasha (2013) argued that high operating cost of internet is also a challenge to online recruitment. He explained that most of the telecommunication companies in Africa are operating between 3G and 4G which require reliable internet bundle which is quite expensive for many people below the bottom line. In this regard, the predisposition that many people cannot afford credit for internet bundle is high which could consequently hinder social networking recruitment.

In addition to the high poverty and low-income levels of people, Jonathan et al. (2019) identified lack of consistent power supply in most developing countries as a challenge to online recruitment activities. They further explained that, in most parts of developing countries, power supply is not reliable, and this implies that those living in these areas may find it difficult to use their ICT gadgets and facilities even if these facilities and gadgets are available. Therefore, adopting online recruitment could deny qualified candidates which could consequently affect the human capital intensity of organizations. In spite of these challenges mentioned above, the significance of adoption and usage of social networking websites for recruitment and selection purposes is needful.

5   Methodological Approach to Data Gathering

This study gathered empirical data from interviews of human resource managers in some multinational corporations (MNCs) in Ghana. By this, we employed the qualitative methodology research design which makes use of interviews to collect information from the target participants. Interviews are considered most appropriate for this study to unearth the lived experiences of HR managers who are in-charge of recruitment and selection practices in the organization. The interviewers' behavioral, emotional, and social meanings attributed to their experiences in HR policies, and recruitment and selection of workforce in their respective institutions were considered very significant to this study. Accordingly, information with respect to the points of views on the extent to which social networking websites are used for recruitment and selection of employees is appropriate as data gathering source. Hence, the use of semi-structured interviews on HR managers of MNCs in Ghana.

6 Sampling Design

To focus on the right sample for this study, we contacted only HR Managers who are directly involved in the recruitment and selection of employees in the various companies as the sample for this research. This sample was appropriate because these HR managers are responsible for all recruitment processes and procedures in the various companies. Therefore, they suitably assisted the researchers in understanding the processes and dynamics involved in the identification and attraction of candidates to a vacant position, how they conduct background checks, screening of candidates as well as assessing person- job fit through the utilization of social networking websites. In all, twenty (20) Multi-national corporations were selected as the sample size from which twenty (20) HR managers of these selected MNCs were interviewed. MNCs are noted to speedily adopt new technologies in their operations due to their large size and large capital base; and hence, they spread or introduce their practices to their subsidiaries globally. Additionally, due to the interconnected of businesses arising from globalization, MNCs have increasingly become influential actors in people management in the subsidiaries. Hence, the choice of HR managers of selected MNCs were interviewed. All respondents from each multinational company had their identity coded with the initial "MNC" and assigned numbers as

Table 1 Characteristics of respondents

Respondent's code	Respondent's gender	Multinational sector
MNC 1	Male	Manufacturing
MNC 2	Female	Oil and gas
MNC 3	Female	Financial
MNC 4	Male	Financial
MNC 5	Male	Engineering
MNC 6	Male	Manufacturing
MNC 7	Male	Manufacturing
MNC 8	Female	Aviation
MNC 9	Male	ICT
MNC 10	Female	Manufacturing
MNC 11	Male	Management consultancy
MNC 12	Male	Telecommunication
MNC 13	Female	ICT
MNC 14	Male	Non-profit/humanitarian
MNC 15	Male	Manufacturing
MNC 16	Male	ICT
MNC 17	Male	Hospitality
MNC 18	Male	Education
MNC 19	Female	Telecommunication
MNC 20	Male	Telecommunication

Source: Authors' construct

presented in Table 1. This coding was to offer anonymity to both companies and participants in the research process.

7 Method of Analyzing the Interview Data

We analyzed the interview data using content analysis. Content analysis attempts to identify the quantitative patterns and meanings that are commonly associated with the topic and research theme through transcription of the raw data. By this, we first coded the data generated from the transcribed interviews, and then transformed these coded data into written text. The codes were developed inductively from the empirical data themselves to form categories or main thematic groupings presented in Table 2.

8 Results and Discussions of Findings

8.1 Usage and Application of Social Networking Websites in Staffing Organizational Manpower

The interview results realized a greater extent of social networking usage as source of manpower recruitment for organizations. Most of the interviewees accepted that social network has become the order of the day, and therefore, most institutions have seized the opportunity to use it as a window for procuring institutional manpower since the youth of today rely very much on all sorts of social media. Managers therefore see social networking websites as a social basket where young and talented people can be observed and sampled for organizational usage. From the results, we gathered the different types of social media that our sampled institutions use as a base for their search and recruitment of staff. Among the different types of social networking websites employed by the institutions include LinkedIn, Facebook, WhatsApp, Twitter, Instagram, Weibo, WeChat, Xing, Google +, YouTube, Skype, Stack Overflow, GitHub, Yama, Wat and Evo. These websites are presented in Fig. 1.

Table 2 Themes emerged from the study

Themes/categories	
1.	Usage and application of social networking websites in staffing organizations
2.	Institutional approach to social media usage
3.	Advantages of social media networking websites as online recruitment and selection practice for staffing organizational HR
4.	Challenges of using social networking websites in recruitment of candidates

Source: Authors' construct

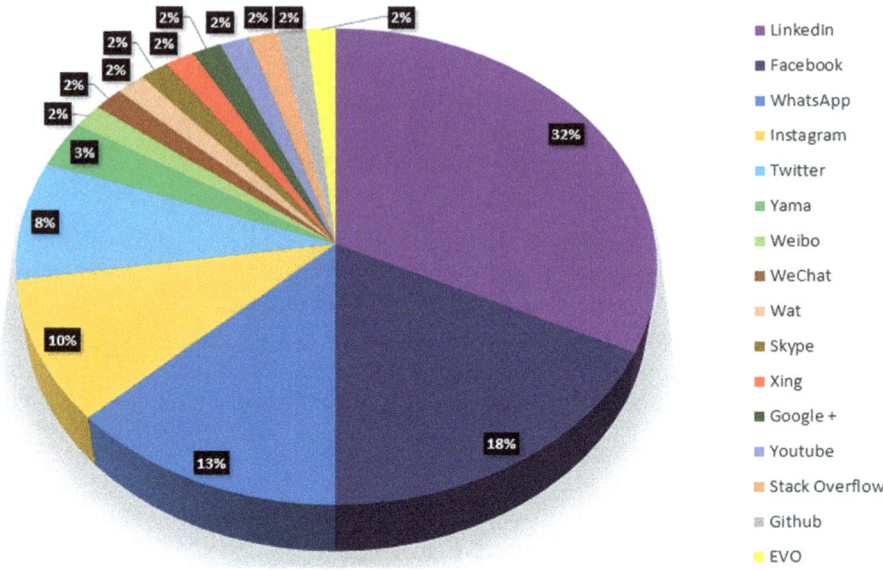

Fig. 1 Pie chart of types of social networking websites used in recruitment and selection of employees

From the lived experiences of all respondents, it is evident that multinational companies are adopting social networking websites as a recruitment tool to identify and attract the needed human resources. Thus, human resource managers are constantly devising recruitment strategies through the utilization of widely used and available technology to hire talents.

8.2 Institutional Approach to Social Media Usage

As part of our investigation of the use of social media networking as HRM practice, we solicited views of various HR managers who participated in the interview on the approaches and ways in which their various organizations or institutions incorporate social media as an HR practice. Most of the participants revealed that the social network media were used whenever recruitment and selection activities had been initiated by the organization. This means, when organizations are desirous of procuring human skills to aid in organizational activities, they resort to their social media websites to see which young people are trending with their skills. The assertion below was highlighted by one of the interviewees:

> Social networking websites are used by our company as at when there is a need to recruit people, but there are some roles that we keep recruiting for every day, for example, customer service agents. This category of people keep leaving because they are hired as

contract staff. So, they mostly leave without notice, but the job advertisement must be running. (MNC 20)

In addition to this, we discovered from the results that the frequent use of social networking websites in recruitment and selection of employees by some multinational companies are influenced by the company's policy on recruitment. Accordingly, any vacant positions that is to be sourced externally must be advertised on the social networking websites of the company. This is supported by a remark from an interviewee:

From entry roles to mid-senior roles, we advertise on LinkedIn. There is a policy to that effect; if we don't put it on LinkedIn, we don't recruit. Unless we want to keep it internal, if not, it must be put on LinkedIn. (MNC, 15)

Hence, organizations or institutions would use social media as at when and how they (corporations) believe the social media websites would aide their course of operations. Institutions are also looking at the direction of competition and playing accordingly. If social media has become a choice for many organizations and people to communicate their views, then that becomes an approach to leverage the benefits of recruitment and selection of personnel.

8.2.1   Social Media Websites Used as Assessment and Screening Tools for Recruitment

From the analysis of the interviews collected, most of the interviewees reported that they use their social media website to search for information about potential candidates. The social media websites enable them to gain some insights about the potential candidates in ways that the traditional modes of selection methods do not afford them such opportunity. The information gathered on the candidates forms part of the screening process during the selection stage, and this assists them to shortlist qualified candidates they prefer for further assessments. Thus, the information obtained from these websites serve as background checks of the candidates without their prior knowledge. In using these sites as source of background information, some of the interviewees agreed that they also use Google as a gateway to candidates' social networking website profiles to obtain the needed information. Hence, personal social websites of candidates serve as background checks and assessment of candidates for recruitment processes. To buttress this assertion, a respondent remarked that:

Social networking websites are used for some background checks because information on social networking websites gives an independent opinion about who the candidate is. This is because no one is under any form of duress to post information about himself on Facebook. People voluntarily post things on social networking websites about themselves, and we as searchers rely on this information as background of potential candidates. (MNC, 18)

Narratives of the interviewees also indicated that information obtained from social media about candidates was used to form impressions about the candidates' thought patterns, opinions about issues, likes and dislikes, hobbies, and character. Hence, information gathered during the search does influence the employment decision made about the candidate. The words of this respondent below clearly exemplify this:

> In our line of business, what an employee does affects the brand. So, we take a critical look at what potential candidates post on their sites. When we analyse their posts and these are deemed offensive, and which may affect our brand operations, then we reject that candidate. (MNC, 12)

From the above discussion, information obtained from social networking websites about potential candidates are used to form either negative or positive impression which can influence the hiring decisions about the candidate based on the sensitive role of the jobholder, and the company's policy on recruitment of employees.

8.3   Advantages of Social Media Networking Websites as Online Recruitment and Selection Practice for Staffing Organizational Human Resource

All respondents explained that using social networking websites in the recruitment and selection of employees had enormous benefits. The benefits outlined by the interviewees are discussed in the following sub-themes:

8.3.1   Social Media Websites Draws on Large and Diverse Pool of Applicants

An Added benefit outlined by interviewees of this study is the attraction of a large and diverse pool of applicants for recruitment when they use or advertise their recruitment through social media. Narratives from respondents revealed that using social networking websites during recruitment and selection enabled human resource managers to reach a greater pool of interested persons faster than the traditional mainstream communication media. Participants claimed that as the internet has no geographical boundary, and the fact that many people are found to be more active on social networking websites than other communication media, job advertisement spreads faster on social networking websites platforms by attracting applicants from all over the world with diverse skills and nationality. This benefit is deemed very significant for companies that aim at diversifying their workforce. The following excerpts from respondents exemplify this benefit:

> The dimension and spread of social media cannot be contested. You get access to a wide range of people. They are easily accessible because most people are there morning, afternoon, evening. We are able to get to the kind of people we want especially for an organization

*like ours, where we have lots of millennials. Therefore, social networking websites are one of the best places to get the millennials apart from career fairs. (**MNC, 19**)*

*It enables us to create a large pool of young graduates. Thus, in the future, we may add twitter to our recruitment search. (**MNC, 3**)*

Likewise, the respondent from MNC 14 remarked that:

*Social media gives us access to a diverse pool of talents. Our Social networking websites have helped to improve upon our diversity policy in recruitment, both in terms of cultural background and nationality. (**MNC, 14**)*

8.3.2   Social Media Websites Decreases the Recruitment Time Process

One important advantage in the adoption of information technology is the speed that comes with its usage. All participants in the interview agreed that social networking website usage in recruitment and selection purposes reduces the amount of time it takes them to find candidates to fill a vacant position. Interviewees said there was an increase in speed of their recruitment processes, and they could easily identify and attract candidates faster with social networking websites. For some of the online networking sites such as WhatsApp, respondents shared job advertisements among employees and other individuals in order to disseminate the information faster and quicker. The quicker dissemination of information helped reduce the recruitment time and cost. The following excerpt from MNC 13 typify this:

*The time it takes to recruit for a role is now shorter with the use of social networking websites. Recruitment usually took about three months to complete but with the use of LinkedIn for example, it has helped reduced the recruitment time. LinkedIn usage assist us to easily identify top-notch candidates that could fill the role within a month. With this, I don't need to wait for applications to come in. All I need is to poach the person for the position. (**MNC, 13**)*

8.4   Challenges of Using Social Networking Websites in Recruitment of Candidates

From the results, interviewees contended that in spite of the many advantages of social media usage for recruitment and selection of organizational manpower, social media usage has some challenges especially in the context of sub-Saharan Africa. Interviewees identified the following challenges of recruitment of employees through social media which are discussed under the following sub-themes:

8.4.1 Challenges of Dishonesty and Inaccurate Presentation of Personal Information on Social Networking Websites

Some interviewees revealed that a lot of people do create fake or pseudo profiles on social networking websites and do provide deficient and inaccurate information. Hence, most information sought for from potential candidates do not initially reflect the true self of the candidate. False and inaccurate information of potential candidates drawn from social networking websites could lead to the hiring of wrong candidates if strong precautions are not taken by the search team. The following remarks by respondents explained this challenge:

> You may not get accurate information on social networking websites because people create pseudo names and fake profiles. Therefore, the filtering becomes expensive and you may not get the people you want. You then have to start the recruitment process all over again. **(MNC, 7)**

> Social networking websites use for job advertisement exposes the company to fraudulent activities. Because some fraudsters create a whole social networking website page and advertise the vacancy with the aim defrauding desperate and gullible job seekers, thereby extorting money from them. **(MNC, 3)**

Accordingly, inaccurate and dishonesty of persons have led to increase in internet fraud which affects recruitment and selection of job candidates. There is therefore a high amount of dishonesty and misinformation perpetuated by fraudsters who sometimes even impersonate very senior managers or even the company just to swindle unsuspecting job seekers. This challenge sometimes discourages potential candidates who may not respond to genuine job advertisement from companies with the view that everything from the internet is a scam.

8.4.2 Large T Social Media

Interviewees contented that job advertisements circulated through social media comes along with the challenges of overwhelming and uncontrollable applicants. There is a huge volume of applications that sometimes, it becomes a nuisance to the recruitment process or the recruitment team on how to sort out good applicants from bad applicants. Sometimes, applications continue to come even after the deadlines or submission have elapsed. In some instances, the challenge emanates from individuals who tend to delete the stated deadline for a job application before disseminating the job advertisement to others or displaying the advertisement on their personal pages or statuses. Therefore, making the circulation of such advertisements difficult to control since recruiters may not know how far such information might have reached, and whether the right information sent out may not have been tampered with. Thus, recruiters or the company may find it difficult to retract or pull back the information because those advertisements were shared by others but not from the companies. A participant illustrates this point in the following words:

For me, one major challenge of social media is that; once the advertisement is dissemi-
nated, it becomes difficult to retract. Once it is out there, it will continue to circulate.
Sometimes after a deadline, people are still sending applications. Social media travels too
far for comfort. **(MNC, 2)**

8.4.3   Challenges Posed by Restrictions and Policies of the Parent Company

Another major challenge identified from this study findings is organizational policy
or restrictions placed by companies on the use of social media for recruitment and
selection practices. Some of the interviewees stated that their companies had some
restrictions or guidelines about the usage and application of social media. As multinational companies, subsidiaries are limited by power to go all out and resort to the
application of social media in whatever form without permission from the parent
company or headquarters. Depending on the restrictions from headquarters or policies on recruitment practices, subsidiary units cannot on their own use some of these
social media websites to engage people on official communication. This poses a
great challenge on the autonomy of companies desiring the usage of social media
for recruitment and selection of applicants in organizations. The assertion below
illustrates this challenge by an interviewee:

We have realized that LinkedIn is a good avenue for recruitment but, we do not have a
corporate LinkedIn account. However, the Parent company has a LinkedIn account and
when we wanted to create one here, we were told we must obtain permission from the parent
company before. Until now, we rely on our contract workers' private LinkedIn to get us
people if we need some. **(MNC, 1)**

8.4.4   Challenges of Internet Accessibility to Potential Recruiters

Another major challenge to using digital or social media particularly in developing
countries is the difficulty of access to internet. Though the internet has become
worldwide tool to access information, most developing countries are still suffering
from active access to internet facilities. Most of the interviewees lamented over the
access of these digital space by potential recruiters. They argued that due to accessibility and high cost of internet, most potential adults may not be captured during
the search for employees due to lack of access to information. An interviewee from
MNC 1 demonstrated this in the words below:

Internet accessibility poses a challenge to social media recruitment. There was a time, the
internet connectivity became a problem to many companies, we don't know what actually
happened but, I think Vodafone as our internet source had some problems. Even companies
are having problems with their internet connectivity and operations, what about young
adults who are not working, yet we expect them to have these facilities to access informa-
tion. **(MNC, 1)**

9 Discussions of Findings

In this chapter, we examined recruitment and selection of employees in the digital era with focus on social media networking websites. This was achieved through a qualitative analysis of interviews of 20 HR personnel from 20 multinational companies (MNC) in Ghana. The first purpose of the study was to identify the use and application of social networking websites in recruitment and selection of Ghanaian corporations. The results indicated largely that many MNCs in Ghana are taking advantage of the new technology of social media networking to beef up their recruitment policies. By this, almost all MNCs sampled for this study use and apply social networking websites as a medium to recruit and select their workforce for organizational practice. The findings also showed that Ghanaian corporations use different and multiple types of social media for their recruitment and selection practices.

The second purpose of this study was to investigate how and when social networking websites are employed as recruitment and selection practice by Ghanaian corporations. The results from the study showed that Ghanaian corporations or MNCs display different approaches to the use and type of social media for recruitment and selection of their workforce. By this, MNCs rely on the prevailing environmental factors and market competition to resort to the type or kind of social media that can give them a leverage on their recruitment practices. Third, this study found that social media websites are used as assessment tools for screening potential employees during recruitment and selection. Also, the results of the study showed that there are both advantages and disadvantages of the use of social media and social networking websites as recruitment and selection practice. These advantages and disadvantages of social media usage are cataloged in the results section of this chapter.

10 Theoretical Implications

A number of theoretical contributions are emanating from this study. First, this study provides a basis for understanding the use and application of online and social media network for recruitment and selection practices and the implications for MNCs' HR managers and prospective employees in developing countries like Ghana.

Second, this study sheds light on a critical element of human resource management practice of attracting skilled people to fill existing or projected job openings in organizations. The study adopts the social media network perspective as new media in information technology. In doing so, our results contribute and extends the application of e-HRM and digitalization of people management by validating and highlighting the importance of incorporating scientific fields like information technology (new media) and HRM, and the need to integrate them to enhance the recruitment practices of corporations in developing countries. Consequently, the chapter makes a significant contribution to the global digital divide—where developing economies are encouraged to accelerate their institutional access to new information and communication technologies for people management.

Third, this chapter contributes to the growing body of literature on technological diffusion through the usage and application of social media networking websites by Ghanaian corporations. In doing so, the chapter validates the different social media types that are in use as HRM recruitment practice by MNCs in Ghana. Among the different social media networks used by Ghanaian corporations include LinkedIn, Facebook, WhatsApp, Twitter, Instagram, Weibo, WeChat, Xing, Google +, YouTube, Skype, Stack Overflow, GitHub, Yama, Wat, and Evo. The implication is that choosing the right kind of social media channel is critical to achieving efficient recruitment and selection goals as well as HRM goals of corporations.

11   Conclusion

This chapter discussed the use of social media networking websites for recruitment and selection of employees for MNCs' operations in Ghana, with its broader implications of digitalization of HRM including its benefits and challenges in developing economies. Social networking websites are recent phenomena adopted as online and digital recruitment tools. Social networking sites are among the most prevalent social media applications and platforms on the internet today, used by corporate bodies. Thus, this chapter advocates the importance of considering digitizing the procurement aspects of HRM practices (recruitment and selection of employees) through social media networking sites as significant sources of recruitment and selection of staff. A social media network perspective of recruitment and selection practice establishes the dynamics of multiple channels of dialog and platforms of communication between employers and prospective employees.

References

Acikgoz, Y. (2019). Employee recruitment and job search: Towards a multi-level integration. *Human Resource Management Review, 29*(1), 1–13.

Acikgoz, Y., & Bergman, S. M. (2016). Social media and employee recruitment: Chasing the runaway bandwagon. In *Social media in employee selection and recruitment* (pp. 175–195). Cham: Springer.

Adeola, M. M., & Adebiyi, S. O. (2016). Employee motivation, recruitment practices and banks performance in Nigeria. *International Journal of Entrepreneurial Knowledge, 4*(2), 70–94.

Aguado, D., Rico, R., Rubio, V. J., & Fernández, L. (2016). Applicant reactions to social network web use in personnel selection and assessment. *Revista de Psicología del Trabajo y de las Organizaciones, 32*(3), 183–190.

Alabi, E., Afolabi, M. A., & Adeyemo, S. A. (2015). Influence of E-recruitment on organizational performance in Nigeria. In *The Academic Conference of African Scholar Publications & Research International on Achieving Unprecedented Transformation in a fastmoving World: Agenda for Sub-Sahara Africa* (Vol. 3, no. 3).

Boyd, D. M., & Ellison, N. M. (2008). Social network sites: Definition, history and scholarship. *Journal of Computer-Mediated Communication, 13*(1), 210–230.

Bratton, J., & Gold, J. (2003). *Human resource management* (4th ed.). New York.

Breaugh, J. A. (2008). Employee recruitment: Current knowledge and important areas for future research. *Human Resource Management Review, 18*(3), 103–118.

Breaugh, J. A. (2013). Employee recruitment. *Annual Review of Psychology, 64*, 389–416.

Brown, V. R., & Vaughn, E. D. (2011). The writing on the (Facebook) wall: The use of social networking sites in hiring decisions. *Journal of Business and Psychology, 26*(2), 219–225.

Caers, R., & Castelyns, V. (2011). LinkedIn and Facebook in Belgium: The influences and biases of social network sites in recruitment and selection procedures. *Social Science Computer Review, 29*(4), 437–448.

Curtis, B. L. (2014). Social networking and online recruiting for HIV research: Ethical challenges. *Journal of Empirical Research on Human Research Ethics, 9*(1), 58–70.

Daniel, C. O. (2018). E-recruitment and its effects on organizational creativity and innovation in Nigerian manufacturing firms. *Nile Journal of Business and Economics, 4*(8), 3–12.

Doherty, R. (2010). Getting social with recruitment. *Strategic HR Review, 9*(6), 11–15.

Dutta, D. (2014). Tweet your tune — Social media, the new pied Piper in talent acquisition. *Vilkapa, 39*(3), 93–104.

El Ouirdi, A., El Ouirdi, M., Segers, J., & Henderickx, E. (2015). Employees' use of social media technologies: A methodological and thematic review. *Behaviour & Information Technology, 34*(5), 454–464.

Foot, M., & Hook, C. (2011). *Introducing human resources management* (6th ed.). Essex: Pearson Education.

Fosu, A. K. (2017). Growth, inequality, and poverty reduction in developing countries: Recent global evidence. *Research in Economics, 71*(2), 306–336.

Hada, B., & Gairola, S. (2015). Opportunities & challenges of E-recruitment. *Journal of Management Engineering and Information Technology, 2*(2), 1–4.

Hunt, S. T. (2014). *Common sense talent management: Using strategic human resources to improve company performance.* San Francisco, CA: Wiley.

Jobvite. (2016). Jobvite Recruiter Nation Report. 2016. Retrieved from https://www.jobvite.com/wp-content/uploads/2016/09/RecruiterNation2016.pdf

Jonathan, T., Peihua, F., Bah, T., Souleymanou, A., & Emmanuelle, N. Y. H. (2019). Eg hrm in Cameroon Africa. *Archives of Business Administration and Management, 2*, 132.

Kaplan, A. M., & Haenlein, M. (2010). Users of the world, unite! The challenges and opportunities of social media. *Business Horizons, 53*, 59–68.

Kapp, J. M., Peters, C., & Oliver, D. P. (2013). Research recruitment using Facebook advertising: Big potential, big challenges. *Journal of Cancer Education, 28*(1), 134–137.

Kietzmann, J. H., Hermkens, K., McCarthy, I. P., & Silvestre, B. S. (2011). Social media? Get serious! Understanding the functional building blocks of social media. *Business Horizons, 54*(3), 241–251.

Kluemper, D. H., & Rosen, P. A. (2009). Future employment selection methods: Evaluating social networking web sites. *Journal of Managerial Psychology, 24*(6), 567–580.

Kumar, M. A., & Priyanka, S. (2014). A study on adoption of E-recruitment using technology acceptance model (TAM) with reference to graduating students in universities in Bahrain. *International Journal of Advance Research in Computer Science and Management Studies, 2*(9), 377–383.

Madera, J. M. (2012). Using social networking websites as a selection tool: The role of selection process fairness and job pursuit intentions. *International Journal of Hospitality Management, 31*(4), 1276–1282.

ManpowerGroup (Firm). (2013). 2013 Talent Shortage Survey: Research Results. Retrieved December 20, 2020, from http://www.manpowergroup.com/wps/wcm/connect/587d2b45-c47a-4647-a7c1e7a74f68fb85/2013_Talent_Shortage_Survey_Results_US_high+res.pdf?MOD=AJPERES

Masa'd, F. M. (2015). Deployment of social Media in the Recruitment Process. *Journal of Knowledge Management, Economics and Information Technology, 1*, 1–24.

Melanthiou, Y., Pavlou, F., & Constantinou, E. (2015). The use of social network sites as an E-recruitment tool. *Journal of Transnational Management, 20*(1), 31–49.

Mwasha, N. (2013). An over-view of online recruitment: The case of public and private sectors in Tanzania. *European Journal of Business and Management, 5*(32).

Nikolaou, I. (2014). Social networking web sites in job search and employee recruitment. *International Journal of Selection and Assessment, 22*(2), 179–189.

Pavon, F., & Brown, I. (2010). Factors influencing the adoption of the world wide web for job-seeking in South Africa. *South African Journal of Information Management, 12*(1), 1–9.

Rahman, M., Mordi, C., & Nwagbara, U. (2018). Factors influencing E-HRM implementation in government organisations. *Journal of Enterprise Information Management, 31*(2), 247–275.

Sanusi, A., & Martadha, A. M. (2011). Public sector reforms and E-recruitment in Nigeria: Will good governance count. *European Journal of Social Sciences, 26*(4), 611–620.

Uzair, S., Kanwal, S., & Haleem, R. (2017). The use of social media in the recruitment process: A study on Karachi. *International Journal of Multidisciplinary and Current Research, 5*, 360–364.

Zottoli, M. A., & Wanous, J. P. (2000). Recruitment source research: Current status and future directions. *Human Resource Management Review, 10*, 353–382.

Gender and Rural Entrepreneurship in Digitizing Sub-Saharan Africa

Lettice Kinunda Rutashobya, Linley Chiwona-Karltun, Merezia Wilson, Mesia Ilomo, and Mohamed Semkunde

1 Introduction

Rural entrepreneurship is increasingly recognized as a major contributor to regional and rural development in most of sub-Saharan African (SSA) countries. Defined as entrepreneurial activities that warrant value addition to rural resources as well as other activities that focus mainly on using locally available resources (Korsgaard et al. 2015; McKeever et al. 2015), rural entrepreneurship contributes in changing the quality of life of the rural population, minimizing rural–urban migration, reduce unemployment and fight abject poverty (Lekhanya 2018). Needless to add, these entrepreneurial undertakings act as seedbeds for entrepreneurial talents (Makombe 2006), and in some instances, they promote the use of new technologies, which increase the entrepreneurial outputs (Gaddefors et al. 2019). These rural entrepreneurial activities, which are characterized mainly by informal and small-scale businesses emanating from agricultural and related businesses, have been the engine of economic growth and have contributed to uplifting the well-being of rural communities. This is because the nature of the context within which these entrepreneurial engagements happen creates an intimate relation between entrepreneurial activity and the place (Gaddefors and Anderson 2019; Korsgaard et al. 2015). As the mainstay of rural economy, agriculture provides the most important resource for rural entrepreneurship.

In SSA, the contribution of the agricultural sector to rural entrepreneurship is unquestionable. As a major occupation for rural households in these countries,

L. K. Rutashobya (✉) · M. Wilson · M. Ilomo · M. Semkunde
University of Dar es Salaam Business School, Dar es Salaam, Tanzania

L. Chiwona-Karltun
Swedish University of Agricultural Sciences, Uppsala, Sweden
e-mail: Linley.chiwona.karltun@slu.se

agriculture employs more than half of the total labor force (Nelson 2013). For example, in Burundi, Burkina Faso, and Madagascar, more than 80% of the labor force works in agriculture (Shimeles et al. 2018). In Tanzania, more than 70% of the total population lives in rural areas out of which, about 75% of the work force is engaged in agricultural activities (United Republic of Tanzania 2020). In most of the rural areas, the percentage of women engaged in agricultural activities goes up to 98% (Nelson 2013) as agriculture comprises a greater part of women's economic activity than men's.

While rural entrepreneurship seems promising as argued above, sustainability of these activities and their potential outcomes however are still hampered by many gender-specific constraints (Amine and Staub 2009; Langevang et al. 2018). Gender inequality, a major problem in most SSA countries (Spring and Rutashobya 2009), hinders both social and economic development. Such inequalities, which are particularly evident in the agricultural sector, which employs majority of rural women and men in these countries as observed above, have potential to stifle the benefits that rural entrepreneurship promise.

For many years, entrepreneurship literature has taken gender for granted. Ahl and Marlow (2012) call for the use of feminist perspective to analyze existing and future body of entrepreneurial research to illustrate how gender is performed within this field. The influence of gender on rural entrepreneurship stems from the fact that economic activities including entrepreneurship are embedded social processes highly influenced by the social, institutional, business, and spatial structures (Granovetter 1985; Langevang et al. 2018; Rutashobya et al. 2009; Welter 2011). Acting together, these factors determine the success or failure in entrepreneurial engagements.

In most rural areas of SSA, women are reported to be the most disadvantaged group when it comes to entrepreneurial engagements (Langevang et al. 2018; Quisumbing and Pandolfelli 2010; Rutashobya 2001). Among other factors, gendered socio-cultural-spatial factors such as mobility, infrastructural challenges embedded with rurality, stereotypes against women, and access to resources have been shown to hinder women's engagement into rural entrepreneurship (Kodithuwakku and Rosa 2002; Quisumbing et al. 2014). More importantly, the prevailing informal institutional and patriarchal relations in SSA legitimizes men's and women's roles to the disadvantage of women. Women bear triple roles—productive, reproductive, and community roles (Langevang et al. 2018; Rutashobya 1998), which limit their ability to engage in entrepreneurial activities (Akyoo and Lazaro 2007; Dolan 2001). As a result, women are mostly found to engage in agricultural primary production while their engagement in upgraded business-related activities is limited (Quisumbing et al. 2014; SOFA Team and Doss 2011).

Normative institutions characterizing many SSA countries appear to shape the unequal participation of women and men in economic activities and their subsequent outcomes, as well as implying unequal access to and control over resources (Langevang et al. 2018; Njeru and Njoka 2001). Such institutions also limit women mobility (both spatial and social mobility), which subsequently limits their access to distant input as well as output markets. The situation is even more challenging for poor rural women engaged in perishable products, with short value chains such as horticultural products.

Given the gendered constrains, it remains a fact that realization of the potential that rural entrepreneurship present in SSA requires an urgent transformation of the agricultural-based rural entrepreneurship. Emergent literature point to digitalization of rural entrepreneurial processes and adaptation of modern technologies as being among the key solutions to these challenges (FAO 2019; Lekhanya 2018; Ughetto et al. 2019). That is, digitalization has significant possibilities of minimizing these barriers (Bouwman et al. 2018; Lekhanya 2018; Schelenz and Schopp 2018; Siemens 2017). According to Lekhanya (2018), effective rural entrepreneurial engagements can only be achieved by digitalization of the process. Digitalization presents a huge potential to address the liabilities of remoteness and sparseness of population that characterize many rural areas in SSA. The potentials can unlock the social and spatial immobility facing rural women in particular, given their multiple roles in society. Promoting women's access to digital technology should enhance women's productivity and output in rural entrepreneurship (Lekhanya 2018: 42).

While academic research is starting to analyze the role that digital technologies play in entrepreneurial ecosystems (Brush et al. 2019), the gender dimensions of digitalization and rural entrepreneurship remain largely unexplored (Rajahonka and Villman 2019; Ughetto et al. 2019). Similar analysis focusing on rural entrepreneurship particularly in Sub-Saharan Africa is scanty. Significant research gap still exists in exploring how and to what extent digitalization enhances women's rural entrepreneurial activities as well as how it addresses the gendered constraints in entrepreneurial activities. Knowledge about gendered dimensions of digitalization especially for rural women entrepreneurs is inadequate to fully understand the dynamics at play. More specifically, knowledge concerning the benefits of digitalizing rural businesses, its contributions in enhancing rural women's entrepreneurial engagements and optimizing agricultural productivity remains mostly assumptive among professionals and policymakers. This chapter attempts to fill this knowledge gap. Understanding how digitalization addresses gender constraints facing rural women entrepreneurs and the extent to which it enhances their entrepreneurial activities is of key importance as it may be a key differentiator between successful and unsuccessful rural entrepreneurship. The new knowledge is also useful in shaping rural entrepreneurship policy and practices, which should contribute to sustainable rural development. Consequently, this chapter contributes to the entrepreneurship, gender, and digitalization literature. We extend our analysis to examine spatial and gender digital divide, which may retard the potential digitalization gains in rural entrepreneurship.

We achieve our objectives with the aid of two case studies of rural women entrepreneurs in the agricultural sector in Tanzania. The case studies help us to explore how digitalization enables women to minimize the gender constraints and succeed in their entrepreneurial engagements. We also use documentary evidence and own viewpoints. The viewpoint approach is used on the basis of the authors' awareness and understanding of the Sub-Saharan African countries' context, Tanzania in particular.

The rest of the chapter is organized as follows: The next section presents a brief literature on how digitalization addresses the gender constraints to enhance rural entrepreneurship, as well as the challenges of digital divide and their implications on gender and rural entrepreneurship. This is followed by a brief methodology section. Findings on digital divide, which potentially pose as constraint to what digitalization promise and on how digitalization enhances rural entrepreneurship (using two case studies) are presented next. Finally, the discussion of the findings, theoretical implications, future research as well as policy recommendations are outlined.

2 Role of Digitalization in Enhancing Entrepreneurial Activities and Addressing Gender Constraints

Emergent literature focusing on analyzing the role of digitalization in entrepreneurial processes and performance show conflicting results. A good number of scholars agree that the application of digital technologies in the context of entrepreneurship and small- and medium-sized enterprises has revolutionized organizations around the globe (Celuch et al. 2014; Ziyae et al. 2014). Ughetto et al. (2019), for example, argue that digitalization, particularly new mobile technologies and applications, is transforming the entrepreneurial field through expanding the possibilities for start-ups and potential entrepreneurs. New digital patterns have transformed the way people work and interact, and modified the way of doing business (Autio et al. 2018; Sussan and Acs 2017; Ughetto et al. 2019). Yet others have argued that access to digital technology does not automatically translate into access to opportunities arising from digitalization. According to Cigna (2018), the literature pointing to the benefits of digitalization assumes that digitalization addresses inequality. He calls this a simplistic assumption, pointing out further that the availability of digital technology cannot close the gender gap in skills and capital distribution. Unfortunately, this kind of argument has not received much attention in the digitalization literature and hence the need for further research. Even where attempts have been made, the results are mixed. On the one hand, some believe that digitalization can enhance gender equality and create more income opportunities for women. For instance, Manello et al. (2019) investigated on how digital networks can boost female entrepreneurial outcomes, focusing on the different technological dimensions of their business in the Italian context. They found that firms with female leaders are, on average, associated with lower levels of technical efficiency. However, the observed performance significantly increases when they participate in formal networking through digital platforms.

Yet other studies have painted a gloomy picture. For example, Oggero et al. (2019) explored on how digital channel improves the impact of financial education and in choosing entrepreneurship as an occupational choice. They looked at the context of Italian households to identify how financial literacy and digital skills are related with the prospect of being an entrepreneur, observing differences between men and women based on cultural and institutional factors. Their results showed that men have clear benefits of being more financially educated and gifted with digital skills than women by using the same factors. Subsequently, women found to be not leaned for being into business. They concluded that financial and digital knowledge do not act as gender equalizers particularly in entrepreneurship. Similarly, cyber-feminist researchers have argued that offline gender inequalities are reflected in the online environment. This is probably because of the digital divide, more so the gender digital divide, which we discuss in this chapter.

3   Digital Divide

Although digitalization appears promising, digital divide seems to interact with existing forms of inequality, especially inequality in access and use of digital technology. The new digital opportunities are not evenly distributed and accessed across the globe and kinds of people. There is thus a digital divide, a term introduced in mid-1990s, a gap between those who have access to ICT and the skills to use it and those who do not have ICT access and skills (Nour 2017; OECD 2001; Van Dijk 2002). Digital divide could be associated with several factors including availability and level of infrastructural investments, socioeconomic status, knowledge and skills, psychological factors and culture, institutional structure and type of government, and price, speed, content, and quality of service (Srinuan and Bohlin 2011). Subsequently several gaps in digitalization are found: There is a digital gap between countries (global divide), especially, developed versus developing countries, gap in access to digital technology between different group of society (social divide/gender divide), a gap between those who use or those not using digital technology (democratic), as well as spatial divide (rural-urban divide) (OECD 2001). While studies exploring digital divide at global level have proliferated, studies focusing on developing countries are limited (Srinuan and Bohlin 2011). Apart from exploring the contribution of digitalization to rural entrepreneurship and addressing gender constraints, this chapter also looks at digital divide in SSAs, a subregion known to have lower access to ICT and digital skills than the rest of the globe (Graham 2011).

4   Digitalization and the Digital Era in Africa

Over the past two decades, African countries like other countries around the globe have witnessed a huge wave of digitalization through globalized ICT (Schelenz and Schopp 2018; Siemens 2017; Songwe 2019). ICT has affected all forms of global development and gives Africa the opportunity to leapfrog over the gap of under development (Polikanov and Abramova 2003). On the other hand, there are also pessimist who argue that progress in ICT will further deepen the digital divide and leave some countries behind. Some arguments that have prevailed indicated that rural people in Africa were more concerned about food and their daily needs than connection to ICT (Mutula 2005). However, there are also realists who argue that any technology intended for the good of society inevitably gets adopted even in conditions of marginalization, because the technology is intended to serve society (Wilson et al. 2003). Although some regions of Africa remain relatively low in terms of connectivity as compared to other regions elsewhere, adoption in terms of use of ICT's, the number of users has grown exponentially compared to a baseline of "zero" (Polikanov and Abramova 2003). Many African countries are catching up in the global effort to build a digital planet (Schelenz and Schopp 2018). In 1996, only 11 countries had internet connectivity, and already by 2003, all 54 countries were connected to some degree. While the original concentrations of connectivity and internet users were associated with being rich males, English speaking and living in the cities, it did not take long before rural areas achieved connectivity although with some challenges (ibid). Rural Africa though challenged sets itself apart, with its shared access practices (the small number of telephones, TV, and radio sets prepared Africans to share the little that was available). For example, sharing helps to split costs among the large number of users, thus diminishing individual expenditures (Polikanov and Abramova 2003).

Development in Africa's ICT sector is largely attributed to the expansion of digital mobile services through telecom companies. The existence of multinational telecommunication companies such as South African-based MTN, French-owned Orange SA, and Indian Bharti Airtel remains the biggest providers of internet infrastructure in Africa with few government-run companies (Evans 2018; Schelenz and Schopp 2018). Availability of cheap mobile phones with fourth-generation internet connectivity has facilitated fast and effective increase in internet penetration in both rural and urban areas, hence promoting digital access (Evans 2018; Ndung'u 2018). The efforts to improve digital access are in many African countries and already have had an impact, with the cost of mobile internet in Africa dropping by 30% since 2015 (Kah 2020). One of the consequences of mobile revolution in SSA was the creation of "mobile money services" such as M-Pesa, Airtel money, eazy pesa, and tigo pesa. These services are part of the bottom-up therapy to the widespread lack of access to formal and informal banking and financial services particularly in rural areas. By the year 2018, the SSA region had approximately half of global mobile money accounts (Bahia and Suardi 2019).

Despite the above developments, it remains a fact that internet usage in most SSA is lower when compared to the rest of the world. For example, Fig. 1 indicates that five of six selected SSA countries have internet use below 20%, whereas usage of most developed countries is above 60%.[1] By 2016, only 10% of household in Africa had computers at home, which is far below the global average (at 47%). It is low in sub-Saharan Africa and much lower in rural areas of these countries.

---

[1] Statistics by International Telecommunication Union (ITU), available at https://www.itu.int/en/ITU-D/Statistics/Pages/stat/default.aspx

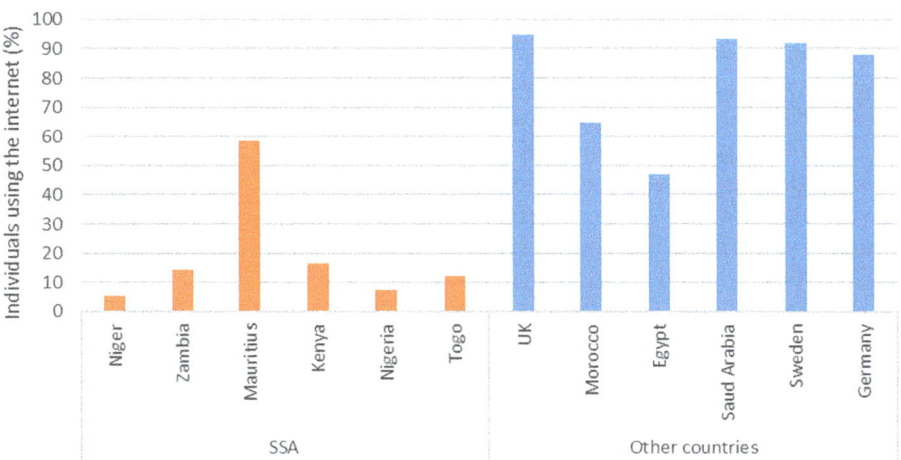

Fig. 1 Percentage of individuals using internet in selected SSA and the rest of the world. (Source: ITU, accessed on June 24, 2020)

Whereas mobile communications through cellular networks have increased exponentially in Africa, internet access in rural areas is still low (Seretse et al. 2018). There are different factors that affect internet access, among others include gender relations, economic status, education level and individual skills. Literature in the area of internet adoption in Africa point out that digital skills and literacy levels are demand-side issues that significantly affect internet use for both users and non-users of smart devices (Lucini 2016; Schelenz and Schopp 2018). As stated earlier, access to digital technology in rural Africa is not the one and only challenge. The ICT services in rural areas is also unreliable, thereby exacerbating digital divide.

5 Methodology

The methodology used in writing this chapter included documentary review, two case studies of rural women entrepreneurs generated from field work in Tanzania as well as researchers' own viewpoints. We opted to use cases of rural women entrepreneurs only because they are the most marginalized gender in African societies. As alluded to earlier, we also used the viewpoint approach based on the authors' awareness and understanding of the Sub-Saharan African countries' context, Tanzania in particular. Our own experience contributed in generating insights, especially about the intersection of informal normative institutions and digitalization in SSAs. As Rabe (2003) pointed out, researchers' own experiences can be a very helpful tool in social science researches as it gives the researcher an insider-knowledge advantage that researchers from outside the particular context do not have.

Likewise, as Sutton and Austin (2015) noted, researchers' experience does not mean to reduce the quality or significance of the analysis process since every researcher has his or her own experience. Conversely, by explicitly acknowledging researchers' own experience as part of the materials and analysis process, the researchers make it easy for readers to contextualize their work.

Apart from researchers' own experiences, the use of qualitative case study design (Yin 2014) in gathering empirical materials provided for a closer observation of social process and interactions as women engage in rural entrepreneurship. The two cases combined with documentary review were useful in generating empirical insights necessary in understanding the phenomena under study (Amaratunga and Baldry 2001; Gillham 2000).

6   Findings and Analysis

6.1   Digital Divide

Regular and effective access to ICT is important (Furuholt and Kristiansen 2007) especially in entrepreneurship. While development of digital technology across the globe has taken place at considerable speed, this has not been at an even pace within all places (Graham 2011; Riddlesden and Singleton 2014). Broadly explained in terms of availability, use, and quality (Otioma et al. 2019), digitalization concerns access and use, which is influenced by skills, access to technology, education, and related factors (ibid). Digital divide thus refers to the unequal access and use of such technology. Such divide is observed at different levels and groups including regions, countries, parts of the country, and by gender. There has been a fundamental un-evenness to the delivery of digital technology in all its forms that has been shaped by existing geographic and social inequalities (Graham et al. 2012; Townsend et al. 2013), which has, in turn, shaped the characteristics of new inequalities (hence digital divide). While many studies examine digital divide around the globe, the implications of digital divide for rural entrepreneurship in SSA is less documented. This section attempts to map and discuss such divide by geography as well as by economic and social milieu, which includes the engendering of digitalization.

Extant literature has revealed that technology is not a scale-neutral (Fischer 2016) and gender-neutral (Bergman Lodin et al. 2012; Doss 2001). Smallholder farmers and small firms may have less access to technology than large-scale farmers and entrepreneurs. Fewer women than men may adopt new technologies (Doss 2001; Quisumbing and Pandolfelli 2010). Financially strong people may have better access to technology and are likely to benefit more than their counterparts. Rural population often include people who are financially constrained. Fewer rural people may have access to digital gadgets. Rural areas also have underdeveloped infrastructures to support digitalization. While this is the case around the globe, the level of underdevelopment is vivid in most sub-Saharan African countries (ITU 2018).

Substantial digital divide analyses between developed and developing economies have been undertaken and documented elsewhere. In this chapter, we opt to focus on digital divide within countries, viz. rural–urban and gender divide.

6.1.1 Urban–Rural Digital Divide

The urban–rural digital inequality to the disadvantage of rural population presents a serious paradox, in the sense that rural communities are most in need of improved digital connectivity to compensate for their remoteness, but they are least connected and included. Globally, urban areas are well served with internet while rural areas are underserved, implying a spatial digital divide (Salemink et al. 2017). Topography, low population density, electrification, economy, poor infrastructure, and distance may render inefficient investments, thereby discouraging telecommunication investments. Across SSA, while mobile money and mobile data are prevalent throughout the continent, broadband internet connection is scarce and concentrated in urban areas (Lekhanya 2018). In some rural areas, people have to climb the hills or go far from home to access the internet connection. This discourages both suppliers and users of digital gadgets such as smartphones. Consequently, urban population have better access to ICT infrastructure and skills to use it (Henry 2019; Metcalf et al. 2010; Ogbo et al. 2017) than rural population. Figure 2 presents the differences in digitalization between urban and rural areas in selected SSA countries.

Given that the costs for internet access in rural areas constitute a significant percentage of a user's income, and coupled with the nature of subsistence economies in such areas, many people especially women and other vulnerable groups have no access to internet (Henry 2019; Metcalf et al. 2010). Generally, rural women have less access to ICT than urban women (Ponge 2016).

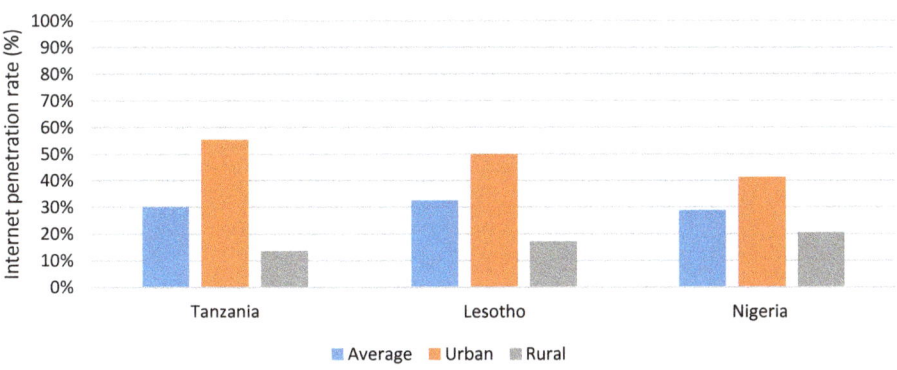

Fig. 2 Internet penetration in selected SSA (%). (Source: RIA After access survey data, 2017)

6.1.2   Gender Digital Divide

Gender digital divide in this case refers to differences between women and men in rural areas in terms of access and use of ICT. Generally, more men than women tend to have better access to technology and its corresponding services (Doss 2001; Quisumbing and Pandolfelli 2010). The gender gap seems to be higher for advanced skills compared to the gap in basic skills (see Fig. 3). The low general literacy level of women implies low digital literacy for them, which may be acute in rural areas (Gurung 2018).

It is clear from Fig. 4 that a higher proportion of men than women in SSA use internet. The gap between women and men is large in some countries such as Malawi and Togo and small in other countries such as Zambia and Mauritius, including countries that are considered to have reached gender equality such as

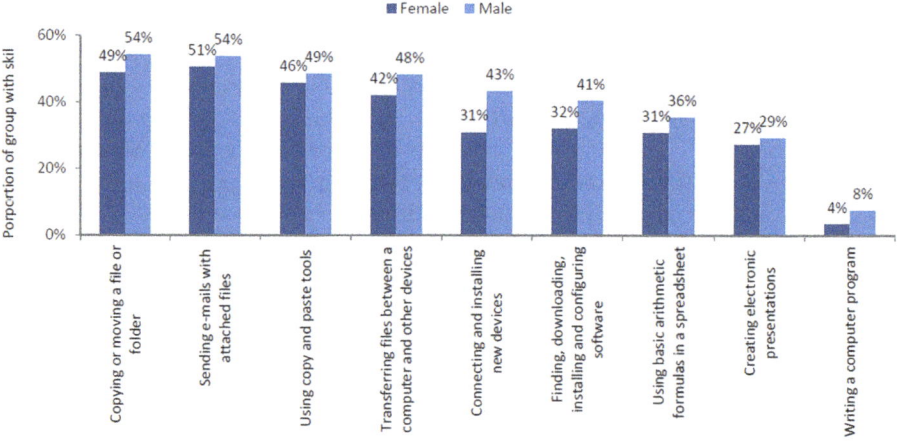

Fig. 3 Gender differences in digital skills. (Source: ITU (2018))

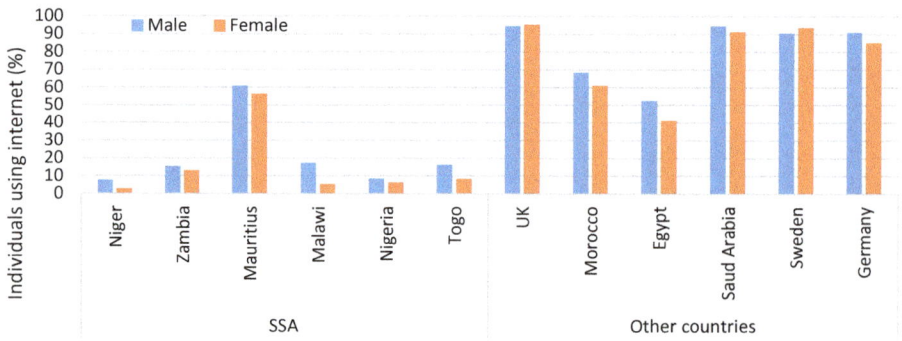

Fig. 4 Gender digital divide in selected SSA countries and rest of the world. (Source: ITU World Telecommunication/ICT Indicators database (accessed on June 9, 2020))

Rwanda (Mumporeze and Prieler 2017). While Mauritius level of internet use is comparable to north-African countries and other countries beyond Africa, the gender digital gap is similar to other SSA countries.

While access to digital technology is now among the rights for all (Amrein and Flotron 2020), rural women entrepreneurs suffer triple divides, namely regional (developed versus developing economies), spatial divide (rural versus urban), and gender divide (women versus men), which also cuts across the first and second divide. Rural women also suffer income divide.

Women's access to ICT in Africa is constrained by social, economic, and cultural factors. Women have less time in accessing ICT than men due to socio-cultural factors (especially the dominant patriarchal structures), which have led to women's multiple roles and heavy domestic responsibilities. These responsibilities also limit their movements. Furthermore, spatial distance also limits women mobility to big cities and rural centers where most of the mobile phone shops are located.

As head of household, men tend to control when, how, and for what purpose other family members may use digital device (Ponge 2016). African women thus tend to have less access to smartphones which can enable them to access internet (Fröhlich 2019; Gillwald et al. 2010) (see Table 1 that shows proportions of mobile phone ownership by gender in selected African countries).

Women's low literacy rate when compared to men also affects their access to appropriate skills and exposure in using digital gadgets such as smart phones (GIZ 2017; Rowntree 2019). Apart from their low smartphone ownership, men tend to control and monitor their wives' communication and interactions. Often married women with smartphones get into problems with a jealous husband when they receive messages or photos perceived to imply intimacy (Fröhlich 2019). Few men have attempted to destroy women's phone because of suspicious conversation, which is often a mere allegation than real. It is thus common for many rural families to have one device, say a single mobile phone. Men have more economic muscles and exposure because of access to education and therefore can afford the technology and are able to gain appropriate skills to use internet (GIZ 2017; Henry 2019).

Gender digital divide seems to amplify gender inequalities in other sectors including economic sector. Rural entrepreneurship is not an exception. Rural women entrepreneurs tend to be disadvantaged compared to rural

Table 1 Percentage of population owning mobile phones

Country	Male	Female
South Africa	83%	87%
Nigeria	71%	68%
Ghana	82%	69%
Kenya	92%	83%
Tanzania	66%	57%
Rwanda	62%	39%

Source: RIA After access survey data, 2017; Nour (2017)

male entrepreneurs for the same reason.[2] Because of cultural norms pervasive in rural SSA, rural women interacting with men in business can still impair the image of good wives. Rural business men interacting with women entrepreneurs for the same reasons do not undergo the same assessment. Unfortunately, such practices constrain rural women entrepreneurs to unlock their full potential, thus reinforcing the existing income and social inequality.

Despite the many gender challenges women face in respect of access to and use of digital technology, some empirical evidence from Tanzania has shown some potential contributions of ICT to rural entrepreneurship. In the following section, we discuss these issues with the aid of some case studies.

6.2 How Digitalization Enhances Women's Engagement in Rural Entrepreneurship

The following section presents the findings on how digitalization enhances rural entrepreneurship. We do this with the help of two case studies.

6.2.1 Connectivity and Efficient Distribution

The first case in Box 1 shows how rural women entrepreneurs exploited mobile phone technology to access large distant markets and increase their business engagements. The two women entrepreneurs in the case study were able to receive orders, sell vegetables to distant markets, and receive the payments without traveling out of their village. In this case, digital technology enabled the women to navigate both social and spatial divides, considering the gender stereotypes, cultural norms and multiple roles that confine women at home.

6.2.2 Reduction of Post-harvest Losses

Information from case 1 show that connectivity has reduced vegetable post-harvest losses. Farmers who are engaged in perishable products such as vegetables and fruits such as Halima and Asha can (though not always the case) get information of

---

[2] Consistently, sex-disaggregated data for SSA are not readily available. For example, only 11 countries out of 48 SSA countries in ITU World Telecommunication/ICT Indicators database have sex-disaggregated data. Further, these statistics cannot be easily comparable as the pace of updating them differs by country, where 2016 is the latest year for some countries' reported statistics in UN agency for telecommunication (ITU). This may limit some potential usefulness, say at regional level. All EAC countries except Burundi did report data on individuals using the internet. Networked Readiness Index would be an alternative data source but the indicators are less comparable over time as they regularly change in structures. For example, the structure of 2019 is different from other years and thus difficult to undertake longitudinal analysis (https://networkreadinessindex.org/nri-2019-countries/)

the demand trends and plan in advance on when to farm or when to harvest. With enabled access to information on demand projections, farmers can plan ahead on what, when, and how much to cultivate and harvest. With effective use of ICT such as mobile phones, mass production may no longer be an issue. Vegetable cultivation and related businesses can be done through crop planning, rotation, and advance ordering. Such arrangements, though done at micro levels, can have significant impact in ensuring sustainability of the agricultural value chain more so for perishable agricultural products.

6.2.3 Connectivity to Export Markets

Case 2 (Box 2) reveals that digital connection through WhatsApp platforms is helping farmers in rice business to connect with markets within and across countries. The direct link to the market place is important for rural entrepreneurship and sustainability of rural businesses. Through information shared on WhatsApp platforms, farmers and entrepreneurs get to know what is needed in the market and the going prices. Consequently, profit levels are enhanced by bypassing some intermediaries who may withhold some important market information.

6.2.4 Alertness to Climate Change Issues and Impact on Post-harvest Losses

WhatsApp platform facilitates information flow on various contemporary issues. For instance, case 2 indicates that women were informing each other on how to take advantage of the rains that came earlier than expected. Subsequently, women advised each other to use drought-resistant seeds for unforeseen climatic changes. Through such initiative, group members put climate change adaptation strategies in place to ensure sustainable farming for both business continuity and food security. Digital connectivity enables these women to share climate change adaptation strategies so as to increase agricultural outputs.

6.2.5 Financial Security

Information from the first case study reveals that cash payment was unnecessary. Vegetable buyers can pay both in cash and through mobile money transfers. Apart from making business transactions easy, mobile transfers also help in protecting money from thefts and loss. Despite the financial charges accompanying mobile transactions, the benefits outweigh the costs.

Box 1 Rural Digital Connection to Distant Large Markets
Halima and Asha represent women of Mavumo village who engage in a number of entrepreneurial activities besides farming. The two women who are both in their early 40s engage in vegetable farming, trading, and brokering. Using their mobile phones, they collect vegetable orders from large nearby and distant markets. Sometimes, they receive orders in excess of what they produce, and often times, they receive orders for other types of vegetables different from what they cultivate. To meet the excess demand, Halima and Asha usually collect vegetables from other farmers, thus acting as brokers between fellow farmers and buyers at large distant markets. They collect vegetables from different places and either transport them to the buyers through cargo trucks or pack them ready for the buyers' trucks to come and collect.

To ensure that they receive and service the orders timely, Halima and Asha maintain constant contact with farmers from different parts of the village and mostly from the remote rural areas. They keep themselves updated with the type and amount of vegetables available from other farmers. This makes easier communication with the buyers. Likewise, orders are received a week or two in advance of the actual collection. Halima and Asha often keep themselves informed of demand and seasonality trends. This enables them to forecast and inform other farmers of what will be demanded in the coming few months.

The two women use motorbike taxis to pick up collected vegetables from interior places where it is difficult to reach farmers through mobile phones. Farmers who can be reached through mobile phones are usually organized to make deliveries at vegetables collection points within the village.

Those buyers who physically come to collect vegetables from the village usually make cash payments while distant buyers pay through mobile money transfers.

Box 2 Organizing Rural Business Through Digitalization
Kashishi is the village in Lake Zone Tanzania where women engage in rural entrepreneurship through collective action. Usually, the business activities are organized in groups of 6–30 women. The women engage in rice production and marketing. During the field work, researchers admired how these women organized their business activities through ICT. A visit to one of the groups known as "Tumaini Letu" a Swahili word for "Our Hope" found that members of this group were using WhatsApp platform for business processes. WhatsApp links them with other actors in the value chain, namely suppliers of inputs, customers and business development service providers. For example, researchers were able to see one conversations in the WhatsApp chats

where a member of the group was encouraging fellow women not to wait until the regular cultivation season starts. Instead, they should take advantage of the rains that came before the usual season. She advised them to use short-term seeds to avoid unexpected rain cut-off or droughts. She even produced a short 1-minute video clip of herself kneeling deep in her rice paddy field when she was preparing it.

Tumaini Letu has two WhatsApp groups. The first group connects only members of the farming and trading group. It is designed for members to share ideas about their activities and to discuss opportunities for further business growth. The second group links the first group with other groups and agricultural marketing cooperative society (AMCOS) in the district. Only three members of the first group represent others in the second group. Important information from the second group is instantly shared with other members in the first group for discussion and decision-making. Through WhatsApp platform, these women were able to connect directly to urban markets within Tanzania and even to export markets in Rwanda and Uganda. The platform gives them access to price information before physically visiting the markets.

7   Discussion

This section provides discussion of the findings on how digitalization enhances rural entrepreneurship and the gendered dimensions of the digitalization process. We also argue that, realizing the optimal outcomes will require addressing digital divide, especially the gender divide.

7.1   Contribution of Digitalization in Enhancing Rural Entrepreneurship

A disconnect between infrastructure, connectivity, and agricultural supply chains is one of the primary reasons for Africa lagging behind.[3] However, with digitalization, new changing trends are emerging in rural businesses and in the ways different values are delivered and distributed to the markets (Roberts et al. 2017; Salemink et al. 2017). Although our evidence is anecdotal, requiring further research, we agree with Lekhanya (2018) that digitalization benefits rural entrepreneurship by enabling access to distant and global markets, efficient distribution of products, higher brand awareness, and effective business communication. Digitalization has eased

---

[3] https://transformafricasummit.org/ [Accessed June 30, 2020]

challenges of spatial and social mobility facing rural women entrepreneurs, thus promoting gendered participation in rural entrepreneurship. Our analysis contributes to the gender, digitalization, and rural entrepreneurship literature and hopes that it will stimulate further research in this area.

7.2   Spatial and Social Mobility

Findings drawn from the case studies showed that to a certain extent, digitalization of the entrepreneurial process has reduced the periphery of the rural areas by bringing the distant markets closer to rural entrepreneurs. ICT has partly addressed the challenge of spatial mobility. Thus, other things being equal, rural entrepreneurship is no longer an issue of spatial distance rather digital connectivity. As alluded to earlier in this chapter, connectivity has a huge potential in addressing the liabilities of remoteness, sparseness and immobility more so for women who are often constrained by their multiple roles (Bergman Lodin et al. 2019; Mandel 2004), and mobility controls by spouses. Simple technologies like mobile phones with good internet connectivity has helped improve and reduce cost of linking of buyers, sellers, markets, locally and globally. The use of mobile phones in the agricultural systems has led to more informed and engaged producers, consumers and traders. Thus, promoting further access to and use of such technologies could enable rural farmers and rural entrepreneurs to plan and take informed decisions to make them more competitive (World Bank 2019). Self-made videos captured with the mobile phone or advisory digital videos explaining complex systems in the local language can result in smarter farming, trading as well as public servicing.

From our cases, digital connections have also addressed social mobility limitations facing rural women entrepreneurs. It not only has permitted rural women to circumvent physical mobility barriers but has also enabled them to balance work and home commitments (Dhanamalar et al. 2020).

7.3   Financial Inclusion

Apart from the spatial connectivity, digital tools in Africa have played an exceptional role in the banking and financial technologies including financial literacy and ledger technologies for value chain traceability (World Bank 2019). Mobile phone technologies in Africa have enhanced financial inclusion. Rural communities that were hitherto unserviced by banks are now enjoying financial services and mobile money is monopolizing the rural clientele.[4]

---

[4] https://www.economist.com/middle-east-and-africa/2020/05/28/the-covid-19-crisis-is-boosting-mobile-money [Accessed 2020-06-30]

Nevertheless, while digitalization may enhance female entrepreneurship, realizing the optimal outcomes will require addressing digital divide. This entails all kinds of digital divide including developed-developing countries, urban–rural, and gender divide.

8 Policy Recommendations

According to Polikanov and Abramova (2003), Africa must make deliberate and persistent efforts to harness science and technology, physically, and financially. Sub-Saharan Africans will need to be the generators of ideas and not just recipients of the technology as this may cause another form of colonial dependency. To generate ideas and innovations means investing in human resources. The African continent has the most youthful population with a median age of 19.7 years and projected to be 2.5 billion by 2050 if fertility rates remain at present level and the education of girls remains unchanged (World Statistics 2020).

Agribusiness has changed from merely defined as farming to market centric. It is not possible for Africa to engage in agribusiness without applying the latest information technologies, scientific discoveries, and marketing tools in order to maximize returns from the value chain products and services. This is particularly important for rural areas as much of the farming activities need transforming into market centric. Digitalization of rural Africa will make a lot of sense if it covers agriculture, and agribusiness, which employs the majority of rural population, especially women.

In summary, digital technologies offer several opportunities for Africa, but they are not a panacea. As more and more data becomes digitalized, issues such as trust, security, and privacy become increasingly more important. Remote rural areas, marginalized groups, the poor, women, and youth, as well as non-skilled individuals may not be included in some of digitalization opportunities yet acutely suffer the mentioned challenges. Thus, governments' partnership with the private sector, coupled with public policies that protect, and foster inclusion are imperatives. Most importantly, Africa must invest in the education, skilling, re-purposing, re-schooling, and innovations. For example, empowering women in digital era is only feasible by elevating ICT skills (Ponge 2016). Without investing in these, Africa will merely be a recipient of cyber neocolonialism. Given the experience with the coronavirus (Chiwona-Karltun, Amuakwa-Mensah,Wamala-Larsson, et al. 2021) and the observed increased nationalism, enacting the African Continental Free Trade Agreement (AfCFTA) enshrined by the African Union and SMART Africa will fast-track the digitization of rural Africa.

In its agenda on African Unity enshrined in the manifesto "the Africa we want by 2063" of the African Union, ICT, and digital transformation are identified as being key elements for the economic transformation of Africa.[5] For the supply chains to function effectively, there is need to invest in infrastructure and connectivity that can translate into a single digital market economy. This can only be achieved if access to and use of digital services combine digital literacy, skills, innovation, and more importantly that it is affordable. The ultimate goal of AfCFTA established in 2018 is to enable a more inclusive economic development that would see a transformation of rural economies.

9   Future Research

With 60% of Africa's population in rural areas and livelihoods comprising mostly agriculture, it is important to continue discussing the role of ICT in farming and agribusiness, and its gendered patterns.

References

Ahl, H., & Marlow, S. (2012). Exploring the dynamics of gender, feminism and entrepreneurship: advancing debate to escape a dead end? *Organization, 19*(5), 543–562. https://doi.org/10.1177/1350508412448695.

Akyoo, A., & Lazaro, E. (2007). *The spice industry in Tanzania: General profile, supply chain structure, and food standards compliance issues* Retrieved from https://www.econstor.eu/handle/10419/84561

Amaratunga, D., & Baldry, D. (2001). Case study methodology as a means of theory building: performance measurement in facilities management organisations. *Work Study, 50*(3), 95–105. https://doi.org/10.1108/00438020110389227.

Amine, L. S., & Staub, K. M. (2009). Women entrepreneurs in sub-Saharan Africa: An institutional theory analysis from a social marketing point of view. *Entrepreneurship and Regional Development, 21*(2), 183–211. https://doi.org/10.1080/08985620802182144.

Amrein, T., & Flotron, R. (2020). *Digitalization, Rural Development and 'Localness'*. Retrieved from https://www.siliconmountains.unibe.ch

Autio, E., Nambisan, S., Thomas, L. D. W., & Wright, M. (2018). Digital affordances, spatial affordances, and the genesis of entrepreneurial ecosystems. *Strategic Entrepreneurship Journal, 12*(1), 72–95. https://doi.org/10.1002/sej.1266.

Bahia, K., & Suardi, S. (2019). State of Mobile Internet Connectivity Report 2019. Retrieved from https://www.gsma.com

Bergman Lodin, J., Paulson, S., & Mugenyi, M. S. (2012). New seeds, gender norms and labor dynamics in Hoima District, Uganda. *Journal of Eastern African Studies in Agricultural Economics, 6*(3), 405–422. https://doi.org/10.1080/17531055.2012.696889.

Bergman Lodin, J., Tegbaru, A., Bullock, R., Degrande, A., Nkengla, L. W., & Gaya, H. I. (2019). Gendered mobilities and immobilities: Women's and men's capacities for agricultural innovation in Kenya and Nigeria. *Gender, Place and Culture, 26*(12), 1759–1783. https://doi.org/10.1080/0966369x.2019.1618794.

---

[5] https://transformafricasummit.org/ [Accessed June 30, 2020]

Bouwman, H., Nikou, S., Molina-Castillo, F. J., & de Reuver, M. (2018). The impact of digitalization on business models. *Digital Policy, Regulation and Governance, 20*(2), 105–124. https://doi.org/10.1108/dprg-07-2017-0039.

Brush, C., Edelman, L. F., Manolova, T., & Welter, F. (2019). A gendered look at entrepreneurship ecosystems. *Small Business Economics, 53*(2), 393–408. https://doi.org/10.1007/s11187-018-9992-9.

Celuch, K., Bourdeau, B., Saxby, C., & Ehlen, C. (2014). SME internet use: the moderating role of normative influence. *Journal of Small Business Strategy, 24*(2), 69–90.

Chiwona-Karltun, L., Amuakwa-Mensah, F., Wamala-Larsson, C. et al. (2021). COVID-19 (2021): From health crises to food security anxiety and policy implications. Ambio, 50, 794–811. https://doi.org/10.1007/s13280-020-01481-y.

Cigna, L. (2018). Digital inequality in theory and practice: Old and new divides in the broadband era. *Interações: Sociedade e as novas modernidades, 34*, 47–63. https://doi.org/10.31211/interacoes.n34.2018.a3.

Dhanamalar, M., Preethi, S., & Yuvashree, S. (2020). Impact of digitization on women's empowerment: A study of rural and urban regions in India. *Journal of International Women's Studies, 21*(5), 107–112.

Dolan, C. (2001). The 'Good Wife': Struggles over resources in the Kenyan Horticultural Sector. *The Journal of Development Studies, 37*(3), 39–70. https://doi.org/10.1080/00220380412331321961.

Doss, C. R. (2001). Designing Agricultural Technology for African women farmers: Lessons from 25 years of experience. *World Development, 29*(12), 2075–2092.

Evans, O. (2018). Digital Agriculture: Mobile phones, internet and agricultural development in Africa. *Actual Problems of Economics, 7-8*(205–206), 76–90.

FAO. (2019). *Digital technologies in agriculture and rural areas*. Rome. Retrieved from http://www.fao.org/3/ca4985en/ca4985en.pdf

Fischer, K. (2016). Why new crop technology is not scale-neutral—A critique of the expectations for a crop-based African Green Revolution. *Research Policy, 45*(6), 1185–1194. https://doi.org/10.1016/j.respol.2016.03.007.

Fröhlich, S. (2019). Africa's mobile gender gap: Millions of African women still offline. Retrieved from https://www.dw.com/en/africas-mobile-gender-gap-millions-of-african-women-still-offline/a-49969106

Furuholt, B., & Kristiansen, S. (2007). A rural-urban digital divide? Regional aspects of Internet use in Tanzania. *The Electronic Journal of Information Systems in Developing Countries, 31*(1), 1–15.

Gaddefors, J., & Anderson, A. R. (2019). Romancing the rural: Reconceptualizing rural entrepreneurship as engagement with context(s). *The International Journal of Entrepreneurship and Innovation, 20*(3), 159–169. https://doi.org/10.1177/1465750318785545.

Gaddefors, J., Korsgaard, S., & Ingstrup, M. B. (2019). Regional development through entrepreneurial exaptation: Epistemological displacement, affordances, and collective agency in rural regions. *Journal of Rural Studies, 74*, 244–256. https://doi.org/10.1016/j.jrurstud.2019.10.010.

Gillham, B. (2000). *Case study research methods*. London: Bloomsbury Publishing PLC.

Gillwald, A., Milek, A., & Stork, C. (2010). Gender assessment of ICT access and usage in Africa. Towards evidence-based ICT policy and regulation. *1*(5). Retrieved from https://www.eldis.org/document/A67783

GIZ. (2017). Women's pathways to the digital sector: Stories of opportunities and challenges. Bonn. Retrieved from https://www.entreprise-development.org

Graham, M. (2011). Time machines and virtual portals: The spatialities of the digital divide. *Progress in Development Studies, 11*(3), 211–227.

Graham, M., Hale, S., & Stephens, M. (2012). Featured graphic: Digital divide: The geography of internet access. *Environment and Planning A: Economy and Space, 44*(5), 1009–1010. https://doi.org/10.1068/a44497.

Granovetter, M. (1985). Economic action and social structure: The problem of embeddedness. *American Journal of Sociology, 91*(3), 481–510. https://doi.org/10.1086/228311.

Gurung, L. (2018). The digital divide: An inquiry from feminist perspectives. *Dhaulagiri Journal of Sociology and Anthropology, 12*, 50–57.

Henry, L. (2019). *Bridging the urban-rural digital divide and mobilizing technology for poverty eradication: challenges and gaps*. Retrieved from https://www.un.org

ITU. (2018). Measuring the Information Society Report 2018. Retrieved from https://www.itu.int/en/ITU-D/Statistics/Pages/publications/misr2018.aspx

Kah, M. M. O. (2020). Africa is leapfrogging into digital agriculture. Retrieved from https://www.un.org/africarenewal/web-features/africa-leapfrogging-digital-agriculture

Kodithuwakku, S. S., & Rosa, P. (2002). The entrepreneurial process and economic success in a constrained environment. *Journal of Business Venturing, 17*(5), 431–465.

Korsgaard, S., Hanne, S. M., & Tanvig, W. (2015). Rural entrepreneurship or entrepreneurship in the rural – between place and space. *International Journal of Entrepreneurial Behavior & Research, 21*(1), 5–26. https://doi.org/10.1108/IJEBR-11-2013-0205.

Langevang, T., Hansen, M. W., & Rutashobya, L. K. (2018). Navigating institutional complexities: The response strategies of Tanzanian female entrepreneurs. *International Journal of Gender and Entrepreneurship, 10*(4), 224–242. https://doi.org/10.1108/IJGE-02-2018-0015.

Lekhanya, L. M. (2018). The digitalisation of rural entrepreneurship. In S. M. Brito (Ed.), *Entrepreneurship - Trends and challenges*. Rijeka: IntechOpen.

Lucini, B. A. (2016). *Consumer barriers to mobile internet adoption in Asia*. Retrieved from https://www.gsma.com

Makombe, I. A. M. (2006). *Women entrepreneurship development and empowerment in Tanzania: the case of SIDO/UNIDO-supported women microentrepreneurs in the food processing sector* (Doctoral dissertation). University of South Africa.

Mandel, J. L. (2004). Mobility matters: women's livelihood strategies in Porto Novo, Benin. *Gender, Place and Culture, 11*(2), 257–287. https://doi.org/10.1080/0966369042000218482.

Manello, A., Cisi, M., Devicienti, F., & Vannoni, D. (2019). Networking: a business for women. *Small Business Economics, 55*(2), 329–348. https://doi.org/10.1007/s11187-019-00300-3.

McKeever, E., Jack, S., & Anderson, A. (2015). Embedded entrepreneurship in the creative re-construction of place. *Journal of Business Venturing, 30*(1), 50–65. https://doi.org/10.1016/j.jbusvent.2014.07.002.

Metcalf, A., Blanchard, M., McCarthy, T., Phillips, L., Hartup, M., & Burns, J. (2010). *Bridging the Digital Divide: Engaging young people in programs that use information technology to promote civic participation and social connectedness*.

Mumporeze, N., & Prieler, M. (2017). Gender digital divide in Rwanda: A qualitative analysis of socioeconomic factors. *Telematics and Informatics, 34*(7), 1285–1293. https://doi.org/10.1016/j.tele.2017.05.014.

Mutula, S. M. (2005). Peculiarities of the digital divide in sub-Saharan Africa. *Program, 39*(2), 122–138. https://doi.org/10.1108/00330330510595706.

Ndung'u, N. (2018). New frontiers in Africa's digital potential. In *Harnessing Africa's Digital Potential: New Tools for a New Age–Foresight Africa Report*.

Nelson, C. (2013). Case studies of women in Tanzanian Agribusiness, The Women in Public Service Project. Retrieved from http://hdl.handle.net/20.500.12018/2709

Njeru, E. H., & Njoka, J. M. (2001). Women entrepreneurs in Nairobi: The socio-cultural factors influencing their investment patterns. In P. O. Alila & P. O. Pedersen (Eds.), *Negotiating social space: East African Microenterprises* (pp. 141–174). Trenton and Asmara: Africa World Press.

Nour, S. (2017). Africa bridging the digital divides. Nordiska Afrikainstitutet. Retrieved from www.diva-portal.org

OECD. (2001). Understanding the Digital Divide. Paris.Retrieved from http://www.oecd.org/dataoecd/38/57/1888451.pdf

Ogbo, E., Brown, T., & Sicker, D. (2017). *Understanding mobile service substitution and the urban-rural Digital Divide in Nigeria*. SSRN 2944367.

Oggero, N., Rossi, M. C., & Ughetto, E. (2019). Entrepreneurial spirits in women and men. The role of financial literacy and digital skills. *Small Business Economics, 55*(2), 313–327. https://doi.org/10.1007/s11187-019-00299-7.

Otioma, C., Madureira, A. M., & Martinez, J. (2019). Spatial analysis of urban digital divide in Kigali, Rwanda. *GeoJournal, 84*(3), 719–741. https://doi.org/10.1007/s10708-018-9882-3.

Polikanov, D., & Abramova, I. (2003). Africa and ICT: A Chance for Breakthrough? *Information, Communication & Society, 6*(1), 42–56. https://doi.org/10.1080/1369118032000068778.

Ponge, A. (2016). Bridging the gender Digital Divide: challenges in access and utilization of ICTs for development at the devolved level in Kenya. *International Journal of Innovative Research and Development, 5*(7), 328–339.

Quisumbing, A. R., & Pandolfelli, L. (2010). Promising approaches to address the needs of poor female farmers: resources, constraints, and interventions. *World Development, 38*(4), 581–592. https://doi.org/10.1016/j.worlddev.2009.10.006.

Quisumbing, A. R., Rubin, D., Manfre, C., Waithanji, E., Van den Bold, M., Olney, D., & Meinzen-Dick, R. (2014). *Closing the gender asset gap: Learning from value chain development in Africa and Asia* (Vol. 1321). Washington, DC: Intl Food Policy Res Inst.

Rabe, M. (2003). Revisiting 'insiders' and 'outsiders' as social researchers. *African Sociological Review/Revue Africaine de Sociologie, 7*(2), 149–161.

Rajahonka, M., & Villman, K. (2019). Women managers and entrepreneurs and digitalization: on the verge of a new era or a nervous breakdown? *Technology Innovation Management Review, 9*(6), 14–24.

Riddlesden, D., & Singleton, A. D. (2014). Broadband speed equity: A new digital divide? *Applied Geography, 52*, 25–33. https://doi.org/10.1016/j.apgeog.2014.04.008.

Roberts, E., Beel, D., Philip, L., & Townsend, L. (2017). Rural resilience in a digital society: Editorial. *Journal of Rural Studies, 54*, 355–359. https://doi.org/10.1016/j.jrurstud.2017.06.010.

Rowntree, O. (2019). The Mobile Gender Gap Report 2019. Retrieved from https://collaboration.worldbank.org

Rutashobya, L. K. (1998). Female Entrepreneurship in Tanzania: Entry and Performance barriers. *OSSREA Gender Research Series, No. 9.*

Rutashobya, L. K. (2001). Female entrepreneurship in Tanzania: Constraints and strategic considerations. *Business Management Review, 7*(1), 22–32.

Rutashobya, L. K., Allan, I. S., & Nilsson, K. (2009). Gender, social networks, and entrepreneurial outcomes in Tanzania. *Journal of African Business, 10*(1), 67–83. https://doi.org/10.1080/15228910802701387.

Salemink, K., Strijker, D., & Bosworth, G. (2017). Rural development in the digital age: A systematic literature review on unequal ICT availability, adoption, and use in rural areas. *Journal of Rural Studies, 54*, 360–371. https://doi.org/10.1016/j.jrurstud.2015.09.001.

Schelenz, L., & Schopp, K. (2018). Digitalization in Africa: Interdisciplinary perspectives on technology, development, and justice. *International Journal of Digital Society, 9*(4), 1412–1420.

Seretse, M., Chukwuere, J., Lubbe, S., & Klopper, R. (2018). Problems around Accessing Information in Rural Communities. *Alternation Journal, 25*(1), 214–244. https://doi.org/10.29086/2519-5476/2018/v25n1a10.

Shimeles, A., Verdier-Chouchane, A., & Boly, A. (2018). *Building a resilient and sustainable agriculture in Sub-Saharan Africa*. Basingstoke: Springer Nature.

Siemens. (2017). African Digitalization Maturity Report 2017. Retrieved from https://www.siemens.co.za/pool/about_us/Digitalization_Maturity_Report_2017.pdf

SOFA Team, & Doss, C. (2011). *The role of women in agriculture. ESA Working Paper No. 11-02.* Rome: FAO.

Songwe, V. (2019). *A Digital Africa.* Retrieved from https://www.imf.org/external/pubs/ft/fandd/2019/06/digital-africa-songwe.htm

Spring, A., & Rutashobya, L. K. (2009). Gender-related themes in African Entrepreneurship: Introduction to the articles. *Journal of African Business, 10*(1), 1–10. https://doi.org/10.1080/15228910802701270.

Srinuan, C., & Bohlin, E. (2011). *Understanding the digital divide: A literature survey and ways forward.* Retrieved from https://ideas.repec.org/p/zbw/itse11/52191.html

Sussan, F., & Acs, Z. J. (2017). The digital entrepreneurial ecosystem. *Small Business Economics, 49*(1), 55–73. https://doi.org/10.1007/s11187-017-9867-5.

Sutton, J., & Austin, Z. (2015). Qualitative research: Data collection, analysis, and management. *The Canadian Journal of Hospital Pharmacy, 68*(3), 226–231.

Townsend, L., Sathiaseelan, A., Fairhurst, G., & Wallace, C. (2013). Enhanced broadband access as a solution to the social and economic problems of the rural digital divide. *Local Economy: The Journal of the Local Economy Policy Unit, 28*(6), 580–595. https://doi.org/10.1177/0269094213496974.

Ughetto, E., Rossi, M., Audretsch, D., & Lehmann, E. E. (2019). Female entrepreneurship in the digital era. *Small Business Economics.* https://doi.org/10.1007/s11187-019-00298-8.

United Republic of Tanzania. (2020). *2019 Tanzania in Figures.* Retrieved from https://www.nbs.go.tz/index.php/en/tanzania-in-figures/533-tanzania-in-figures-2019

Van Dijk, J. A. G. M. (2002). A framework for digital divide research. *Electronic Journal of Communication, 12*(1), 2.

Welter, F. (2011). Contextualizing entrepreneurship-conceptual challenges and ways forward. *Entrepreneurship Theory and Practice, 35*(1), 165–184. https://doi.org/10.1111/j.1540-6520.2010.00427.x.

Wilson, K. R., Wallin, J. S., & Reiser, C. (2003). Social stratification and the digital divide. *Social Science Computer Review, 21*(2), 133–143. https://doi.org/10.1177/0894439303251554.

World Bank. (2019). *Future of food: Harnessing digital technologies to improve food system outcomes.* Retrieved from https://openknowledge.worldbank.org/handle/10986/31565

Yin, R. K. (2014). *Case study research: Design and methods* (5th ed.). Thoasand Oaks: SAGE.

Ziyae, B., Sajadi, S. M., & Mobaraki, M. H. (2014). The deployment and internationalization speed of e-business in the digital entrepreneurship era. *Journal of Global Entrepreneurship Research, 4*(1), 15.

Social Media and Economic Development: The Role of Instagram in Developing Countries

Bamidele Adekunle and Christine Kajumba

1 Introduction

There is no better way to see the impact of Instagram (IG) than the surge in its use during the COVID-19 pandemic. In the first quarter of 2020, March–June, people from different spheres of life started broadcasting using Instagram live to entertain and educate their followers and other interested viewers. This development further emphasizes the relevance of Instagram to communication, fake and authentic, business development and entertainment. Users of Instagram have been able to use captivating pictures and videos to keep followers and non-followers glued to their screens. Our impression is that this development will continue into the foreseeable future though the surge in Instagram live will decline after COVID-19. This is expected because people will not have the luxury of time they had during lockdown once the pandemic is over. The reversal of the growth of Instagram live is not synonymous with the use of Instagram itself. There are other features on the platform that will make it an important application.

The use of Instagram is so ubiquitous in developing countries to the extent that it is shaping our interactions. For example, Dele Momodu (@DeleMomodu), the publisher of OVATION has interviewed policymakers, including two Nigerian federal ministers, kings, present and former governors, and entrepreneurs on Instagram

B. Adekunle (✉)
SEDRD, University of Guelph, Guelph, ON, Canada

Ted Rogers School of Management, Ryerson University, Toronto, ON, Canada
e-mail: badekunl@uoguelph.ca

C. Kajumba
Independent Consultant, Ottawa, Ontario, Canada

Live[1] in 2020, and this may continue, even though at a reduced frequency, after COVID-19. We have also watched people transmitting different programs on Instagram and discussing different issues on business development in Africa. A typical example is Morayo Afolabi Brown (@morayobrown). COVID-19 led to deaths, layoffs and economic downturn, but if there is anything that has come out of the challenging time, it is the ability of *Homo sapiens* to be resilient and get the best of any bad state of nature. We have become innovative with deliveries, working remotely, non-physical interactions and better use of what we already have in an innovative manner including Instagram Live. Instagram Live is just one among other positive impacts of Instagram to developing countries. Though there is low internet penetration in Africa, the introduction of Instagram has made communication, marketing, business development and dissemination of ideas easy even for the less privileged in Africa (Adekunle and Kajumba 2019, 2021). Access is even better with cheap phones such as Infinix and TECNO that are easily procured in most African countries (Adekunle et al. 2020). To further explore the role of Instagram in developing countries, this chapter presents:

1. The history of Instagram.
2. The relevance of Instagram to entrepreneurship and economic development based on Adekunle and Kajumba (2019, 2021).
3. A conceptual framework which explains why Instagram is the most desirable in the production and marketing of spices by farmers in Zanzibar.
4. Workable and desirable policies that will strengthen the positive role of Instagram and reduce the negative impacts.

This chapter, therefore, explores the relevance of Instagram in developing countries, addressing its genesis and its significance in transforming entrepreneurship.

2   The History of Instagram

The internet has transformed our way of life, and we will continue to witness changes because we always want to learn and develop new ideas. Based on this premise, it is difficult to have a market clearance condition because of equilibrating tendencies (not equilibrium) (Kirzner 1997) and destructive creation (Schumpeter 1934) happening in the exchange of ideas and commodities and the advent of social media such as Instagram. The occurrence of equilibrium leads to zero profit, and there is no incentive for any entrepreneur to operate in such market. Platforms such as Instagram reduce the transaction costs of entrepreneurs as they do their daily activities. The use has removed some of the obstacles faced by entrepreneurs in disadvantaged societies. But Instagram will not happen if smartphones did not

---

[1]Also transmitted concurrently on YouTube, Facebook and Twitter. But the main platform is Instagram Live because you can easily link people from different locations.

appear in 2007, if there was no development of better wireless technology and the promotion of mobile applications was stifled.

Instagram, a photo and video sharing social networking mobile application was founded in 2010 (Ting et al. 2015). Instagram started as a photo sharing platform, growing in popularity to attract a large crowd of followers which led to its creative use by bloggers, marketers and promoters. Just like any other social media platform, the use of IG has been transformed by its users. People especially influencers and brand specialist keep using IG in ways that the developers did not even think about when they initially developed the app. Today, Instagram has moved from photo sharing to video sharing and now live streaming. The lockdown and social distancing experienced in 2020 created a situation where people became innovative with how to remain socially connected while keeping physical distance. This scenario led to the surge of IG live and even YouTube live with guest remotely located which was unthinkable before COVID-19. Instagram has registered a steady growth in the number of registered members to one billion monthly active users (Statista 2019) with individuals spending more time on this platform making it the fastest growing platform (Egan 2015; Goor 2012; Thomas and Akdere 2013). IG was also listed as one of the top apps used in Nigeria in an online survey administered between April 5 and April 30, 2020 (Adekunle et al. 2021). IG has connected more people and created influence through the compelling shared content. Available on Apple iOS, Android and Windows Phone, people can view, comment and like posts shared by their friends, role models, and ascribed leaders on Instagram (Instagram.Com 2019).

Instagram has been used for both small- and large-scale entrepreneurs for continued understanding of the market, which has enabled its modification to meet the market needs (Adekunle and Kajumba 2021). It has progressed into a platform for communication, business ventures and service provision, linking users to service providers through services like home deliveries, transportation and online shopping. Instagram has consequently become a credible platform for product awareness, marketing, advertising and promotion strategies (Hanna, Rohm and Crittenden 2011).

Compared to other social media platforms, Instagram appeals more to the younger generation, making it the most popular social media platform among the youth compared to Facebook which remains popular among the older generation (Adekunle and Kajumba 2021). Although most popular among the youth, Instagram has reached a more diverse society (Ting et al. 2015) and has been adopted by non-traditional users such as women, people with mental illness and other disabilities (Singleton et al. 2016). Moreover, it has played a significant role supporting healthcare delivery (Guidry et al. 2017) especially in the developing economies. People with talents have been discovered because of easy access to and dissemination from the platform. Finally, small businesses, artists including comedians, marketers and advocacy experts will continue to appreciate the impact of IG in the advancement of their livelihoods in the foreseeable future.

3   The Relevance of Instagram to Entrepreneurship and Economic Development

Instagram creates an avenue for innovative thinkers to advance the economic and social development of their communities. Moreover, it is an affordable platform which requires minimal start-up capital yet can reach a large and widespread audience. It is appreciated in terms of product and idea dissemination because of its captivating and well-organized photo setup. As observed in the developed economies, Instagram has been used in developing countries for business development, market analysis, advertisement, promotion, marketing and business implementation (Adekunle and Kajumba 2021). This has been done through the selection of the right influencers to target the right market and understand the market needs and right time for postings. The attributes of IG create a desirable condition for the development of entrepreneurship in most places as seen in the countries such as Nigeria, South Africa, Kenya, Morocco and other countries in Africa.

Entrepreneurship is the cornerstone of economic development, and perceived self-efficacy (Chen et al. 1998) and locus of control (Rotter 1966) are important variables which affect personal agency beliefs of people in each community (Harper 2003). The idea that entrepreneurship can be measured using the psychological construct, personal agency beliefs, was validated by Adekunle (2007, 2011). As seen in these scholarly works, all entrepreneurs need support structures including desirable technology to strengthen their competence (self- efficacy) and ensure that they have internal locus of control—the belief that their actions can be contingent to desirable outcomes. One of such technology is IG as can be seen empirically in the way it has enhanced the career of Toke Makinwa (@tokemakinwa)[2] with 3.6 million followers, Funke Akindele (@funkejenifaakindele) with 10.9 million followers, Ayo Makun (@aycomedian) with 8.6 million followers among others. Using the analytical tool, such as "likes" and "comments", users are able to determine the clientele demographics, behaviours, interests and possible response to a situation leading to a better understanding of the market segmentation (Adekunle and Kajumba 2021). Understanding the market benefits, the entrepreneur not only serves their clients better but also enables precision in meeting the specific needs of each group and potentially find under-served segments to explore. Because of its lower setup costs, Instagram has been quickly adopted as a platform for brand awareness in developing countries, Toke Makinwa is one of the successful entrepreneurs and bloggers who has used her Instagram account as a marketing tool for her products. IG has excelled as a communication and marketing tool, promoting information flow to distant customers and stakeholders at limited costs, and within a short time span. The use of Instagram advertisement like most digital advertisement is much cheaper and more efficient compared to traditional media such as print, broadcast and outdoor advertisement making it an effective and powerful tool for large-, medium- and small-sized companies. The information exchanged is considered more trustworthy

---

[2] Her products, perfumes and bags, are sold out even before they are available.

(Lim and Chung 2014) and is more likely to be adopted by consumers (Influencers the New 2016; Hershman 2018) as these tend to relate to the real life of the followers and not the conventional models who appear to be out of touch with the reality (Influencers the New 2016; Hershman 2018). Instagram, however, needs to be used with caution considering its initial intent as a social platform and not a digital billboard. In South Africa, for example, the account Mr. Price has tactfully utilized Instagram in promoting its fashionable lifestyle while maintaining its social commitment and hence attracting large followers, encouraging engagement and trending hashtags such as "#currentmood" and "#summerfeels".

Apart from brand awareness, volunteer tourists from developing countries have taken ownership of sharing their stories on Instagram, making a livelihood as they become a part of the global conversation through narrations and image circulations (Sin and He 2019). Volunteer tourists are transforming the dominant narrative of developing countries that has for long been controlled by external voices such as news reporters and tourists, typically depicting developing countries as the 'other'. With the use of Instagram, citizens of emerging economies can critique and correct narratives that are misrepresented. This has opened new economic avenues for bloggers who earn a living through storytelling of their lifestyle while promoting brands to ardent and unsuspecting followers. Instagram has also played a major role in political journalism in Africa holding many politically accountable to the responsibilities of their offices, thus promoting freedom of speech. This has given a platform for diverse news and information to most Africans. The platform has aided political aspirants and empowered the politically supressed providing them with a political platform to express their grievances, expose their opponents and share information that would have otherwise never been known to the outside world, so keeping systems in check.

The impact of Instagram on the African economy is also seen in the improved health status of the masses. Africa has for long struggled with the high sensitization costs and poor communication network which has left many remote parts uninformed and economically lagging. The consequences of which include premature deaths of an economically viable population, as treatable or controllable diseases take a toll on the remote masses. With Instagram, meaningful and interactive communication has been established with the public in times of global health crises (Guidry et al. 2017). During the 2014 Ebola virus epidemic, three major health organizations; Center for Disease Control and Prevention (CDC), World Health Organization (WHO) and Doctors Without Borders used Instagram to deliberate on important issues with the public through sharing messages and posts targeted at combating Ebola-related misinformation (Guidry et al. 2017). During the COVID-19 pandemic, Instagram was used to create awareness across communities, relevant and accurate information useful for the reduction of the spread of the disease was provided on this platform and information seekers were engaged by answering their questions. This ability to interactively provide the community with accurate and essential information is particularly important for developing countries that typically lack infrastructure and strong public health agencies.

Sensitization of people on the importance of staying home and staying safe was successfully performed on Instagram. People shared personal experiences and solutions to obstacles that came with prolonged periods of staying home. Instagram was used for more than sharing content, it was used to stay in touch with family and friends as well as make new contacts (Bergstrom and Backman 2013). With the outbreak of COVID-19 and the imposed lockdown, the shopping scenario changed drastically with a definite possibility of a new norm. Innovative entrepreneurs took advantage of the new norm, promoting their businesses on Instagram especially grocery supply, and direct delivery to consumers through partnership with companies such as uber and other independent logistics companies.[3] Even after the COVID-19, the new normal is likely to have entrepreneurs continue house to house delivery of groceries to busy middle-class families.

Similarly, Instagram has been used to overcome the geographic, social and economic isolation of rural smallholder farmers. Farmers are able to obtain the information and services they desperately need, through connecting with other farmers, sharing experiences through shared videos, comments and pictures on new farming techniques, information on seeds, fertilisers, markets and prices. Twiga Foods, with 602 followers, uses Instagram to solve its market issues; other Instagram accounts used to promote agriculture include #africaagriculture, #agricultureafrica to name but a few. Organizations have also used Instagram to support youth start-up careers; Africa's Young Entrepreneurs (AYE) has an Instagram account Africasyoungentrepreneurs, and it prides itself in being the World's Largest Entrepreneurship Network used to fund, train, mentor and empower the youth. ThriveAgric, another start-up, brings together entrepreneurs in the farming field, using the crowdfunding principle to support struggling African farmers while co-farmers benefit from the returns earned. ThriveAgric utilizes Instagram to create awareness and inform the public of their on-going activities, connecting with their current and potential co-farmers. Zanzibar spice farmers too have embraced the use of Instagram to market and promote their products. #zanzibarspices is one of the accounts promoting the Zanzibar spices on Instagram.

Finally, Instagram has made dating easy, and people can now connect in a boundaryless way. While Instagram has helped connect many, there has been an increase in the level of promiscuity as the platform has facilitated connecting with strangers to satisfy adventurous lifestyle because of the ease to get another willing partner by sending a direct message (DM) without leaving your space or incurring huge costs.

---

[3] Thrive Agric has arrangements with delivery agents to deliver food produced by the tech start-up to households in Abuja, Nigeria.

4   Explaining the Role of Instagram in Developing Countries

Digital entrepreneurship has been defined as a process of developing an idea into a business venture (Gawel and Toikko 2014) with either part of or all the business venture in a traditional organization being virtualized at either the production, workplace, marketing or distribution stage (Hull et al. 2007; Turban et al. 2008; Hafezieh et al. 2011). According to Adekunle and Kajumba (2021), digital entrepreneurship comprises four stages: initialization, market analysis, marketing and finally implementation of the business idea. In their conceptualization, four propositions were used to illustrate the nexus between Instagram use and digital entrepreneurship. Proposition 1 posits that the use of Instagram initiates digital entrepreneurship through back and forth chatting with prospective customers usually referred to as followers. This works on the principle of 'following and being followed', meaning that account holders share information with other account holders who they are 'following' through comments, likes and reviews. As the potential entrepreneur shares ideas with the followers, this leads to a better understanding of the followers' interests and possible market demand resulting in an appropriate assessment of the viability of the business.

The next step, Proposition 2, which is market analysis, is done through use of Instagram's unique followers. With the continued chatting, commenting and reviews, the potential entrepreneur can gather information about conditions that affect a marketplace. Using Instagram's analytical tool, they can integrate both quantitative and qualitative data to access and determine the need and market characteristics such as the gender or age group. Once the need is determined and the market identified, then the strategies for brand promotion are put in place. Proposition 3 shows how advertisement, promotion and marketing are done using Instagram to sway followers towards a brand. Through comments, likes, appealing photos and videos, and hash tags, Instagram influencers advertise, promote and market brands and tactfully sway sceptical followers (Wei and Lu 2013). Consumers are more likely to adopt from an Instagram follower as they see them as fellow consumers rather than the models in the traditional advertisement who are considered as actors. They trust the products promoted by their influencers (Long-Crowell 2016) believing they cannot abuse their position of fame[4] (Djafarora and Rushwoth 2017). Similarly, consumers would likely be associated to their favourite follower's lifestyle.

Proposition 4 shows how Instagram is used for business implementation through the use of Instagram's royal customers and knowledgeable influencers with high engagement rates who do an excellent job at information diffusion leading to increased sales (Johansen 2019). Likewise, they have a stronger persuasive position and can control peer opinion, validate perception and convince followers (Teng et al. 2014; Cheung et al. 2009) through comments and chats. Furthermore,

---

[4] Due to the challenges of hidden information, influencers are expected to indicate whether they were paid to promote a product (brand) or not.

innovative features like the 'Contact' buttons and an inbuilt analytics tool in the business accounts have helped improve target markets and sales (ThriveHive 2015), enabling Instagram users to execute their business from start to completion without having to exit the platform.

Instagram use for entrepreneurship has continued to grow in Africa, and to further stimulate use in developing countries, Instagram has released a slimmed-down version of their app to appeal to an even wider audience. This new app is called Instagram Lite, and it caters to the needs of those living in the developing world (Dotsquares 2018). This new version of Instagram, while still containing the core features of the original version takes up less space on the user's phone, uses less data, for areas where mobile coverage is irregular and data is expensive (Dotsquares 2018). With continued novelties in Instagram, more entrepreneurs are using the platform. Below we present a conceptual framework illustrating the impact of social media on the Zanzibar spice industry, elaborating the farmers' perspective on Instagram and Facebook.

The conceptual framework below (Fig. 1) illustrates how social media has been used by the spice industry in Zanzibar and how the spice farmers relate to Instagram use compared to Facebook. The spice industry of Zanzibar produces spices like vanilla, peppers and cloves. Zanzibar's vanilla and pepper marketing are mainly managed by cooperatives while the state has a monopoly over the clove market, limiting the farmers' role in its market dynamics. To improve sales and strengthen the presence of these spices in the spice industry, it is essential for farmers to embrace use of social media such as Instagram and Facebook to promote their sales.

With high-speed internet and social apps like Instagram and Facebook, Zanzibar farmers are able to create and share content, maintain connections while discovering new contacts much easier and hence attracting more entrepreneurs. Although introduced much later (2010), Instagram is quickly gaining ground and popularity. New spice farmers and new start-up businesses and many millennials prefer Instagram while Facebook is more popular among the more established businesses, scaling up businesses (Adekunle and Kajumba 2021) and the older generation who have a higher income and higher spending power (Poushter et al. 2018; Endres 2013).

Illustrated in the conceptual framework is the fact that use of Instagram is considered easier to navigate and more user friendly and gives a clearer more appealing picture. The Instagram picture display is less cluttered, making its appearance more professional, and the added notification feature facilitates easier identification and marketing of products. Use of the extra bio-data feature in Instagram provides details such as age and gender which helps one understand, access and target a specific clientele, strengthening its position in identifying the best clientele. Facebook, on the other hand, was considered crowded and not suitable for marketing but was described as more personal with less wide-scale public exposure (Fischer and Reuber 2011).

Knowing and understanding these attributes helps Zanzibar spice farmers appreciate the value of being cognizant of the target market when selecting an appropriate platform to promote and raise awareness about their business. Agri vanilla and spices company for example uses Instagram to promote and raise awareness about

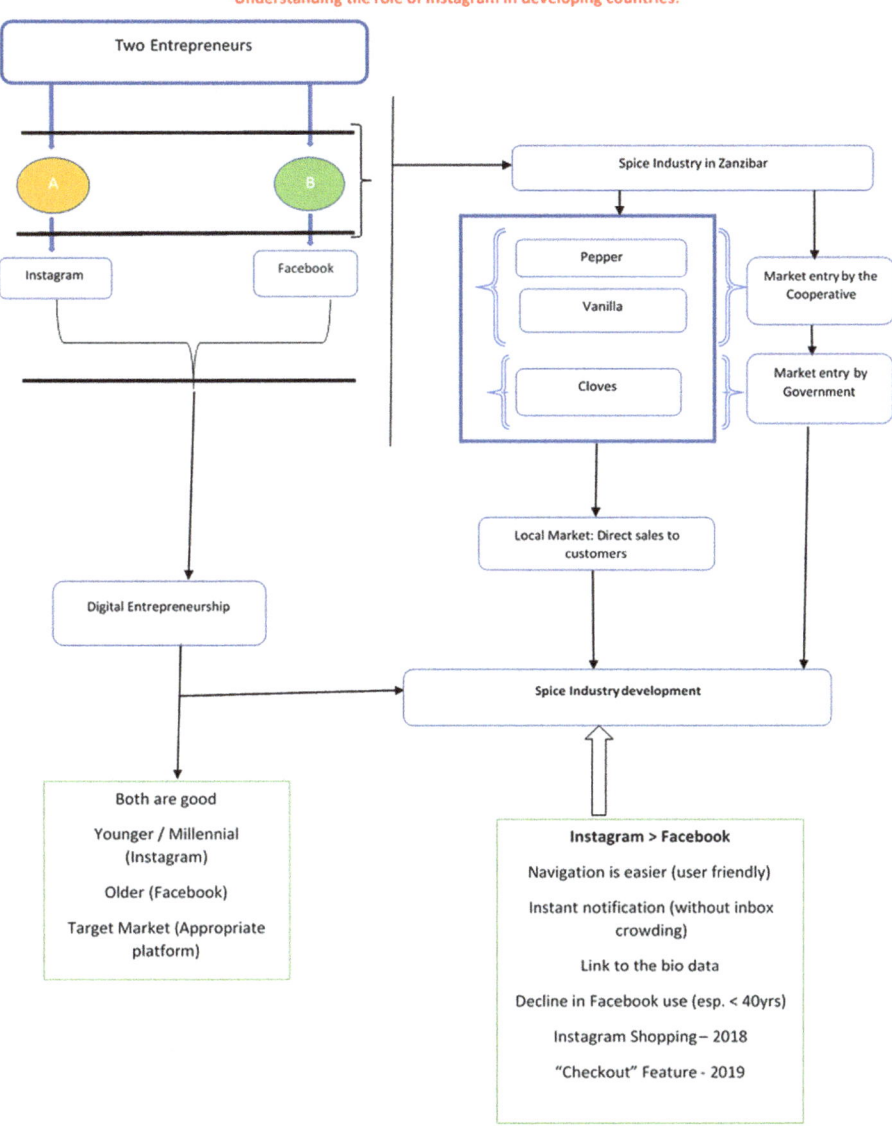

Source: Adekunle and Kajumba (2020)

Fig. 1 A conceptual framework illustrating the role of Instagram in the production and marketing of spices in Zanzibar. (Source: Adekunle and Kajumba (2021))

vanilla activities they are involved in, using hash tags like #coffee #vanilla #spices to reach even more targets. Social media has played an important role in the direct sales of the spices to customers, therefore increased use of social media marketing will activate the spice Industry development and boost production, thus increasing revenue. Further growth is anticipated with the introduction of the Instagram shopping in 2018 and the Instagram Checkout feature (2019).

Although social media use continues to rise in developing countries (Poushter et al. 2018), this is reflected more in private entrepreneurs while African states still lag in social media marketing and promotion. Zanzibar state is no exception, yet the state has a monopoly in the clove marketing system; therefore, it is a possibility that social media marketing of cloves might be minimal. The state monopoly in the clove marketing has been criticized for negatively impacting the Zanzibar spice market, resulting in a steady decline in the Zanzibar clove market from an average of 16,000 tons/year in the 1970s to a 3500 tons/year (ZACPO 2013). The impact of states' minimal involvement in social media marketing can be elaborated by the decline in the Zanzibar clove industry.

The conceptual framework shows that social media use, such as Instagram, among Zanzibar farmers has a positive impact on the direct sales of the local spice market to customers and eventually to the spice industry development. This is true for many entrepreneurs in Africa who have embraced use of Instagram; however, this does not eliminate the challenges faced by digital entrepreneurs in Africa as they struggle with the growing mobile industry.

The mobile industry is very important to the economy by contributing directly to government taxes, generation of the continent's GDP and creation of jobs (Dahir 2016). The African mobile industry relies predominantly on smartphones which are minicomputers equipped with a high-resolution touch screen. These smartphones possess a strong photo system which has enabled high profile photo taking and video recording in addition to texting and talking. With internet connection, smartphones are used to search the net, communicate through e-mails, determine one's direction and location and enhance the use of apps such as WhatsApp, Instagram and Facebook—the popular platforms. In Africa, smartphones are the platform for digital entrepreneurship because only the privileged own a laptop or tablet.

Smartphone ownership is highest in developed economies but has remained at its lowest in Sub-Saharan Africa. Since most access to the internet is through smartphones, low smartphone ownership limits access to the internet hence low social media usage among potential entrepreneurs. This has incapacitated Africa's global communication, connection and use of apps, which in turn has affected the economic development. The low ownership has been attributed to the high digital illiteracy levels as well as the costly smartphones which are taxed highly as they are considered a luxury. To improve smartphone availability in Africa, companies like TECNO and Infinix have advanced production and supply of affordable Android phones to the continent.

5 Workable and Desirable Policies That Will Strengthen the Positive Role of Instagram and Reduce the Negative Impacts

While Africa still lags in smartphone ownership, there is a registered increase of 65% over the past 5 years, which is twice the global average (Poushter et al. 2018). The steady increase in smartphone ownership has been a result of a decrease in smartphone prices, from an average of $230 in 2012 to $160 in 2015 (GSMA Report 2015). With increased ownership, more people will be able to access the internet, henceforth improving service provision in sectors like health, agriculture and education (Dahir 2016). It is important for African governments to ensure increased supply of smartphones/mobile devices through start-up capital, or soft loans to facilitate and encourage entrepreneurial investment in manufacturing mobile devices. Pan-African conglomerate Mara Group for example opened a factory in Rwanda that will produce Mara smartphones, the first of its kind in Africa (Collins 2019). African governments should also think of creating tax holidays to stimulate foreign investment as well as encourage and support more local entrepreneurs' partnership with foreign manufacturers for importation of good quality and affordable mobile devices. Some local companies are already in these partnerships like Safaricom which has partnered with Google to introduce the Lipa Mdogo programme which, enables Kenyans to buy 4G smartphone devices at affordable rates.

Although Africa has recorded a growth in smartphone use, it is still challenged with internet accessibility and affordability with an average penetration rate of 39% as compared to 88% in Europe and 95% in North America (Internet World Stats 2020). Internet concentration is mainly in the major urban centres with only a small minority accessing the internet in their homes (de Lanerolle 2013). Majority of users access the internet mainly through their phones, while others access the internet through shared space like cyber cafes, WIFI in major malls, schools, colleges and workplaces. The implication of this is that the rural majority, the backbone of the economy, is left with no access or very poor access to the internet.

The government needs to facilitate the expansion of the internet to greater parts of the rural areas to support development in these areas and ensure the cost of the data is affordable through initiation of affordable pay plans to inspire more subscription to innovative internet 4G and eventually 5G. Governments should similarly invest in literacy in website and mobile apps development and promote tech firm that offer training in software development like the Andela, a Zuckerberg Chan-sponsored tech company in Nigeria, Kenya, Rwanda, Uganda and the United States as well as the Lipa Mdogo in Kenya which develops websites, mobile apps and intelligent digital marketing strategies.

Even with the steady increase in the internet and social media use in Sub-Saharan Africa, there is a difference in usage according to age, education, income and gender, creating the digital divide. Internet and social media use are higher among the younger generation, those with higher education, higher incomes (Silver 2019) and in Africa, the gender gap is apparent with men more likely than women to use the internet (Poushter et al. 2018). Although, according to Silver (2019), gender has played a limited role in the adoption of this technology, in fact a recent study indicates that the ratio of active participants is equal between the two genders (Adekunle et al. 2021).

Youths and millennials between the ages of 15 and 30 years are the highest users of social media (Adekunle and Kajumba 2021; Ephraim 2013), and both men and women are equal participants (Silver 2019; Adekunle et al. 2021). With majority of Africa's population under the age of 25 years and women known to play a major role in agriculture, health and education, it is important that governments address the issues of microeconomic characteristics (gender, age, income inequality) as these impact internet accessibility hence limiting IG use. African governments should play their role in creating an enabling environment that promotes the development of social goods as well as set favourable policies that will eliminate exclusion of the disadvantaged yet talented majority. The government should similarly facilitate and create amenities that promote innovation and creativity thus promoting new ideas, and technology that meet the needs of the locals—an example is the development of the app Instagram lite.

On another note, there is a need to minimize the tax burden on services, equipment and users of social media. Policies should favour rather than deter development. As we proceed digitally in this twenty-first century, government policies should be desirable, and licencing of telecommunication companies should be fair and based on expertise. These prerequisites should be in place if Africa wants to harness the benefits and curtail the downsides, of social media especially IG.

6   Summary

This chapter addresses the role of IG in developing countries, outlining its use in digital entrepreneurship. It examines Instagram use in business initialization and implementation, promotion and marketing of brands as well as communication, citing the example of IG live video streaming, which was enhanced during the COVID-19 lockdown. The chapter shows how various sectors such as tourism, politics, health and agriculture have benefited from the use of IG, while acknowledging the unintended consequences and the dilemma associated with the use of social media in general. A conceptual framework was developed illustrating the perceptions of Zanzibar spice farmers using social media (Instagram and Facebook). Instagram stands out as a platform of choice by the farmers because of its easy of navigation, user friendliness and the more appealing picture.

In Africa, IG is mainly used on smartphones allowing more people to access and use the platform. The chapter elaborates on the introduction of fast internet and smartphones which have allowed innovative use of IG, hence a reduction in transaction costs as it eliminates infrastructural obstacles and enables entrepreneurial development. Although Instagram is popular in Africa, the continent is still faced with challenges for example internet penetration and affordability of smartphones, impeding the maximization of Instagram usage.

In conclusion, Instagram has played a major role in the African economy by connecting users to resources such as ThriveAgric which connects farmers to funders through crowdfunding. It is also used for training, mentoring and empowering the youth, marketing brands and services as well as communication and promotion of businesses. However, for the continent to fully benefit from the fruits of the platform, governments should develop viable policies that will strengthen its use and curtail its negative externalities.

References

Adekunle, B. (2007). The impact of cooperative thrift and credit societies on entrepreneurship and microenterprise performance. Unpublished doctoral thesis, University of Guelph, Ontario.

Adekunle, B. (2011). Determinants of microenterprise performance in Nigeria. *International Small Business Journal, 29*(4), 360–373.

Adekunle, B. & Kajumba, C. (2019). Digital Entrepreneurship: How Relevant is Instagram. In *A selected paper presented at the IAABD 2019 Annual conference, 8–11 May 2019*, Dar es Salaam, Tanzania.

Adekunle, B., & Kajumba, C. (2021). The Nexus between Instagram and digital entrepreneurship. *Journal of African Development*. Forthcoming.

Adekunle, B., Odularu G., Kajumba, C., Adegboye, F., Oke, J., Ogunnote O., & Akintola T. (2021). Economics of Mobile Applications: Experience from Nigeria. In *A selected paper for the AABD 2020 Annual conference*, McEwan University, Edmonton, Canada.

Bergstrom, T., & Backman, L. (2013). *Marketing and PR in social media: How the utilization of Instagram builds and maintains customer relationships*. Stockholm: Stockholm University.

Chen, C. C., Greene, P. G., & Crick, A. (1998). Does entrepreneurial self-efficacy distinguish entrepreneurs from managers? *Journal of Business Venturing, 13*, 295–316.

Cheung, M. Y., Luo, C., Sia, C. L., & Chen, H. (2009). Credibility of electronic word-of mouth: Informational and normative determinants of on-line consumer recommendations. *International Journal of Electronic Commerce, 13*(4), 9–38.

Collins T. (2019). Mara Group opens Africa's first smartphone factory in Rwanda. *African Business*. Retrieved from https://africanbusinessmagazine.com/region/east-africa/mara-group-opens-africas-first-smartphone-factory-in-rwanda/

Dahir, A. L. (2016). Smartphone use has doubled in Africa in two years. *Quartz Africa*. Retrieved August 3, 2016, from https://qz.com/africa/748354/smartphone-use-has-more-than-doubled-in-africa-in-two-years/

de Lanerolle, I. (2013, August). *The rise of social Media in Africa*. Retrieved May 20, 2020, from https://www.researchgate.net/publication/271205465_The_Rise_of_Social_Media_in_Africa

Djafarora, E., & Rushwoth, C. (2017). Exploring the credibility of online celebrities' Instagram profiles in influencing the purchase decisions of young female users. *Computers in Human Behavior, 68*, 1–7.

Dotsquares. (2018, March 25). Instagram reaches out to developing countries with a new version of its App. Retrieved April 16, 2020, from https://www.dotsquares.com/news_events/instagramreach-out-to-developing-countries-with-a-new-version-of-its-app/

Egan, J. (2015). 14 eye—opening Instagram statistics. Entrepreneur media. Retrieved May 10, 2020, from http://www.entrepreneur.com/article/242659

Endres, H. (2013). *Shreddz a clothing brand: Creating a marketing plan through social media and traditional marketing research*. San Luis Obispo: California Polytechnic State University.

Ephraim, P. E. (2013). African youths and the dangers of social networking: A culture-centered approach to using social media. *Ethics and Information Technology, 15,* 275–284.

Fischer, E., & Reuber, A. R. (2011). Social interaction via new social media: (how) can interactions on twitter affect effectual thinking and behaviour? *Journal of Business Venturing, 26,* 1–18.

Gawel, A., & Toikko, T. (2014). Entrepreneurial processes in new company creation: An examination of private companies in the social service sector. *Journal of Enterprising Communities: People and Places in the Global Economy, 8*(3), 198–216.

Goor, M. (2012). *Instamarketing: A content analysis into marketing on Instagram.* Universiteit van Amsterdam.

GSMA Report. (2015). *Digital inclusion and mobile sector taxation in the Democratic Republic of the Congo.*

Guidry, J., Jin, Y., Orr, C. A., Messner, M., & Meganck, S. (2017). Ebola on Instagram and twitter: How health organizations address the health crisis in their social media engagement. *Public Relations Review, 43*(3), 477–486. https://doi.org/10.1016/j.pubrev.2017.04.009.

Hafezieh, N., Akhavan, P., & Eshraghian, F. (2011). Exploration of process and competitive factors of entrepreneurship in digital space. A multiple case study in Iran. *Education, Business and Society: Contemporary Middle Eastern Issues, 4*(4), 267–279.

Hanna, R., Rohm, A & Crittenden, V. L. (2011). We're all connected: The power of the social media ecosystem. Kelley School of Business, Indiana University. Business Horizon 881-pp 9.

Harper, D. A. (2003). *Foundations of entrepreneurship and economic development.* London: Routledge.

Hershman, B. (2018). Micro-influencers: A growing component of apparel brand strategy. In *Benzinga Newswires.* Benzinga: Newswires.

Hull, C. E., Hung, Y. T. C., Hair, N., Perotti, V., & DeMartino, R. (2007). Taking advantage of digital opportunities: A typology of digital entrepreneurship. *International Journal of Networking and Virtual Organisations, 4*(3).

Influencers the New. (2016). PR Week, p. 29. Retrieved December 15, 2019, from https://www.prweek.com/article/1379310/newinfluencers

Instagram.Com. (2019). What Is Instagram? | Instagram Help Center." Retrieved from help.instagram.com/424737657584573.

Internet World Stats. (2020). Usage and population statistics. Retrieved from https://www.internetworldstats.com/africa.htm

Johansen, S. H. (2019). Makeup mayhem. Documentary 'broken', season 1, episode.

Kirzner, I. (1997). Entrepreneurial discovery and the competitive market process: An Austrian approach. *Journal of Economic Literature, 35*(1), 60–85.

Lim, B. C., & Chung, C. M. Y. (2014). Word-of-mouth: The use of source expertise in the evaluation of familiar and unfamiliar brands. *Asia Pacific Journal of Marketing and Logistics, 26*(1), 39–53. https://doi.org/10.1108/APJML-02-2013-00.

Long-Crowell, E. (2016). The Halo Effect: Definition, Advantages & Disadvantages. http://study.com/academy/lesson/the[1]halo-effect-definitionadvantages-disadvantages.html

Poushter, J., Bishop, C. & Chwe, H. (2018). Social media use continues to rise in developing countries but plateaus across developed ones. Digital divides remain, both within and across countries. Pew Research Center. Global Attitudes & Trends. Retrieved May 15, 2020, from https://www.pewresearch.org/global/2018/06/19/social-media-use-continues-to-rise-in-developing-countries-but-plateaus-across-developed-ones/

Rotter, J. (1966). Generalized experiences for internal versus external control of reinforcement. *Psychological Monographs, 80*(1), 1–28.

Schumpeter, J. (1934). *The theory of economic development.* Cambridge, MA: Harvard University Press.

Silver, L. (2019). Smartphone ownership is growing rapidly around the world, but not always equally. In *Emerging economies, technology use still much more common among young people and the well-educated.* Pew research center. Global attitudes &

trends. Retrieved May 5, 2020, from https://www.pewresearch.org/global/2019/02/05/smartphone-ownership-is-growing-rapidly-around-the-world-but-not-always-equally/

Sin, H. L., & He, S. (2019). Voluntouring on Facebook and Instagram: Photography and social media in constructing the 'third world' experience. *Tourist Studies, 19*(2), 215–237. https://doi.org/10.1177/1468797618815043.

Singleton, A., Abeles, P., & Smith, C. I. (2016). Online social networking and psychological experiences: The perceptions of young people with mental health difficulties. *Computers in Human Behavior, 61*, 394403.

Statista. (2019). Worldwide daily social media usage by region 2019 | Statista.

Teng, S., Khong, K., Goh, W., & Chong, A. (2014). Examining the antecedents of persuasive eWOM messages in social media. *Online Information Review, 38*(6), 746–768.

Thomas, K. J. & Akdere, M. (2013). Social media as collaborative Media in Workplace Learning. *Human Resource Development Review*.

ThriveHive. (2015). Retrieved August 26, 2019, from https://thrivehive.com/how-to-tag-people-on-instagram/

Ting, H., Wong, W. P. M., de Run, E. C., & Choo, S. L. Y. (2015). IRC Publishers 15 Beliefs about the Use of Instagram: An Exploratory Study. *International Journal of Business and Innovation, 2*.

Turban, E., Leidner, D., McLean, E., & Wetherbe, J. (2008). *Information technology for management: Transforming organizations in the digital economy* (6th ed.). Hoboken, NJ: WileyPLUS.

Wei, P., & Lu, H. (2013). An examination of the celebrity endorsements and online customer reviews influence female consumers' shopping behavior. *Computers in Human Behavior, 29*(1), 193–201.

ZACPO. (2013). The Zanzibar clove growers' organisation. Fact sheet—July 2013. Retrieved May 25, 2020.

Part II
Business and Management in Africa in the Digital Era

Franchising in the Gasoline Retail Industry in Cameroon: A Strategic Perspective

Simon P. Sigué and Altante Désirée Biboum

1 Introduction

The distribution of petroleum products in Cameroon remains very regulated despite some liberalization efforts observed in the last two decades. Wholesalers, also known as marketers, are one of the main players in gasoline distribution in Cameroon. They purchase large quantities of gasoline products from the local refiner or importers for sale either to dealers or to final customers, especially via branded service stations. It is possible for marketers to: (1) own and operate their own gas stations, (2) own gas stations and contract their operations to independent dealers, or (3) partner with independent dealers who own and operate retail outlets.

These organizational or contractual forms have different characteristics. For instance, in the first form, marketers invest heavily in gas stations, and hire and pay wages to their employees, but may not be able to motivate these staff enough to perform to the best of their abilities. In the second form, marketers still heavily invest in gas stations. This time, however, the operation of these outlets is given to independent entrepreneurs who bring in the operating capital and manage the stations at their own risk. Finally, beyond the use of marketer brands in the last arrangement, dealers are the main investors in their gas stations, which are also managed at their own risk. The dealers in the last arrangement best corresponds to what is

S. P. Sigué (✉)
Faculty of Business, Athabasca University, Edmonton, AB, Canada
e-mail: simons@athabascau.ca

A. D. Biboum
ESSEC of Douala, CERAME, University of Douala, Douala, Cameroon

known as trademark or traditional franchisees.[1] Marketers give these dealers the right to use their brands and all visual identification elements to sell petroleum products and other related services for their own profit. Obviously, the basic requirements for the implementation of these three organizational forms and their strategic and operational implications for each individual outlet are very different. The question then is: why should marketers own and operate or partner with a dealer to operate a gasoline station in Cameroon in this area of digital technology?

Several previous theoretical and empirical works provide answers relevant to this fundamental research question (see Combs and Ketchen 2003; Combs et al. 2004, 2011 for a review). One of the first explanations for partnering with dealers or franchisees is resource scarcity theory, which stipulates that marketers adopt franchising mainly because they hope to overcome the lack of internal resources (i.e., trained managers, knowledge of local markets, and financial capital) necessary to develop their networks and achieve economies of scale, especially in the early stages of their development (e.g., Caves and Murphy 1976; Oxenfeldt and Kelly 1969). On the other hand, proponents of agency theory offer an alternative answer to the question of whether to own or franchise a unit (e.g., Brickley and Dark 1987; Rubin 1978). They claim that the decision to adopt either organizational form depends on monitoring costs, the partners' risk aversion and incentives, and the decision right associated with each arrangement. According to agency theory, because dealers are the operators or operator-owners of their outlets, their interests can easily align with those of their marketers. They need less monitoring than do company managers unless it is proven that the former can engage in additional opportunistic behaviors such as free-riding on the network image and service quality, or cheating to avoid or reduce ongoing payments. Based on these different monitoring and incentive schemes, several predictions have been made and empirically tested in various industries with mixed results (Combs and Ketchen 2003; Dahlstrom and Nygaard 1994; Dahlstrom et al. 2009; Pénard et al. 2004; Slade 1998). For instance, in this case, gas stations located near corporate monitoring centers will be expected to be owned and operated by marketers, while those located in remote locations should be franchised. Also, gas stations located in areas where there are more repeat purchase opportunities will be expected to be franchised, and those located in areas where repeat purchase opportunities are rare, such as highways, should be owned and operated by marketers.

This literature implicitly assumes that managers play no major role in the choice of a contractual form for a retail outlet, or if they do, their role is determined by the economic, social, and psychological laws that shape their actions. In other words, any reasonable manager responsible for choosing a contractual form for a given outlet, taking these internal and external factors into account, should make the same decision (Combs et al. 2004). Ghoshal (2005) deplores the simplistic and pessimistic view of agency theory, which in this case reduces a complex strategic decision,

---

[1] The term traditional franchising is used rather than business format franchising by which franchisors give the right to franchisees to use not only their brands but also their all business models. This type of franchising is more common in sectors such as fast food, health services, and education services.

such as choosing a contractual form for a gas station, to the monitoring of opportunistic behaviors and the offering of incentives to mechanically align partners' behaviors to the expectations of marketers. Barthélemy (2011) is also of the opinion that agency theory cannot provide a full account of franchise decisions due to its inability to take social factors into account. On the other hand, the existence of company-owned and dealer-operated outlets in this industry challenges some premises of resource scarcity theory. For instance, considering the lack of investment capital argument, marketers should not relinquish the operation of their own units to independent dealers if they are motivated exclusively by the dealers' investment capital contributions.

In this chapter, we propose a strategic perspective of franchising. Unlike the previous two theories, we consider that the role of managers of these organizations is essential in determining the contractual form for a gas station. Particularly, we contend that managers base their decisions on their perceptions, judgments, beliefs, and views on relevant environmental and organizational factors, with the goal of coping with whatever issue they find critical for the success of a gas station. Environmental factors come from two different levels—the general level affects the conduct of business in a country, and the local level is concerned with only a specific gas station. For instance, at the general level, managers who do not trust the country justice system, for various reasons, may find it difficult to franchise any outlet in the country, regardless of their internal resources and the monitoring costs associated to each outlet. This is because the success of some contractual forms may rely more on the credibility of the justice system than do others. As a matter of fact, research commissioned by the African Development Bank (AfDB) found a positive (negative) relationship between the existence of franchising and the rule of law (corruption) in African countries (African Development Bank 2003; Siggel et al. 2006). In addition, according to the same study, the first and most important obstacle to the development of franchising in Africa is the general lack of familiarity with this concept among the private and public sectors, professional organizations, and academics. In such a context, marketers may find it difficult to find financially able investors willing to commit as dealers for long-term business relationships.

At the local environment level, it does matter how marketers perceive the level of competition, market size, customers, and the access to and reliability of the digital infrastructure. We develop four propositions related to the local environment to illustrate the point that, depending on what marketers or their managers perceive or think of the local environment, they can choose a contractual form based on what they know or believe that this form can achieve. For instance, building on the findings of analytical modeling in marketing, we postulate that managers who anticipate intense local competition should favor dealer-owned and operated stations, while those who anticipate moderate and less intense local competition should respectively favor company-owned and dealer-operated, and company-owned and operated stations. Also, the ability to leverage digital technologies that reduce monitoring and transaction costs can also help expand company-owned outlets in remote areas. Several other propositions can be developed following the same rationale.

Finally, at the organizational level, the lack of internal resources can still play a role in the choice of contractual form. However, what matters most in the theory proposed in this chapter is whether marketers or their managers believe that franchising is the best solution to their lack of internal resources to grow networks. This is essential because marketers can consider other available alternatives to obtain these resources in the market (Rubin 1978). A proposition is developed to illustrate this point using financial constraints that are believed to favor the adoption of franchising in the previous literature.

The strategic perspective of franchising proposed in this chapter provides three major benefits. First, it offers a larger scope than that of previous theories, resulting in a better understanding of the choice of contractual forms. Second, this work highlights the relationship between the general business environment of a country and the decisions affecting a local retail outlet. Except for a few works based on institutional theory (e.g., Barthélemy 2011; Hoffman et al. 2016), previous theories, developed mostly in North America, overlook this dimension. They implicitly assume the existence of strong local business-supporting institutions, which allow companies to focus on making optimal private arrangements among them. In developing countries like Cameroon where local business-supporting institutions are weak and ineffective (Sigué and Biboum 2020), managers cannot afford to make contractual arrangements or strategic decisions without considering the shortcomings of these institutions (Rosado-Serrano et al. 2018; Hoffman et al. 2016; Hoskisson et al. 2000). Third, the emphasis on the inputs of managers to the decision on the contractual form for an outlet compels the use of primary data to better understand their choices. This is a significant improvement over previous theories which favor the use of secondary data or proxies that are often unrelated to the original constructs (Combs and Ketchen 2003).

The rest of this chapter is organized as follows. First, we offer a brief description of the gasoline distribution industry in Cameroon. Second, we present our theoretical framework and develop some testable propositions for its validation. Finally, we conclude and discuss the implications of this work.

2   Gasoline Distribution in Cameroon

This section gives a brief overview of the supply and distribution of petroleum products in Cameroon. The sector is heavily regulated and relies on a few key actors. The National Refining Company (NRC), which is the only refiner in the country, is tasked to supply 80% of the domestic market consumption. The other remaining 20% of the national consumption comes from imports. Wholesalers, also known as marketers, purchase products directly from the NRC or via the Hydrocarbons Prices Stabilization Fund (HPSF), a government agency that coordinates tenders for imports. Among others, additional responsibilities of the HPSF include the harmonization and regulation of petroleum product stocks and prices to ensure stability, affordability, and regular supply across the country. In particular, the HPSF sets regional wholesale and retail prices nationwide. The physical distribution and storage of petroleum products throughout the country are the exclusive domains of the Société Camerounaise des Dépôts Pétroliers (SCDP). This company owns and manages a network of 13 depots in 7 regions (Douala, Yaoundé, Bafoussam, Belabo, Bertoua, Ngaoundéré, and Garoua), which allow for full coverage of the national territory. Whether the products are purchased from the NRC or imported, they are made available to the wholesalers at the nearest SCDP depot serving the market where they are to be commercialized, or at the NRC storage, in the case of those commercialized in the south west region where the NRC is located. There are 13 major marketers of petroleum products and over 600 retail outlets or gas stations in the country.

Unlike other countries where refiners can also engage in gasoline retailing, by law, the NRC is restricted to the production and commercialization to independent marketers in Cameroon. Given its position of quasi monopoly, its prices set on the monthly basis depend exclusively on its production costs and establishment agreement with the government of Cameroon. On the other hand, marketers can sell directly to consumers or indirectly using various types of agreements with resellers. Marketers adopt three major types of distribution arrangements in Cameroon for their branded service stations (see Table 1).

2.1   Company-Owned and Operated (COCO) Stations

This arrangement corresponds to what is known as an integrated channel, where the upstream company (marketer) controls downstream activities and sells products or/and offers services directly to consumers. As shown in Table 1, the marketer owns and controls all, including the site, the equipment, gasoline inventory, and auxiliary services. The manager of a gas station is an employee who is paid a salary and, when applicable, receives additional incentives such as bonuses. These stations are generally well maintained and serve as experimental grounds where new marketing ideas and methods can be tested.

Table 1 Major distribution arrangements for branded service stations

	COCO	CODO	DODO
Site ownership (land, buildings, and tanks)	Marketer	Marketer	Dealer
Equipment ownership (pumps and data interfaces)	Marketer	Marketer	Marketer or/and dealer
Gasoline inventory ownership	Marketer	Dealer	Dealer
Auxiliary services (convenience store, car washes, auto repair)	Marketer	Dealer	Dealer

2.2   Company-Owned and Dealer-Operated (CODO) Stations

Under this arrangement, the marketer owns a gas station that has been in service for at least a full year and entrusts its operation to a lessee dealer who operates this gas station in his name, on his behalf, and at his own risk. In return, the dealer pays rent or a royalty to the marketer for the use of the station. Under Cameroonian law, the dealer must be a registered merchant. Typically, the site, equipment, and all intangible assets associated with the station belong to the marketer, while the dealer controls inventories, operations, and the delivery of all services. The duration of this type of agreements is generally a year. It barely exceeds 3 years as marketers prefer to continuously assess the performance of their dealer partners.

2.3   Dealer-Owned and Dealer-Operated (DODO) Stations

In this case, the dealer owns the retail outlet and enters into an agreement to use the marketer's brand and sell her products. In addition, the marketer generally supplies some equipment such as pumps and data interfaces. As an owner of the outlet, the dealer has the freedom to provide additional services other than those normally encountered in marketer-owned outlets such as convenient stores, car washes, and auto repairs.

Finally, we provide in Table 2 the contractual arrangements used by current marketers with more than 10 service stations in Cameroon. This table indicates that only

Table 2   Major marketers and distribution arrangements used

	COCO	CODO	DODO
Africa petroleum	X		
Blessing petroleum	X	X	
BOCOM	X		
CAMOCO	X		
CAPOGCO	X		
Citizen's oil	X		
Confex oil	X		
Green oil	X		
Gulfin	X		
Neptune	X		
Petrolex	X		
PPSM	X	X	X
SOCAMIT	X		
TRADEX		X	
Mrs Corlay	X	X	
Ola energy		X	X
Total oil	X	X	X

a few marketers offer CODO and DODO arrangements. Most marketers, generally smaller in size, exclusively own and operate their gas stations, which proves that the resource scarcity theory cannot explain the use of franchising in such a context.

3 Theoretical Framework

The fundamental idea of the theory proposed in this chapter is that marketers or their managers choose organizational or contractual forms for their gas stations based on their perceptions, judgments, and beliefs about the adequacy of these forms with regard to critical environmental factors and their own organizational resources, capabilities, and goals (see Fig. 1). We build on a premise of the upper echelon theory (UET) that the perspective of top managers or executives is important in understanding their organization's strategic decisions and performance (Hambrick 2007; Hambrick and Mason 1984).

The choice of a contractual form for an outlet in the gasoline retail industry is one of the most important and complex strategic decisions for marketers. It not only determines the level of financial capital that marketers are willing to commit for the unit but also affects the nature of the business relationship they can maintain with their downstream partners, the level of service they offer to consumers, their ability to respond to rival network marketing activities, and their levels of sales and profits.

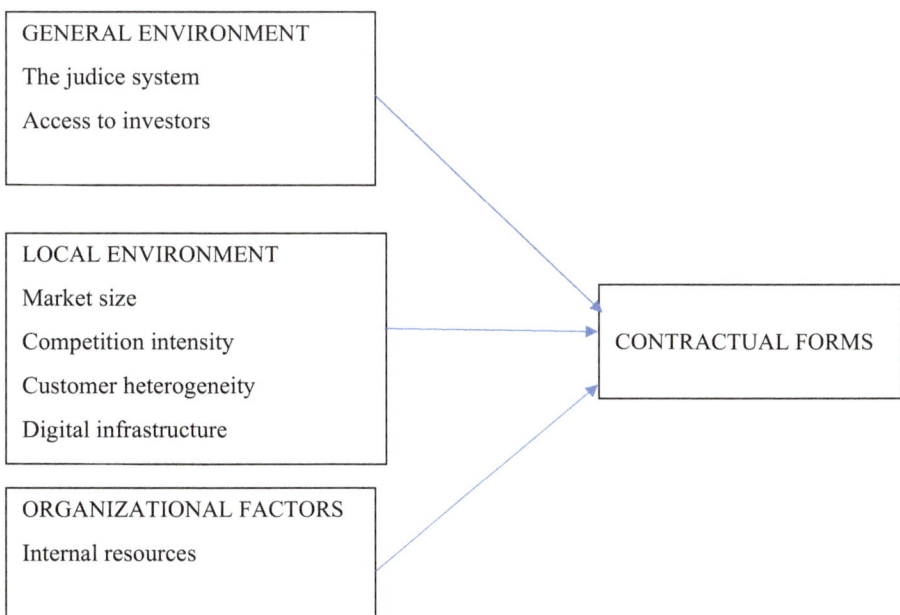

Fig. 1 Theoretical framework

Hambrick and Mason (1984) support the view that these types of complex decisions reflect the decision maker's values, and their knowledge or assumptions about future events, alternatives, and consequences attached to various alternatives. These variables shape their perceptions of the organization's external and internal reality, as well as the actions to be carried out to achieve desired goals.

The influence of the UET on our theoretical framework stops, however, at this level. In fact, Hambrick and Mason (1984) argue that to study organizations' strategic decisions and performance, the focus should be directed toward their top managers' individual characteristics with respect to educational, professional, and social backgrounds. In particular, since the cognitions, values, and perceptions of top managers are difficult to measure, Hambrick and Mason establish a causal relationship between the demographic characteristics of top managers—including age, experience, education, and relevant others—with organizational decisions and outcomes. The demographic characteristics of managers are considered as acceptable proxies for what they think, value, and perceive when studying organizational outcomes. Combs et al. (2004) propose a more faithful application of the UET in the field of franchising.

In this chapter, we move away from the use of managers' demographic proxies. We believe that the key to understanding the choices of contractual forms is to directly study the perceptions, judgments, and beliefs of marketers regarding their ability to cope with the general and local environment of each outlet as well as their internal resources or constraints.

3.1 General Environment

The general environment refers to external factors or forces that shape business opportunities and threats for gasoline marketers in the country, regardless of the location of a specific gasoline retail outlet. The concept is very broad and includes demographic, cultural, economic, institutional, legal, natural, political, social, and technological environments. Despite the importance of the general environment in the international franchising literature, it is often overlooked in domestic franchising (Hoffman et al. 2016; Dant and Grünhagen 2014; Rosado-Serrano et al. 2018; Sashi and Karuppur 2002). Consistent with the international franchising literature, we contend that managers' perceptions of certain factors in these different environments influence the contractual forms they select for their retail outlets in a country. We use the justice system and the availability of investors to illustrate this point. Several other relevant factors may be used to generate additional empirically testable propositions.

3.1.1 Trust in the Justice System

According to Van de Walle (2009), the justice system is a generator of meta-trust as it makes trust in other public institutions possible. For this research, we consider that marketers trust the justice system when they count on its institutions to protect them against opportunistic and harmful behaviors in their business dealings with all stakeholders (Roussey and Deffains 2012). It is believed that people who have confidence in the justice system are less likely to cheat or break the law and contracts. Also, a credible and reliable justice system encourages business partners to avoid litigation costs by finding mutually beneficial out-of-court arrangements (Friedman and Wittman 2007; Roussey and Deffains 2012). In the franchising literature, it is widely recognized that without the rule of law, franchisors (referred in this paper as marketers) have no interest in sharing their various assets, including intellectual property, with dealers who can potentially become competitors or/and damage the value of their brands through opportunistic behaviors. An alternative in this case, assuming the organization decides to invest in the country despite a perceived weak judicial system, would be to own and operate outlets directly, thus avoiding costly litigation due to contract breaks and the need to spend resource monitoring dealers' potential opportunistic behaviors. This is critical in a context like that of Cameroon where there is no franchise association, partners can count on to enforce a code of ethics and resolve certain disputes amicably.

Otherwise, the level of control that marketers exercise over their dealers under the CODO and DODO contractual forms varies considerably. Particularly in CODO, dealers can act opportunistically to increase their profits at the expense of their marketers, but they cannot easily become direct competitors given that the marketers own these outlets. Also, contracts are generally designed to allow marketers to easily terminate these partnerships, limiting the possibility of expensive litigation. DODO agreements, where retailers invest massively in their outlets, are different. Contracts are generally very complex and cover longer periods. Consequently, contract breaks in DODO can lead to very expensive litigation if the justice system is not reliable. As a result, we propose that:

> *P1: Marketers who greatly trust the justice system adopt DODO, while those who moderately and only slightly trust the justice system adopt CODO and COCO, respectively.*

3.1.2 Access to Investors

In the context of this research, an investor is a person or an organization that partners with a marketer to operate a gas station at their own risk with the expectation of achieving profits. An employee whose income is based on salary or commissions is not an investor. As previously discussed, the COCO arrangement relies exclusively on employees, while the success of the CODO and DODO agreements depend on marketers' ability to find investors who can contribute their own resources and effectively operate assigned outlets to the benefit of all distribution channel partners. The resources expected from a potential dealer may be of various types, including knowledge of local markets, management expertise, industry-specific expertise, and capital. For the sake of brevity, below, we focus only on financial resources. In particular, marketers expect CODO and DODO dealers to have enough capital to operate marketer-owned outlets and to build/buy and operate new outlets, respectively. It is common knowledge that the shortage of investment capital is one of the major challenges for micro and small entrepreneurs in Africa, as financial institutions are highly risk averse and do not want to commit to long-term projects. As a result, marketers are constrained by the scarcity of potential dealers able to invest and own a gas station (African Development Bank 2003; Sigué 2012). They are more likely to find CODO dealers who, in principle, only need working capital to operate marketer-owned outlets, as financial institutions are less reluctant to respond to these types of requests. Given these contextual realities, marketers need to be aware of their market power that may enable them to attract the very few financially able investors available. For example, local marketers with weaker brand names may have a harder time convincing investor to partner with them than multinational marketers with established networks and strong brands. This could explain why in Table 2, major multinational marketers such as Ms. Corlay, Ola Energy, and Total Oil have CODO and DODO outlets, while many local marketers only have COCO outlets. We therefore posit that:

> P2: Marketers who believe in their market power to find financially able investors adopt DODO, those who moderately believe in their market power to find financially able investors adopt CODO, and those who do not believe in their market power to find financially able investors adopt COCO.

3.2   Local Environment

The second set of factors affecting the choice of the contractual form belongs to the local environment of the retail outlet. Acknowledging that several local factors may play a role in the management decision on a contractual form, we focus here on four factors, namely market size, the intensity of competition, the heterogeneity of customers, and the digital infrastructure.

3.2.1   Market Size

Here, market size refers to the total sales potential of all services and products of a prospective gas station. It determines the level of investment that either the marketer or the dealer should make to own the station and adequately serve the local market. Beyond agency considerations related to the size of market discussed in previous works (e.g., Dahlstrom et al. 2009), the market potential of an outlet could be used as an indication of its profitability. As a result, a marketer who acts to maximize profits would want to have increased control over retail outlets that are more likely to generate maximum sales. In the case of Cameroon, this is even more critical, because distribution margins and retail prices are regulated. The one remaining way to maximize profits is to sell large quantities. The rationale for this is that managers view most of the costs of owning an outlet as fixed costs that can easily be recouped with sales volume. All other retail outlets will be operated in partnership with dealers under the CODO agreement or the DODO agreement depending on their market size. The following proposition captures this idea:

P3: Marketers adopt DODO when they perceive the outlet's local market as small, otherwise they adopt CODO and COCO when the outlet's local market is perceived as medium and large, respectively.

In the case of the Cameroon where service stations that generate the most sales are generally in urban areas with high population density, one might think that these stations will be DODO or CODO, while those located outside these areas will be DODO. Using agency theory considerations, Dahlstrom and Nygaard (1994) made such a prediction in Norway. However, we refrain from making this type of generalization—what matters is the prospect of selling large quantities, which may in fact be affected by other local environmental factors such as the purchasing power in the surrounding area and the proximity of high-traffic activities.

3.2.2 Competition Intensity

In the economics and marketing literature, competition is largely recognized as affecting contractual arrangements between distribution channel members (e.g., Dahlstrom et al. 2009; McGuire and Staelin 1983; Moorthy 1988; Slade 1998). The underlying idea is that certain contractual forms are more effective than others in dealing with competition. For instance, while it is well-known in bilateral monopoly contexts that COCO arrangements perform better than the other arrangements, due to vertical externalities such as double marginalization, several works have now demonstrated that, in the context of competition between highly substitutable products, DODO arrangements should be preferred (e.g., Coughlan 1985; Martín-Herrán and Sigué 2020; McGuire and Staelin 1983; Moorthy 1988; Trivedi 1998; Wang et al. 2011). These studies support the view that local competition among independent dealers attenuates price and advertising war for highly substitutable products such as those distributed in the gasoline industry to the benefit of the upstream channel partners. Even though retail prices of major gasoline products are exogenously set by a central authority in Cameroon, this argument still holds because a typical gas station sells other non-regulated products and services. Also, members of a gasoline distribution channel have control over other marketing activities that are not regulated. On the other hand, another factor that affects the intensity of local competition is the distance between retail outlets (Martín-Herrán and Sigué 2019, 2020). Everything else being equal, local competition intensifies as the distance between outlets decreases. Following this rationale, we postulate that:

P4: DODO is adopted when managers anticipate intense local competition, otherwise managers adopt CODO and COCO when they anticipate moderate and less intense local competition, respectively.

3.2.3 Customer Heterogeneity

The heterogeneity of customers refers to the existence of different customer segments whose satisfaction can lead the marketer to adopt differentiated marketing
strategies. Assuming that the choice of a contractual arrangement for a retail outlet
is an element of the marketer's marketing strategy, Brickley and Dark (1987) are
among the first to establish a relationship between the existence of heterogenous
customers and this important element of the marketing strategy. They argue that to
ensure consistent quality of service at all outlets in a franchise network, outlets serving regular customers should be franchised (CODO or DODO), while those serving
non-regular customers should be operated by the franchisor (COCO). This is
because franchisees have the incentive to locally lower the quality of service provided to non-regular customers to maximize profits in the short term and may only
suffer from this opportunistic behavior in the long run, as will the whole franchise.
Conversely, regular customers can directly punish opportunistic franchisees by
ceasing to buy from them.

We abandon Brickley and Dark's (1987) pessimistic vision of franchise relationships inspired by agency theory and adopt a marketing perspective that
focuses on satisfying the needs of heterogenous customers. It should be mentioned that Brickley and Dark assume that the success of a franchise network
depends on its ability to offer a standardized assortment of services to all its
customers. Factual observations of gasoline stations in Cameroon, and in other
countries like Canada, reveal that the assortment of services offered in some
franchises in this industry vary considerably from one outlet to another. Some
outlets offer additional services on top of those encountered in typical outlets of
the same franchise network. This practice is part of the desire of marketers to
adapt to the needs of local customers. In such a context, marketers primarily
care about whether a prospective retail outlet should offer either their standard
service assortment or an enhanced or modified assortment designed to better
respond to the needs of local customers. They can implement either undifferen-
tiated or differentiated marketing strategies by allowing partners to respond to
the specific needs of customers in their areas. It is easier to offer standardized
services via one's own outlets (COCO) to maintain uniformity in both marketing and operations, while CODO and DODO outlets can be given some flexibility without jeopardizing the core business of the network and its image. For
instance, in Cameroon, some CODO and DODO outlets offer consumer credit at
the discretion of their operators. Managers of COCO outlets do not generally
have this type of power. In addition, CODO and DODO operators can choose
not to participate in certain promotional activities of the marketer which are,
moreover, compulsory for COCO managers. As discussed earlier, DODO outlets may even combine their gasoline service offering with other services not
typically encountered in other gas stations. As a result, we contend that the
choice of a contractual form is based on the segmentation of the market, which

can be done using various relevant criteria that justify the use of a differentiated marketing strategy to meet local customer needs. Therefore:

P5: COCO is adopted when marketers believe local customers can be served well with their standard offering of services, while CODO and DODO are adopted when marketers believe their standard offer of services should be slightly or significantly altered to satisfy local customers, respectively.

3.2.4 Digital Infrastructure

The role of digital infrastructure in local and international franchising is now well documented (e.g., Hoffman et al. 2016; Paswan et al. 2004; Rosado-Serrano et al. 2018). The digital infrastructure is the basis for the use of digital technologies in several critical aspects in franchise firms. These aspects include, among others, communication, support, monitoring, and the delivery of training and marketing materials to dealers. This has led Hoffman et al. (2016) to postulate, at the international franchise level, that franchise firms are more likely to expand into countries with well-developed Internet infrastructure due to the reduction in monitoring and transaction costs it entails. In the local franchising literature, proponents of agency theory have used the physical distance between monitoring centers and retail outlets as an indicator of how costly it is to monitor local operators. Franchise outlets that are far from monitoring centers are generally advised to reduce their monitoring costs and to own nearby outlets that are not very expensive to monitor (Brickley and Dark 1987; Dahlstrom and Nygaard 1994). If the Internet infrastructure can help marketers reduce transaction and monitoring costs despite distance, then it promotes the expansion of company-owned outlets into remote areas that will naturally be allocated to franchise operators. In other words, in a country like Cameroon where Internet access and its reliability vary considerably from one region outside of the major cities to another, managers should take this into account when choosing a contractual form for each specific remote outlet. We therefore postulate that:

P6: COCO is adopted when marketers believe they can rely on the Internet to manage outlets that are very far from monitoring centers, while CODO and DODO are adopted when marketers believe they cannot rely on the Internet to manage these outlets.

3.3 Organizational Factors

Organizational factors are internal elements that favor or oppose the adoption of a contractual form for a specific outlet. These organizational factors may be circumstantial or structural. Their impact on the selection of a contractual form depends on how mangers perceive and manage them.

3.3.1 Internal Resources

One of the first explanations of the adoption of DODO in a franchise network is the lack of internal resources necessary to support its expansion (Caves and Murphy 1976). Focusing only on financial resources, it is believed that the owner of a distribution network adopts DODO to finance its growth thanks to the capital brought by the dealers. Implicitly, Caves and Murphy (1976) assume that COCO is the best contractual form and that any DODO outlet will ultimately be converted into COCO when financial resource constraints are overcome. This explanation has been criticized because there are other cheaper ways to obtain capital in the market (Rubin 1978). Also, empirical evidence does not support the prediction that the proportion of network-owned units increases as the network matures and overcomes its financial constraints (Combs and Ketchen 2003). As with Caves and Murphy, we believe that the availability/non-availability of internal capital can influence the contractual form choice for a given outlet. However, what matters most is whether marketers see franchising as the best solution to their financial constraints. This perception is important as it influences their decision to invest in owning (or not) the new outlet, and to eventually look for alternative financing opportunities in the market as discussed by Rubin (1978). For instance, Combs and Ketchen (2003) speculate that franchising might be a better financing alternative in times of tight credit. We therefore postulate that:

> P7: Marketers who perceive franchising as the best solution to their financial constraints for growth adopt DODO, while those who do not adopt either COCO or CODO.

4 Conclusion

This chapter proposes a new theoretical perspective of the study of whether a marketer should own and operate or partner with a dealer to operate a gas station in Cameroon. It supports the view that the choice of a contractual form of a retail outlet in this industry is a strategic decision, which depends on the perceptions, judgments, and beliefs that managers of these companies have about the impact of certain organizational and environmental factors on the success or failure of the different alternatives. This new theorization radically differs from the main previous attempts, which undermine the role of managers in this decision and focus on the lack of internal resources and the management of monitoring costs as main decisive factors. In addition, it highlights the influence of the general business environment of the country on this decision, especially in the context where business-supporting institutions such as the justice system and financial institutions are weak or deficient. The importance of the local environment of each retail outlet is also discussed, with a particular emphasis on digital infrastructure, market size, competitive intensity, and customer heterogeneity.

We have purposely chosen to limit the scope of this initial development to the context of a single industry and a specific country to maintain a close relationship with a business reality. We hope, however, that this chapter stimulates more theoretical developments and empirical works in several other industries and countries that focus on understanding the perspective of managers in the choice of a contractual form for a retail outlet. The poor development of network organizations in several African countries, in sectors where franchising excels elsewhere, challenges us all to better understand why their managers do not consider franchising as an alternative or rely more on franchising to speed their growth. For instance, marketers in the gasoline retail industry in Cameroon can still expand their networks as the market is not fully covered, especially outside of the two major cities, Douala and Yaoundé. Based on our framework, a potential explanation of what prevents some of these marketers from relying on franchised outlets to expand their market coverage could be the difficulties they anticipate or encounter in the hiring of investors with the necessary resources.

We have kept this initial framework very simple. It could be expanded in several ways. For example, interactions among some of the factors identified here or additional other factors can be introduced. Also, even with this simple framework, several other testable propositions can be developed. A multidisciplinary approach would probably be richer. Because of our background, the reader may have identified a bias toward marketing. Finally, as a theoretical development effort, the loop will be closed when our predictions are empirically validated. This would require collecting and analyzing primary data from marketers.

Acknowledgments The first author acknowledges the financial support from Athabasca University. The research was conducted when he was on a Research and Study Leave in Cameroon. The authors thank Dr. Pierre Boubou, Mr. Donatien Kodog, Mr. André Kwam, Mr. Isaac Nyouma, Mr. Jean Pierre Tchoutezo, and all the members of ESSEC 2A9 for their multidimensional assistance during this research.

References

African Development Bank. (2003). *Enhancing development in Africa - franchising report.* Retrieved from https://www.afdb.org/fileadmin/uploads/afdb/Documents/Generic-Documents/003_FRANCHISING.pdf

Barthélemy, J. (2011). Agency and institutional influences on franchising decisions. *Journal of Business Venturing, 26,* 93–103.

Brickley, J. A., & Dark, F. H. (1987). The choice of organizational form: The case of franchising. *Journal of Financial Economics, 18,* 401–420.

Caves, R. E., & Murphy, W. F. (1976). Franchising: Firms, markets, and intangible assets. *Southern Journal of Economics, 42,* 572–586.

Combs, J. G., & Ketchen, D. J. (2003). Why do firms use franchising as an entrepreneurial strategy? A meta-analysis. *Journal of Management, 29*(3), 443–465.

Combs, J. G., Michael, S. C., & Castrogiovanni, G. J. (2004). Franchising: A review and avenues to greater theoretical diversity. *Journal of Management, 30*(6), 907–931.

Combs, J. G., Ketchen, D. J., Shook, C. L., & Short, J. C. (2011). Antecedents and conse-quences of franchising: Past accomplishments and future challenges. *Journal of Management, 37*(1), 99–126.

Coughlan, A. T. (1985). Competition and cooperation in marketing channel choice: Theory and applications. *Marketing Science, 4*, 110–129.

Dahlstrom, R., & Nygaard, A. (1994). A preliminary investigation of franchised oil distribution in Norway. *Journal of Retailing, 70*(2), 179–191.

Dahlstrom, R., Haugland, S. A., Nygaard, A., & Rokkan, A. S. (2009). Governance structures in the hotel industry. *Journal of Business Research, 62*, 841–847.

Dant, R. P., & Grünhagen, M. (2014). International franchising research: Some thoughts on the what, where, when, and how. *Journal of Marketing Channels, 21*, 124–132.

Friedman, D., & Wittman, D. (2007). Litigation with symmetric bargaining and two-sided incom-plete information. *Journal of Law, Economics, and Organization, 23*(1), 98–126.

Ghoshal, S. (2005). Bad management theories are destroying good management practices. *Academy of Management Learning & Education, 4*(1), 75–91.

Hambrick, D. C. (2007). Upper echelons theory: An update. *Academy of Management Review, 32*(2), 334–343.

Hambrick, D. C., & Mason, P. A. (1984). Upper echelons: The organization as a reflection of its top managers. *Academy of Management Review, 9*(2), 193–206.

Hoffman, R. C., Munemo, J., & Watson, S. (2016). International franchise expansion: The role of institutions and transaction costs. *Journal of International Management, 22*, 101–114.

Hoskisson, R., Eden, L., Lau, C., & Wright, M. (2000). Strategy in emerging economies. *Academy of Management Journal, 43*(3), 249–267.

Martín-Herrán, G., & Sigué, S. P. (2019). Offensive and defensive marketing in spatial competi-tion. *Journal of Service Research, 22*(2), 189–201.

Martín-Herrán, G., & Sigué, S. P. (2020). Manufacturer offensive and defensive advertising in competing distribution channels. *International Transactions in Operational Research, 27*(2), 958–983.

McGuire, T., & Staelin, R. (1983). An industry equilibrium analysis of downstream vertical inte-gration. *Marketing Science, 2*, 161–192.

Moorthy, K. S. (1988). Strategic decentralization in channels. *Marketing Science, 7*, 335–355.

Oxenfeldt, A. R., & Kelly, A. O. (1969). Will successful franchise systems ultimately become wholly-owned chains? *Journal of Retailing, 44*(4), 69–83.

Paswan, A. K., Wittmann, C. M., & Young, Y. A. (2004). Intra, extra, and internets in franchise network organizations. *Journal of Business to-Business Marketing, 11*(1/2), 103–127.

Pénard, T., Raynaud, E., & Saussier, S. (2004). Théories des contrats et réseaux de franchise. *Revue Française d'Économie, 18*(4), 151–191.

Rosado-Serrano, A., Paul, J., & Dikova, D. (2018). International franchising: A literature review and research agenda. *Journal of Business Research, 85*, 238–257.

Roussey, L., & Deffains, B. (2012). Trust in judicial institutions: An empirical approach. *Journal of Institutional Economics, 8*(3), 351–369.

Rubin, P. (1978). *The theory of the firm and the structure of franchise contracts* (Vol. 21, pp. 223–232). Journal of Law and Economics.

Sashi, C. M., & Karuppur, D. P. (2002). Franchising in global markets: Towards a conceptual framework. *International Marketing Review, 19*(5), 499–524.

Siggel, E., Maisonneuve, P., & Fortin, E. (2006). Franchising and the potential for economic devel-opment in Africa. *Canadian Journal of Development Study, 27*(2), 223–238.

Sigué, S. P. (2012). The promises of franchising in Africa: The need for a critical examination. *Journal of African Business, 13*(3), 168–171.

Sigué, S. P., & Biboum, A. D. (2020). Entrepreneurial marketing and social networking in small and medium service enterprises: A case study into business dealings in Cameroon. *Journal of African Business, 21*(3), 338–354.

Slade, M. E. (1998). Strategic motives for vertical separation: Evidence from gasoline markets. *The Journal of Law, Economics, & Organization, 14*(1), 84–96.

Trivedi, M. (1998). Distribution channels: An extension of exclusive retailership. *Management Science, 48*(7), 896–909.

Van de Walle, S. (2009). Trust in the justice system: A comparative view across Europe. *Prison Service Journal, 183*, 22–26.

Wang, C.-J., Chen, Y.-J., & Wu, C.-C. (2011). Advertising competition and industry channel structure. *Marketing Letters, 22*, 79–99.

Supply Chain Management Systems in Africa: Insights from Nigeria

Ade Oyedijo, Kweku Adams, and Serge Koukpaki

1 Introduction

Over the past two decades, firms have heavily relied on supply chain collaboration (SCC) to gain competitive advantage and to develop internal and external opportunities (Cao and Zhang 2011; Um and Kim 2019). The strategic value of SCC has been recognised as firms try to enter new markets (Chen et al. 2017) and for higher efficiencies in their procurement, planning, manufacturing and distribution (Soosay and Hyland 2015). However, today's supply chains (SC) operate in more dynamic environments characterised by the intense level of competition, high level of uncertainty, demanding and unpredictable customers, globalisation, and fast developing technologies (Liu et al. 2020). As a result, there are increasing structural and nonstructural barriers which may influence SCC resulting in the need for more collaborative efforts (Busse et al. 2016).

Although several studies have investigated the concept of SCC (e.g. Fawcett et al. 2012; Liu et al. 2020), there are still a number of gaps which require scholarly attention. For instance, past studies on SCC have tried to establish a solid definition of the concept, determine its benefits and outcomes, conduct a systematic review, or

A. Oyedijo
Department of Logistics and Management Systems, Hull University Business School, University of Hull, Hull, UK
e-mail: A.Oyedijo@hull.ac.uk

K. Adams (✉)
Department of Management, Huddersfield Business School, University of Huddersfield, Queensgate, UK
e-mail: k.adams@hud.ac.uk

S. Koukpaki
York Business School, York St John University, York, UK

J. B. Abugre et al. (eds.), *Business in Africa in the Era of Digital Technology*,
Advances in Theory and Practice of Emerging Markets,
https://doi.org/10.1007/978-3-030-70538-1_8

examine its performance impact, all from either a single (one-sided) or dyadic per-spective (Nyaga et al. 2013; Panahifar et al. 2018). However, there is a dearth of research on the barriers and driving factors that impact SCC and some possible approaches for improvement (Soosay and Hyland 2015). Second, the majority of the studies on SCC and general supply chain management (SCM) have mainly focused on developed countries often omitting developing economies and emerging markets. Third, past studies have rarely considered the impact of digital technolo-gies on collaboration between SC partners in Africa. This is a crucial topic for aca-demics and practitioners as it offers new and interesting insights regarding how supply chains can flourish with the aid of digital technologies in such settings. Responding to broader requests in the literature for knowledge development about SCC in context-specific settings (Ramanathan and Gunasekaran 2014), this research focuses on Nigeria.

So far, only a few studies (e.g. Adebanjo et al. 2013; Ojadi et al. 2017) have con-sidered Nigeria in the examination of SC-related subjects. This is rather surprising because the economy of Africa is constantly evolving, and Nigeria is playing an increasing role in Africa's evolving economy because of its role as a supplier of some major commodities (Muogboh and Ojadi 2018). Nigeria is also the seventh most populous nation in the world (United Nations, 2019), and the largest economy in Africa (International Monetary Fund 2019). Similar to other developing coun-tries, it is difficult to manage SCs in Nigeria due to the level of complexity and vari-ous manufacturers, retailers, suppliers, and third-party providers responding to the demand of a growing population of over 200 million people (Orji et al. 2019). Although the literature has stressed on the importance of SC collaborative activities for improving firm and SC performance (Nyaga et al. 2010), however, whether this is the case in a developing economy warrants an investigation. Thus, it is unclear whether the conceptual frameworks proposed in the pertinent literature are appli-cable in the Nigerian setting. It is also unclear how SCC in Nigeria can improve through the adoption of digital technology. Based on the gaps in the literature, we ask the following research questions:

RQ1.   *What ways do barriers and driving forces impact SCC in the Nigerian context?*

RQ2.   *How can the challenges associated with SCC in Nigeria be effectively managed?*

We contribute to the literature by providing new insights into the continuing challenges that supply chains face in developing countries like Nigeria. The atten-tion on Nigeria is warranted considering that it is an emerging and increasingly globalised market (Muogboh and Ojadi 2018), which depicts an area that is not well 'understood' about the discourse on SCM (Ojadi et al. 2017). Thus, we provide an empirically rich and unique context to understand this subject matter. Specifically, the focus on SCC within the food and beverage (F&B) sector in Nigeria is because it plays a major role in the regional and global economy in Africa by meeting the needs of people (World Bank 2018).

For theory, it contributes to the literature on SCM and SCC by revealing the barriers and drivers of SCC from the perspective of an emerging market. Second, it extends and tests the significance of supply chain collaborative activities in a different setting with structural and non-structural barriers. Thus, this study develops an integrated model which links three levels of barriers and driving forces of SCC together. Third, it contributes to the buyer–supplier collaboration literature by using the dyad as a unit of analysis and studying how different parties cope with SSC challenges.

For practice, it reveals new approaches to managing supply chains and developing a strong collaboration between supply chain partners in developing economies like Nigeria. This knowledge is vital for sustaining SCC in such contexts. Second, it helps practitioners categorise the different issues affecting SCC based on the integrative model proposed in this study. Thus, the insights from this study provide managers with clear evidence to develop approaches and invest in key areas that would enable them to compete globally, especially in a digitised market.

The next section presents a review of the literature and provides a background to the research context. Then, the methodology of the research is described with the qualitative and quantitative studies. Next, we discuss the research findings and implications. Finally, we conclude the chapter with some suggestions for future research based on the limitations.

2 Literature Review

2.1 Supply Chain Collaboration

Collaborative activities represent each party's willingness to give and take in the relationship this allows the relationship to adapt over time and creates an avenue for on-going administration of the exchange (Simatupang and Sridharan 2008). Srinivasan and Brush (2006) stated that these activities promote cooperative behaviour and increase the potential value of the exchange relationship. We consider three types of collaborative activities in this study: information sharing, joint relationship effort, and dedicated investment as they represent value-adding relational norms. Each of these activities is defined below.

Information sharing has become an important aspect among organisations as the value-creating factors are shifting from the physical and financial assets towards intangible assets (Koçoğlu et al. 2011). Information sharing refers to the extent that critical information is conveyed to a party's relationship partners (Kembro and Näslund 2014). This may include involving other parties in early stages of product design, opening the books and sharing cost information, discussing future product development plans, or jointly providing supply and demand forecast (Cannon and Perreault Jr 1999). Information sharing is considered one of the five building blocks that characterise a solid SCC (Lalonde 1998), and a critical factor to bring forth competitive advantage in the long run (Li and Lin 2006).

Joint relationship effort is critical for SCC as SC partners need to work together to plan, coordinate activities, and resolve problems (Nyaga et al. 2010). Joint relationship effort consisting of joint decision-making and joint problem-solving is perceived as a natural extension and largely dependent upon information sharing between SC partners (Min et al. 2005). Joint planning is essential in SC relationships to co-align operations and capacities which has a positive influence on relationship quality (Min et al. 2005). The importance of joint problem-solving has also been recognised to result in mutually developed process improvement (Min et al. 2005). A joint effort between SC partners such as planning, goal setting, performance measurement and problem-solving is significant for a successful SCC (Soosay et al. 2008).

Dedicated investments refer to investments made that are dedicated to collaboration by SC partners (Heide and John 1990). Dedicated investments are also critical for SCC as they offer tangible evidence that a partner can be believed, cares for the collaboration, and willing to go the extra mile with such investments (Ganesan 1994). These investments have been recognised to communicate a strong commitment to the collaboration, because of the economic consequences that the other party will incur if the relationship ends (Nyaga et al. 2010).

2.2 Collaborative Activities, Supply Chain Relationship and Performance

Past studies recognised the benefits of collaborative activities between SC partners to include risk sharing, cost reduction, enhanced rapid learning capacity, knowledge transfer and sustainable competitive advantage (Li et al. 2006). Dedicated investments offer tangible evidence of a partner's commitment to a relationship, which will in turn increase the level of trust and greater satisfaction in the relationship (Jap and Ganesan 2000). Kwon and Suh (2005) state that inter-firm communication is essential in the trust-building process since sharing of critical information and communication allow businesses to develop a mutual understanding of each other's routines and develop mechanisms for resolving conflicts, which indicates that the partner is trustworthy. The sharing of high-level information minimises uncertainty which results in improved levels of trust and commitment between SC partners in a relationship. Several studies suggest that joint relationship efforts enable partners to co-align their operations and processes, make joint decisions, which enhances the relationship by building trust (Nyaga et al. 2010), commitment to the relationship (Jap and Ganesan 2000) and relationship satisfaction.

Besides the benefits that collaborative activities offer to relationships between SC partners, collaborative activities also have significant advantages for performance (Cao and Zhang 2011). Collaborative practices and long-term relationships with supply chain partners are also expected to yield organisation-specific benefits and have a positive influence on a firm's market share, return on investment and advance overall competitive position (Cai et al. 2013).

3 Industry Background

3.1 The Nigerian Setting

Putting this research into context, it is important to start by providing some background into the Nigerian context. Nigeria is the most populous black nation in the world with a fast-rising population that is rapidly reaching 200 million people. It is considered as the biggest economy in Africa with a GDP of US$484.9 billion (International Monetary Fund 2019). In 2008, a report published by Goldman Sachs stated that Nigeria could become one of the largest 20 economies by 2025, which drove the Nigerian government to inaugurate a strategic movement to enable Nigeria to consolidate its leadership role in Africa termed 'Vision 2020'. Observing Nigeria's position now and its previous GDP positions over the past decade, this target may become a reality.

However, the commercial environment in Nigeria has also grown in the past decade to become highly uncertain for businesses to operate (Oyedijo 2011; Oyedijo et al. 2011; Didia and Nwokah 2015). Despite its solid resources, oil-rich Nigeria has been affected adversely by several detrimental factors such as gigantic corruption at all levels, feeble corporate governance, an inconsistent regulatory environment, restrictive trade policies, unreliable dispute resolution mechanisms, fragmented relationships between shareholders and stakeholders (Adams et al. 2019), devaluation of the Nigerian naira, drop in global oil price, weakened consumer confidence and an insurgency in the Northern geographic area for almost a decade (Central Intelligence Agency 2020). These factors have impacted the Nigerian economy adversely which ultimately led to a decline in the business market and an economic recession in 2016 for the first time in almost three decades (International Monetary Fund 2019).

Likewise, the business environment in Nigeria could be highly unstructured and does not follow the distinct configurations utilised in the global industrialised settings (Adebanjo et al. 2013). These issues also include bad roads and transportation links, distorted electricity supply, poor government support, etc. Several manufacturing firms have also ceased to operate in Nigeria while those who stayed manufacture goods at costs relatively higher than other competitors in different countries (Ojadi et al. 2017). Some of these issues are also internal issues, partially because of fraudulent practices in purchasing and supply chain arrangements (Ugoani 2019). Although several initiatives were developed to resolve these business issues in Nigeria (Okonjo-Iweala and Osafo-Kwaako 2007), firms are still seeking opportunities to minimise operating costs, improving product and service quality and developing continuous relationships with supply chain partners as mechanisms to remain competitive (Oyedijo 2011; Njoku 2019). The Nigerian context is similar to several African countries that embarked on IMF economic reform programmes (Adams et al. 2014) to privatise state-owned supply chain enterprises to improve efficiency. In many ways, insights from Nigeria present a fairly accurate reflection of realities in other African countries, at least, in West Africa.

3.2 The Food and Beverage Sector in Nigeria

The food and beverage (F&B) sector represent 22.5% of Nigeria's manufacturing industry, 66% of total consumer expenditure, and an aggregate industry output valued at about $20.55 billion equivalent to 4.6% of gross domestic product (GDP), SC costs are very high, negatively impacting performance (Adebayo 2012). The persistent structural and policy challenges and a wide infrastructural gap have been highlighted as overarching issues (International Monetary Fund 2019). Different issues may influence SCC such as weak visibility, poor information sharing, insufficient joint relationship effort and minimal dedicated investment between SC partners.

Likewise, heavy vehicular traffic, accidents and breakdowns on several intra- and inter-city highways result in a lot of delays which affect lead times and product deliveries, and in turn, increasing costs of operations and minimising efficiency and product delivery levels. Most manufacturers sell their final products only to businesses (third parties), who sell to other actors along with the SC such as retailers, transporters/distributors and end consumers. These distributors are referred to as 'middlemen', who stand in the gap between manufacturers and end consumers in the form of third-party providers (see Fig. 1).

The top manufacturers in the industry include Guinness Nigeria Plc, Consolidated Breweries, Nigerian Bottling Company Ltd., Cadbury Plc, Nigerian Breweries, Fan Milk Plc, 7UP Bottling Company Plc and Coca-Cola Nigeria Plc. The manufacturers often outsource some of the core activities highlighted in Fig. 1. The third parties often undertake the relationship management function which involves feeding back to manufacturers regarding customer needs and concerns about their products. The collaboration between the third parties and other actors in the SC is often fragmented. Thus, this study attempts to examine the challenges encountered in the food and beverage manufacturing SC in Nigeria, and how these challenges can be managed effectively.

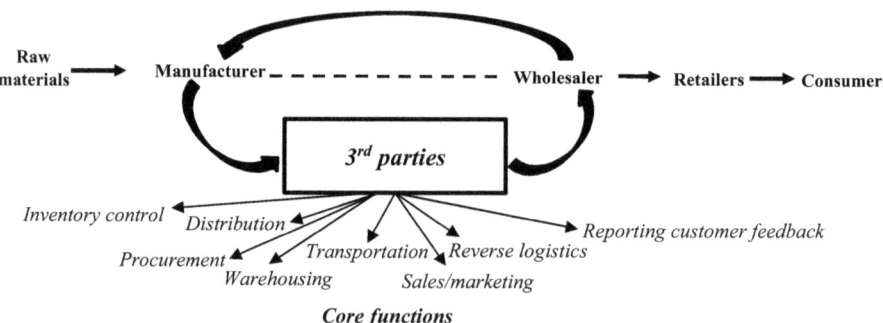

Fig. 1 Supply chain in Nigeria's food and beverage sector

4 Research Method

4.1 Research Design

To empirically explore the challenges associated with SCM systems in Nigeria and identify how to improve the SCM system based on these current challenges, an exploratory research design was adopted based on its emphasis on detail, depth and explanation (Patton 2015). Thus, a qualitative method (Silverman 2014) was used to develop a theory about barriers and driving forces that impact SCC and how to manage them effectively. This approach was selected to elaborate on the existing SCC theory (Lee et al. 1999), particularly because most studies on this subject have not been conducted in a developing country's context. Theoretically, this approach also helps in laying the groundwork that will lead to future research based on the results of this study since, practically, it helps in gaining first-hand insights from practitioners about the subject.

4.2 Data Collection

The target respondents are purchasing and SC managers in the F&B manufacturing supply chain across Nigeria. We collected the data for this phase using semi-structured interviews. We obtained a list of F&B manufacturers in Nigeria from the Nigerian Association of Chambers of Commerce, Industry, Mines and Agriculture (NACCIMA) and the Lagos Chamber of Commerce and Industry (LCCI). We also established contact with the manufacturers through visits to their plants and offices in different parts of Nigeria. We established contact with these firms using an initial invitation letter which stated the aim and objectives of our research. We also had a few follow-up telephone calls to arrange interview dates. All interview respondents were asked to be kept anonymous.

The interviews were held with 22 purchasing and supply executives, and their positions are displayed in Table 1. All the interviews conducted lasted for more than 45 min. We utilised a standard interview guide which was developed from a review of the relevant literature. The interview guide helped us develop questions which were divided into two main themes: *barriers and driving forces which impact SCC in Nigerian context; and how the challenges associated with SCC in Nigeria can be effectively managed*. We also pre-tested the interview guide with academics and practitioners in the industry familiar with the subject matter. The interview guide was semi-structured in nature to allow for flexibility during the interview to explore new issues introduced by the participants. All interviews began with general questions about the background information of the interviewee and their history of the dealings with their supply chain partners. The questions were kept broad as a deliberate act to give the respondents freedom in their answers (Saunders et al. 2009).

We recorded and transcribed the interviews through an ethical procedure with anonymity promised to all the participants to allow for a detailed analysis (Patton

Table 1 Interview details and respondents' features

Position of the interviewee	Interview length (min)	Classification	Educational level	Location	Years of experience
Procurement Manager A	50	Food	Master's degree	Lagos State	9
Sales Manager B	60	Dairy	Master's degree	Lagos State	11
Commercial Manager C	45	Food	Master's degree	Lagos State	14
Merchandise Manager D	45	Food	Master's degree	Ogun State	8
Purchasing Director E	50	Beverage	Master's degree	Lagos State	9
Supply Executive F	60	Beverage	First degree	Ogun State	6
General Manager G	65	Beverage	Master's degree	Lagos State	17
Sales and Distribution Manager H	50	Beverage	Master's degree	Oyo State	10
Supply Chain Manager I	45	Dairy	Master's degree	Lagos State	8
Logistics Manager J	45	Food	First degree	Abuja FCT	12
Supply Chain Project Manager K	50	Beverage	Master's degree	Osun State	7
Project Manager L	45	Food	First degree	Lagos State	6
Logistics Manager M	60	Dairy	First degree	Ogun State	13
Supply and Delivery Manager N	45	Dairy	Master's degree	Kano State	8
Product Delivery Manager O	50	Beverage	Master's degree	Osun State	6
Warehouse Manager P	48	Beverage	First degree	Lagos State	5
Logistics Operations Manager Q	52	Food	First degree	Edo state	4
Inventory Manager R	45	Food	First degree	Anambra State	7
Supply Director S	50	Food	Master's degree	Lagos State	14
Plant Manager T	40	Beverage	Master's degree	Kwara State	10
Distribution Manager U	45	Beverage	First degree	Osun State	7
Supply Chain Manager V	45	Food	Master's degree	Benue State	9

2015). The transcribed interviews were validated with informants by asking for feedback, clarification of any points and final approval (Yin 2009). With qualitative data being difficult to analyse, the findings were cross-checked by an anonymous outsider with experience in analysing qualitative interviews, to help achieve reliability of data. The interviews provided an in-depth view of SCM in Nigeria and the challenges associated with SCC.

Ethical concerns are an important aspect of conducting research (Silverman 2014). Ethical approval was obtained from the relevant University Ethics Committee before the data collection commenced. After each interview, it was explained that their insights would be transcribed, and a copy would be sent back to them to validate, which gave the respondents a chance to edit the transcript (Yin 2009).

4.3 Data Analysis

The interviews were analysed using the thematic analysis method, and we presented all themes by categorising emerging sub-themes (Easterby-Smith et al. 2012; Koukpaki et al. 2020). We followed three key steps endorsed by Miles and Huberman (1994): data reduction, data display and conclusion. We deducted the data to quotes or sentences (first-order codes) that were found related to the research questions. Then, we grouped all the first-order codes into second-order descriptive codes such as 'self-interest seeking and unethical practices', 'rigid structure and governance' and 'bad transport linkage'.

We were able to unravel specific details on the factors that impact SCM in general. Subsequently, we were able to divide and summarise the second-order codes, the challenges, into main aspects such as internal related issues, SC-related issues, and external related issues, which formed the third-order codes.

5 Findings

The research findings show results from the interviews drawing out the main themes from the research questions: why SCCs encounter challenges, as well as how the challenges can be effectively managed.

5.1 The Challenges Associated with SCC in Nigeria

5.1.1 External Level: Governance Support System

We found that the challenges that businesses face are numerous as managers highlighted a long list. Our interactions with managers revealed that many companies believe that their collaboration with SC partners could improve but due to many issues which are encountered, SC collaboration is difficult to actualise. The challenges encountered are structural and non-structural factors, which may be often out of their control. Many of the issues identified are sources of uncertainty and complexity in the manufacturing sector which have an adverse impact on the success of SCCs and reduce the prospects of high levels of relationship quality.

Some of the results derived also confirm the results of a study by Simangunsong et al. (2012) which identified sources of uncertainty in the SC. One main issue that was highlighted by the interviewees is the current structure and governance in the industry. For SC, governance and control play a key role in effectively managing businesses involved both at the SC level and at the industrial level. Individual firms need to have an element of governance and structure in place to achieve the objectives of the SC. Likewise, the arm of government in charge of business developments needs to be able to oversee the affairs of the industry and businesses involved which would increase aspects such as fair competition and business support, with significant effects on the wider economy.

An example of a critical challenge was highlighted by Procurement Manager A, who stated:

> The structures are somewhat fragmented, to be honest, and this affects efficiency. I worked in Europe for several years where the structures on governance are very rigid. So, I think there's a need for a stronger structure that aims to attain high performance for the industry and the economy at large.

Likewise, Commercial Manager C also emphasised the point by stating:

> We need to set up mechanisms that can improve how we operate currently. This new implementation needs to have a long-term vision to develop the manufacturing sector and grow businesses with potentials. Many businesses struggle because of the lack of structure and rigid governance in place to control and oversee the affairs of the industry effectively.

Based on the above evidence, the structure and governance in the industry need to be re-evaluated because of the impact on SC. All stakeholders in the SC need to divert adequate resources for reducing this challenge.

5.1.2   External: Weak Infrastructure

It is a common understanding that poor infrastructure has been a major challenge for the development of Nigeria. Our findings reveal key factors which influence the SCM such as poor transport links and networks, security and safety issues, poor power and electricity supply, and weak government support and investment. These points were highlighted by Supply Chain Manager I who stated that:

> The transport links can be a big issue. There are also a lot of road accidents that occur every time which cause heavy road traffic impacting our delivery schedules. We also spend a lot of money on insurance costs due to the high probability of road accident or vehicle breakdown.

There were also concerns about the high costs incurred by regular repairs and maintenance of trucks due to bad roads. Likewise, interviewees complained that the poor transport systems make it difficult to meet the requirements of the SC partner which affects the relationship quality between them. The weak infrastructural facilities in Nigeria were also highlighted by Sales and Distribution Manager H and Logistics Manager J who stated that:

Our roads are very bad. We spent a lot of money on vehicular repairs and maintenance. I feel this element also affects our ability to meet some of the demands agreed with our supplier.

A major challenge for our supply chain is the poor transport network. It costs us a fortune to manage the logistics aspect due to bad roads, regular traffic jams, and severe auto crash sometimes where people even die. But this is mainly because the roads need fixing and the transport links need to be upgraded.

5.1.3 Internal Level: Human Behaviour and People

We also found that behavioural issues and lack of accountability on the individual level have a negative impact on the prospects of having a successful SCC. These findings endorse the point that human behaviour is critical in SCM and has the potential of disrupting the SCC process. This was also indicated by Merchandise Manager D who stated that:

We also have people who just make things very complicated and often affect the management aspect of the collaborations.

Likewise, Purchasing Director E also mentioned how human behavioural factors can influence collaboration in the SC:

Many of the personnel we deal with regularly who clearly need a lot of training and knowledge on how to deal with SC members. Some people act as if they are not willing to collaborate or we are forcing them to partner with us.

These findings above emphasise the significance and role of people and human behaviour in SCCs. Firm representatives in the F&B manufacturing SCs in Nigeria need to improve their technical know-how for their SC collaborations to become effective. This point was emphasised by Supply Executive F:

The relationship often becomes difficult to handle due to some of the unrealistic demands that our suppliers give. Some people act and behave in a very irrational way especially when making critical decisions on the relationship.

5.1.4 Supply Chain Level: Weak Digital Technology

Likewise, technology advancement was highlighted as a major issue that impacts the collaboration between SC partners and SCM. Respondents stressed the need for a digitalised technological landscape which promotes the use of advanced systems to improve supply chain collaborative activities such as information sharing and communication and to improve dedicated investments to the SCC. The lack of advanced digital technology weakens the process of undertaking other key activities related to fulfilling the requirements of end consumers such as forecasting and inventory management and also slows down the overall decision-making process. These points were highlighted by Supply Director S who stated that:

> There are no optimization systems available to share critical information on-time with our supply chain members on critical aspects such as product modification and changes to orders. So, we spend a lot on purchasing internet Wi-Fi and telephone minutes to enable communication via email and telephone.

The importance of digital technology was also emphasised by Inventory Manager R who stated that:

> We lack advanced ICT systems that can support our decision making on aspects of the supply chain management process such as forecasting, planning and control, distribution, and inventory management.

5.1.5 Supply Chain Level: Ethical Issues

In addition, we also found that current ethical culture is a restraining factor or barrier that impacts SCC in Nigeria. We particularly identified factors such as corruption, bribery, fraud, insider abuse and negative use of bargaining and purchasing power as key elements that impact effective collaboration between SC partners. Some SC partners portray behaviours that are unethical and socially unsustainable. This seems to be a big issue in developing economies and in Nigeria in particular. The following illustrative quote by Supply Chain Project Manager K explains this:

> Corruption, bribery, and other fraudulent practices are also factors that affect our ability to perform well. Some companies bribe to get specific favours and superiority from manufacturing firms which produces unfair competition.

Other challenges associated with managing F&B manufacturing SCs in Nigeria are divided into three categories: internal, supply chain and external level.

5.2   Managing the Challenges Associated with SCC in Nigeria

5.2.1   External: Government Support, Investment and Reforms

Managers also shared some possible solutions to the identified challenges. Most managers stated that many challenges that affect their SC are out of their control as individual businesses. Thus, there is a need for stronger governmental support to resolve some of these challenges. The government is encouraged to introduce reforms that will improve the business environment. These reforms should tackle issues relating to poor governance, poor infrastructure, investment in technology and security issues. These recommendations were emphasised by Commercial Manager C who stated that:

> The weak corporate SC governance can be dealt with by introducing rules and regulations that industry professionals and companies can abide by. We have some structures in place,

but they are too weak in my opinion and they create avenues for different practices that are on the long-run damaging to the longevity of collaborations.

Other managers stressed that these government-level investments should focus on enabling business collaboration and inter-firm trade by concentrating on important aspects such as involving stakeholders in the reformation process, industry-level engagement and resolving issues of power failure, which would foster technology expansion. For example, Sales and Distribution Manager H stated that:

There needs to be an environment that enables collaboration through investments in people, industry, technology, power, security, infrastructure, and regulatory bodies.

By implementing reforms and policies and increasing support level, the government has the potential to reduce some of the unethical, corrupt, fraudulent acts, negative use of power and other security issues in the business environment.

5.2.2   Internal: Investment in Training and Development

To manage the highlighted challenges, managers also referred to factors categorised as internal to the focal firms and their SCs. These factors include investing in the training and development of SC personnel to improve their relationship management approach and behaviour. For example, Supply Executive F explained in the following illustrative quote:

I feel a lot of training and knowledge is needed on how SC collaborations can benefit individual businesses but also the economy at large. When businesses are doing well in a growing economy such as Nigeria, this also benefits the government and living standards.

SC professionals in Nigeria are urged to undertake regular assessment measures to improve their existing technical know-how on the value of collaboration and how to deliver value through the entire SC. Thus, focal manufacturing firms should invest in developing their firm SC practitioners (boundary spanners) and their third-party providers through methods such as supplier evaluation, selection and supplier development programmes. This would promote collaboration between F&B manufacturers and their SC members. The following illustrative quote by Logistics Sales Manager M explains this point:

Collaboration is often difficult to carry out due to some SC members hoard critical information in order to gain a competitive advantage over supply chain partners whom they see as competitors instead of partners. So, a lot of investment needs to be made on training and development.

Similarly, firms are encouraged to focus on collaborative activities to overcome some of the challenges faced. For example, managers mentioned that a higher collaborative effort towards information sharing between the F&B manufacturers and third-party providers is crucial. Other activities such as joint relationship effort between chain members which can help in managing unforeseen challenges dedicated investments to the SC (e.g. innovation) and joint meetings which would help in formulating beneficial terms of trade and increase in flexibility between chain partners. For example, the following illustrative quote by Procurement Manager A and Logistics Manager J highlights the points:

> *Uncertainties also arise as a result of the supplier's inability to meets its initial promises. Cases as such require some form of flexibility on our part and some joint problem solving but stricter supplier selection process for future suppliers.*

> *I think we also need to invest together in technology and innovation and development for our SC collaborations to succeed. Many firms in the SC rarely invest in people which affects the overall quality because people are not well trained.*

5.2.3   Supply Chain Level: Investment in Supply Chain Collaborative Activities

Our findings reveal the importance of collaborative activities in the SC regardless of the challenging context which they operate in. Thus, firms are encouraged to focus on collaborative activities to overcome some of the challenges faced. These collaborative activities (e.g. information sharing could improve visibility by sharing forecast, order information, shipping notes, maintenance plans or even pursue CPFR) can help them resolve issues quickly and manage each other's expectations. The following illustrative quote by Distribution Manager U illustrates this point:

> *We often lack coordination which is due to lack of timely communication. But we also lack systems that would facilitate communication. So, for now, we are trying our best to ensure we have regular meetings with our key supply chain partners especially the members close to the end-consumers.*

Our findings also reveal that commitment and dedication between the two parties can lead to more willingness to share information, work closely and solve problems. This can improve trust levels in the long run and develop a strong relationship. The following illustrative quote by a Supply Chain Manager V explains this point:

> *Our collaboration can also benefit a lot from commitment and dedication that the collaboration can benefit all. More trusting other parties to carry out their duties without any thoughts that we will be cheated in some way can help the collaboration.*

Our data indicate that to manage such challenges associated with SCC in Nigeria, SC partners need to pay attention to joint investment and invest in the joint initiative that will improve other aspects of their collaboration. The following illustrative quote by a Procurement Manager A explains this point:

> *Uncertainties also arise as a result of the supplier's inability to meets its initial promises. Cases as such require some form of flexibility on our part and some joint problem solving but stricter supplier selection process for future suppliers.*

Some other solutions to the challenges associated with managing F&B manufacturing SCs in Nigeria are highlighted in the findings and discussion section.

6   Discussion of Findings and Conclusion

This study attempted to investigate the ways barriers and driving forces impact SCC in the Nigerian context, and how the challenges associated with SCC in Nigeria can be effectively managed. This research is important as it considers a neglected context (Nigeria) and adds to the literature on barriers and drivers of SCC (Fawcett et al. 2008, 2015). Thus, interesting findings were revealed about the nature of SCM in general and how factors which act as barriers of SCC in Nigeria (see Fig. 2 for a summary of research findings). The findings also suggest possible strategies that could be implemented as driving forces of SCC in Nigeria and similar developing contexts. Thus, the following contributions are made to the relevant literature.

Our research demonstrates that supply chains in Nigeria operate in a highly volatile environment, and SCCs are regularly encountering several structural and non-structural challenges. These challenges were classified into three main levels: external, internal and supply chain level. *At the external level*, supply chain partners have to deal with issues that are often out of their control as individual entities or as a supply chain. These issues are mostly related to the nature of the environment and business market in Nigeria which comprises of numerous structural barriers which affect the potential for effective inter-organisational collaboration.

At the internal level, our findings reveal that factors within the control of individual firms also serve as barriers to SCC. For example, issues such as human behaviour, ethical concerns and the role of people, all play a key role in fostering SCC. Extending the current knowledge on SCM in Africa and the associated

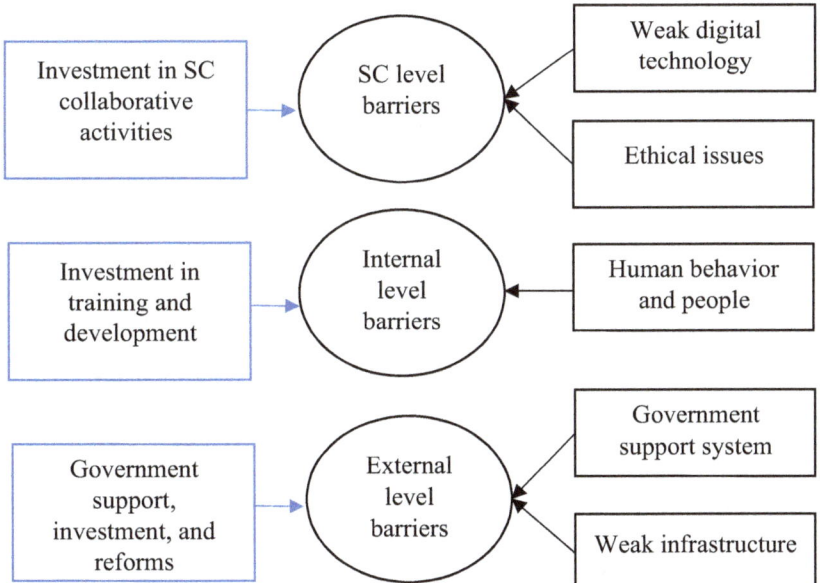

Fig. 2 The driving forces and barriers of supply chain collaboration in Nigeria

challenges, our research shows that people and their behavioural issues influence the prospects of a solid collaboration between supply chain partners. This is in support of the existing literature which has recognised the role of people and human behaviour in SCM (Schorsch et al. 2017; Gligor et al. 2019). However, this issue is pertinent in a setting like Nigeria considering the different cultures and individual beliefs held by people (Aluko 2003; Oyedijo 2011).

At the supply chain level, our findings show that supply chain members in Nigeria lack adequate digital technologies and IT infrastructure as well as the training to support their collaborative activities such as data exchange and communication. This is a generic issue with SCM in developing countries which impacts the effectiveness of SCC due to the lack of technology to perform activities such as collaborative planning. The literature (e.g. Gunasekaran and Ngai 2004; Prajogo and Olhager 2012; Gunasekaran et al. 2017) has also stressed the importance of IT systems and big data analytics in integrating and developing SCC. Thus, our research suggests the need for investment in digital technology at the focal firm and supply chain level to improve aspects such as optimisation of SC processes, joint forecasting, joint planning, inventory management and risk management. Although the value of technology in building sustainable SCM has been revealed (DeGroote and Marx 2013; Saberi et al. 2019), however, our findings show that SCs in Nigeria are still struggling with digital technological advancements like blockchain technology which can improve issues pertinent to the Nigerian context such as transparency, traceability and security (Kimani et al. 2020). Our data further suggest that fraudulent activities at the SC level such as bribery, corruption and insider abuse have a negative influence on SCC. This is another unique finding which is specific to the Nigerian context but has not appeared repeatedly in the pertinent literature on SCM. Though past studies (e.g. Svensson and Bååth 2008; Eriksson and Svensson 2016) have considered ethical issues and social responsibility in supply chains, they neglected issues such as fraud in the SC context.

This study demonstrates that the identified challenges associated with managing SCs in Nigeria can be addressed from the three related levels: internal, supply chain and external. *At the external level*, our findings indicate that government support, investment and reforms can help the general environment and SCs function effectively and efficiently. This issue is important since many businesses require a suitable environment to function. This finding is also unique because government support initiatives are not often included in the SCM debate. Thus, this insight adds to the on-going debate in the literature (e.g. Herczeg et al. 2018; Pakdeechoho and Sukhotu 2018) concerning the critical role that governments play in creating a suitable business environment. *At the internal level*, our findings suggest that focal firms need to pay close attention to internal activities and practices that can develop firm representatives in the supply chain to reduce behavioural issues and issues related to unethical practice. Individual firms in the SC need to take some responsibility in managing their own processes by undertaking regular process evaluations and investing in training and development to improve the effectiveness of the SCC. *At the supply chain level*, our findings indicate that SC partners need to pay close attention to their collaborative activities such as joint meetings, commitment to the relationship, dedicated investment to the relationship, to improve their SCC. Such collaborative activities were revealed to improve the relationship quality between supply chain partners through improved trust levels, high commitment and dedication to the SCC, and overall satisfaction in the SCC. Overall, the findings of this research may also apply to similar developing countries especially in Africa (Hamisi 2011; Ambe and Badenhorst-Weiss 2012).

7   Avenues for Future Research

Issues that may have an impact on the relationship between SC partners in the F&B manufacturing sector in Nigeria have not been captured in this chapter. However, future research may consider the factors that play a significant role within the upstream and downstream sides of the supply chain. While this chapter critically explores the F&B manufacturing industry in Nigeria, we do not suggest that the findings are universally applicable across different sectors in various countries or regions, aside similar markets such as Sub-Saharan Africa. Unlike the oil and gas industry that exports largely, the F&B manufacturing industry in Nigeria is still a growing sector. As a result, there is a possibility that different sectors might have different factors such as industry features, culture and institutional norms that may influence the SCC. Future studies may consider how African governments could improve SCC by investing in training and development for supply chain professionals. Finally, it is crucial for future studies to examine how blockchain and digital technology can improve SCC in Africa.

Acknowledgements   A special thanks to Late Professor Ade Oyedijo, our co-author and the former Dean of the Faculty of Management Sciences at Lagos State University who sadly passed away on the 11th of January 2016. He served as a valuable resource person and gate keeper for the data collection process of this research in Nigeria.

References

Adams, K., Debrah, Y. A., Williams, K., & Mmieh, F. (2014). Causes of financial FDI inflows into sub-Saharan Africa (SSA): Evidence from Ghana. *Thunderbird International Business Review, 56*(5), 439–459.

Adams, D., Ullah, S., Akhtar, P., Adams, K., & Saidi, S. (2019). The role of country-level institutional factors in escaping the natural resource curse: Insights from Ghana. *Resources Policy, 61*, 433–440.

Adebanjo, D., Ojadi, F., Laosirihongthong, T., & Tickle, M. (2013). A case study of supplier selection in developing economies: A perspective on institutional theory and corporate social responsibility. *Supply Chain Management: An International Journal, 18*(5), 553–566.

Adebayo, I. T. (2012). Supply chain management (SCM) practices in Nigeria today: Impact on SCM performance. *European Journal of Business and Social Sciences, 18*(6), 107–115.

Aluko, M. A. O. (2003). The impact of culture on organizational performance in selected textile firms in Nigeria. *Nordic Journal of African Studies, 12*(2), 16–16.

Ambe, I. M., & Badenhorst-Weiss, J. A. (2012). Supply chain management challenges in the South African public sector. *African Journal of Business Management, 6*(44), 11003.

Busse, C., Schleper, M. C., Niu, M., & Wagner, S. M. (2016). Supplier development for sustainability: Contextual barriers in global supply chains. *International Journal of Physical Distribution & Logistics Management, 46*(5), 442–468.

Cai, S., Goh, M., De Souza, R., & Li, G. (2013). Knowledge sharing in collaborative supply chains: Twin effects of trust and power. *International Journal of Production Research, 51*(7), 2060–2076.

Cannon, J. P., & Perreault, W. D., Jr. (1999). Buyer-seller relationships in business markets. *Journal of Marketing Research, 36*(4), 439–460.

Cao, M., & Zhang, Q. (2011). Supply chain collaboration: Impact on collaborative advantage and firm performance. *Journal of Operations Management., 29*(3), 163–180.

Central Intelligence Agency. (2020). *The world fact book: Africa, Nigeria.* Retrieved August 10, 2020, from https://www.cia.gov/library/publications/the-world-factbook/geos/ni.html

Chen, L., Zhao, X., Tang, O., Price, L., Zhang, S., & Zhu, W. (2017). Supply chain collaboration for sustainability: A literature review and future research agenda. *International Journal of Production Economics, 94*, 73–87.

DeGroote, S. E., & Marx, T. G. (2013). The impact of IT on supply chain agility and firm performance: An empirical investigation. *International Journal of Information Management, 33*(6), 909–916.

Didia, J. U. D., & Nwokah, N. G. (2015). Supply chain integration and business performance in the telecommunication industry in Nigeria. *International Journal of Supply Chain Management, 4*(2), 81–89.

Easterby-Smith, M., Thorpe, R., & Jackson, P. R. (2012). *Management research* (4th ed.). London: Sage.

Eriksson, D., & Svensson, G. (2016). The process of responsibility, decoupling point, and disengagement of moral and social responsibility in supply chains: Empirical findings and prescriptive thoughts. *Journal of Business Ethics, 134*(2), 281–298.

Fawcett, S. E., Magnan, G. M., & McCarter, M. W. (2008). Benefits, barriers and bridges to effective supply chain management. *Supply Chain Management: An International Journal, 13*(1), 35–48.

Fawcett, S. E., Fawcett, A. M., Watson, B. J., & Magnan, G. M. (2012). Peeking inside the black box: Toward an understanding of supply chain collaboration dynamics. *Journal of Supply Chain Management, 48*(1), 44–72.

Fawcett, S. E., McCarter, M. W., Fawcett, A. M., Webb, G. S., & Magnan, G. M. (2015). Why supply chain collaboration fails: The socio-structural view of resistance to relational strategies. *Supply Chain Management: An International Journal, 20*(6), 648–663.

Ganesan, S. (1994). Determinants of long-term orientation in buyer-seller relationships. *Journal of Marketing, 58*(2), 1–19.

Gligor, D., Bozkurt, S., Russo, I., & Omar, A. (2019). A look into the past and future: Theories within supply chain management, marketing and management. *Supply Chain Management: An International Journal, 24*(1), 170–186.

Gunasekaran, A., & Ngai, E. W. (2004). Information systems in supply chain integration and management. *European Journal of Operational Research, 159*(2), 269–295.

Gunasekaran, A., Papadopoulos, T., Dubey, R., Wamba, S. F., Childe, S. J., Hazen, B., & Akter, S. (2017). Big data and predictive analytics for supply chain and organizational performance. *Journal of Business Research, 70*, 308–317.

Hamisi, S. (2011). Challenges and opportunities of Tanzanian SMEs in adapting supply chain management. *African Journal of Business Management, 5*(4), 1266.

Heide, J. B., & John, G. (1990). Alliances in industrial purchasing: The determinants of joint action in buyer-supplier relationships. *Journal of Marketing Research, 27*(1), 24–36.

Herczeg, G., Akkerman, R., & Hauschild, M. Z. (2018). Supply chain collaboration in industrial symbiosis networks. *Journal of Cleaner Production, 171*, 1058–1067.

International Monetary Fund. (2019). *World economic outlook database*. Retrieved October 11, 2019, from http://www.imf.org/en/publications/weo

Jap, S. D., & Ganesan, S. (2000). Control mechanisms and the relationship life cycle: Implications for safeguarding specific investments and developing commitment. *Journal of Marketing Research, 37*(2), 227–245.

Kembro, J., & Näslund, D. (2014). Information sharing in supply chains, myth or reality? A critical analysis of empirical literature. *International Journal of Physical Distribution and Logistics Management, 44*(3), 179–200.

Kimani, D., Adams, K., Attah-Boakye, R., Ullah, S., Frecknall-Hughes, J., & Kim, J. (2020). Blockchain, business and the fourth industrial revolution: Whence, whither, wherefore and how? *Technological Forecasting and Social Change, 161*, 120254.

Koçoğlu, İ., İmamoğlu, S. Z., İnce, H., & Keskin, H. (2011). The effect of supply chain integration on information sharing: Enhancing the supply chain performance. *Procedia-Social and Behavioral Sciences, 24*, 1630–1649.

Koukpaki, A. S., Adams, K., & Oyedijo, A. (2020). The contribution of human resource development managers to organisational branding in the hotel industry in India and South East Asia (ISEA): A dynamic capabilities perspective. *Employee Relations: The International Journal*. https://doi.org/10.1108/ER-09-2019-0375

Kwon, I. G., & Suh, T. (2005). Trust, commitment and relationships in supply chain management: A path analysis. *Supply Chain Management: An International Journal, 10*(1), 26–33.

Lalonde, B. J. (1998). Building a supply chain relationship. *Supply Chain Management Review, 2*(2), 7–8.

Lee, T. W., Mitchell, T. R., & Sablynski, C. J. (1999). Qualitative research in organizational and vocational psychology, 1979–1999. *Journal of Vocational Behavior, 55*(2), 161–187.

Li, S., & Lin, B. (2006). Accessing information sharing and information quality in supply chain management. *Decision Support Systems, 42*(3), 1641–1656.

Li, J., Sikora, R., Shaw, M. J., & Tan, G. W. (2006). A strategic analysis of inter organizational information sharing. *Decision Support Systems, 42*(1), 251–266.

Liu, W., Yan, X., Si, C., Xie, D., & Wang, J. (2020). Effect of buyer-supplier supply chain strategic collaboration on operating performance: Evidence from Chinese companies. *Supply Chain Management: An International Journal, 25*(6), 823–839.

Miles, M. B., & Huberman, A. M. (1994). *Qualitative data analysis: An expanded sourcebook*. Thousand Oaks/London: Sage Publications.

Min, S., Roath, A. S., Daugherty, P. J., Genchev, S. E., Chen, H., Arndt, A. D., & Glenn Richey, R. (2005). Supply chain collaboration: What's happening? *The International Journal of Logistics Management, 16*(2), 237–256.

Muogboh, O. S., & Ojadi, F. (2018). *Indigenous logistics and supply chain management practice in Africa, indigenous management practices in Africa* (Advanced series in management, Vol. 20, pp. 47–70). Emerald Publishing Limited.

Njoku, C. (2019). *Here are 5 security challenges Nigeria's leader must tackle*. World Economic Forum. Retrieved November 15, 2019, from https://www.weforum.org/agenda/2019/02/5-security-challenges-facing-nigerias-leadership/

Nyaga, G. N., Whipple, J. M., & Lynch, D. F. (2010). Examining supply chain relationships: Do buyer and supplier perspectives on collaborative relationships differ? *Journal of Operations Management, 28*(2), 101–114.

Nyaga, G. N., Lynch, D. F., Marshall, D., & Ambrose, E. (2013). Power asymmetry, adaptation and collaboration in dyadic relationships involving a powerful partner. *Journal of Supply Chain Management, 49*(3), 42–65.

Ojadi, F., Tickle, M., Adebanjo, D., Laosirihongthong, T., & Boon-itt, S. (2017). Supplier qualification for high-value goods and services in Nigeria: A comparison of qualified and non-qualified suppliers. *International Journal of Logistics Research and Applications, 20*(3), 201–216.

Okonjo-Iweala, N., & Osafo-Kwaako, P. (2007). *Nigeria's economic reforms: Progress and challenges* (Brookings Global Economy and Development Working Paper, 6).

Orji, I. J., Kusi-Sarpong, S., Gupta, H., & Okwu, M. (2019). Evaluating challenges to implementing eco-innovation for freight logistics sustainability in Nigeria. *Transportation Research Part A: Policy and Practice, 129*, 288–305.

Oyedijo, A. (2011). Gaining a competitive marketing advantage in an era of globalization: Some challenges for indigenous firms in developing countries. *The Nigerian Journal, 5*(1), 45–61.

Oyedijo, A., Akinlabi, B., & Awoniyi, B. (2011). Corruption, foreign direct investment and economic growth in Nigeria: An empirical investigation. *Journal of Research in International Business and Management, 1*(9), 278–292.

Pakdeechoho, N., & Sukhotu, V. (2018). Sustainable supply chain collaboration: Incentives in emerging economies. *Journal of Manufacturing Technology Management, 29*(2), 273–294.

Panahifar, F., Byrne, P. J., Salam, M. A., & Heavey, C. (2018). Supply chain collaboration and firm's performance: The critical role of information sharing and trust. *Journal of Enterprise Information Management, 31*(3), 358–379.

Patton, M. Q. (2015). *Qualitative research & evaluation methods: Integrating theory and practice* (4th ed.). Saint Paul, MN: Utilization Focused Evaluation.

Prajogo, D., & Olhager, J. (2012). Supply chain integration and performance: The effects of long-term relationships, information technology and sharing, and logistics integration. *International Journal of Production Economics, 135*(1), 514–522.

Ramanathan, U., & Gunasekaran, A. (2014). Supply chain collaboration: Impact of success in long-term partnerships. *International Journal of Production Economics, 147*, 252–259.

Saberi, S., Kouhizadeh, M., Sarkis, J., & Shen, L. (2019). Blockchain technology and its relationships to sustainable supply chain management. *International Journal of Production Research, 57*(7), 2117–2135.

Saunders, M., Lewis, P., & Thornhill, A. (2009). Research methods for business students, 4th ed. Essex: Pearson Education.

Schorsch, T., Wallenburg, C. M., & Wieland, A. (2017). The human factor in SCM: Introducing a meta-theory of behavioral supply chain management. *International Journal of Physical Distribution & Logistics Management, 47*(4), 238–262.

Silverman, D. (2014). *Interpreting qualitative data* (5th ed.). London: Sage.

Simangunsong, E., Hendry, L. C., & Stevenson, M. (2012). Supply-chain uncertainty: A review and theoretical foundation for future research. *International Journal of Production Research, 50*(16), 4493–4523.

Simatupang, T. M., & Sridharan, R. (2008). Design for supply chain collaboration. *Business Process Management Journal, 14*(3), 401–418.

Soosay, C. A., & Hyland, P. (2015). A decade of supply chain collaboration and directions for future research. *Supply Chain Management: An International Journal, 20*(6), 613–630.

Soosay, C. A., Hyland, P. W., & Ferrer, M. (2008). Supply chain collaboration: Capabilities for continuous innovation. *Supply Chain Management: An International Journal, 13*(2), 160–169.

Srinivasan, R., & Brush, T. H. (2006). Supplier performance in vertical alliances: The effects of self-enforcing agreements and enforceable contracts. *Organization Science, 17*(4), 436–452.

Svensson, G., & Bååth, H. (2008). Supply chain management ethics: Conceptual framework and illustration. *Supply Chain Management: An International Journal., 13*(6), 398–405.

Ugoani, J. (2019). Role of purchasing and supply management in manufacturing profitability in Nigeria. *American Journal of Marketing Research, 5*(1), 10–18.

Um, K. H., & Kim, S. M. (2019). The effects of supply chain collaboration on performance and transaction cost advantage: The moderation and nonlinear effects of governance mechanisms. *International Journal of Production Economics, 217*, 97–111.

United Nations (UN). (2019). *World population prospects 2019*, Retrieved October 15, 2019, from World Population Prospects 2019.

World Bank. (2018). *Food, beverages and tobacco (% of value added in manufacturing)*. Retrieved October 24, 2018, from https://data.worldbank.org/indicator/NV.MNF.FBTO.ZS.UN?end=201 8&start=2018&view=map&year=2018

Yin, R. K. (2009). *Case study research: Design and methods* (4th ed.). Thousand Oaks, CA: Sage.

Understanding Rural Micro and Small Business Marketing Practices in Ghana

Charles Blankson and Peter Renner

1 Introduction

> Though it is important to investigate all relevant issues, new information on the effectiveness of the application of market orientation would be useful addition to the knowledge of how businesses pursue marketing.
>
> —William K. Darley & Robert E. Smith (1993)

There is ongoing interest in the potential contribution of small businesses to rural economic development around the world (North and Smallbone 1996). While review of the literature reveals an increasing interest in the adoption of market orientation concept for managerial application in sub-Saharan African market settings (Kuada and Buatsi 2005), the backbone of economic growth and job creation in sub-Saharan Africa, which is the employment of the market orientation concept and marketing practices in the small business domain (Boohene 2009), appears overlooked.

In spite of the large stream of literature on market orientation and the growing interest in market orientation in the sub-Saharan African context and, more specifically, Ghana (see Kuada and Buatsi 2005), these studies do not examine systematically the market orientation of micro and small businesses in Ghana. In addition, not only have extant studies focused on large organizations, notably, those in developed economies, but data and knowledge on market orientation of micro and small

C. Blankson (✉)
Department of Marketing, Logistics and Operations Management, The G. Brint Ryan College of Business, University of North Texas, Denton, TX, USA
e-mail: Charles.Blankson@unt.edu

P. Renner
New York Life Insurance Company, New York, NY, USA
e-mail: Peter_Renner@newyorklife.com

J. B. Abugre et al. (eds.), *Business in Africa in the Era of Digital Technology*,
Advances in Theory and Practice of Emerging Markets,
https://doi.org/10.1007/978-3-030-70538-1_9

businesses in sub-Saharan African economies such as Ghana have been overlooked by scholars. Correspondingly, despite growing activities and interest in micro and small business development in sub-Saharan African countries (Mambula 2002; Benzing and Chu 2009; Urban and Naidoo 2012) and Ghana in particular (Tagoe et al. 2005; Robson et al. 2009), the study of rural micro and small businesses is not considered. Instead, researchers pay attention to the urban Ghanaian small business environment (see Tagoe et al. 2005) to the exclusion of rural micro and small business. Evidently, urban small businesses have access to better infrastructure and affluent markets compared to their rural counterparts (Masakure et al. 2009). Interestingly, the majority of Ghanaians live in small towns and villages.

Moreover, digital technologies are spreading across Africa—with a potential of transforming the continent (Ndemo and Weiss 2017). The hope is that as Africa embraces the digital age, businesses will adapt and ultimately create and disperse technological innovations across societies (Ndemo and Weiss 2017). Ng and Wakenshaw (2017: 3) write that "digitization is the conversion of analog information in any form such as text, images, sound or physical attributes to a digital format so that the information can be processed, stored, and transmitted through digital circuits, devices, and networks." Put simply, digitization makes it easier to store, access, share, and process information. More importantly, digitization does not happen in a vacuum but is rather contingent on prevailing favorable economic, organizational, political, social, and cultural development of an environment (Ndemo and Weiss 2017). Although Ghana's macroeconomic policies continue to be the envy of other African countries (Benzing and Chu 2009; Blankson and Nukpezah 2019), leading to the reduction of poverty levels, still, few studies examine the implications of rural micro and small business marketing practices in the Ghanaian digital milieu.

Further, observations in rural Ghana reveal that micro and small businesses face more pressing challenges relating to their business expansion and profitability and consequently give the so-called era of digital technology a low priority (Blankson et al. 2018; Blankson and Nukpezah 2019). This is painful to realize despite the increasing attention to the emerging digital transformation of African markets (Ndemo and Weiss 2017). These gaps in the literature provided the inspiration for this study and for this chapter.

The purpose of this chapter is to examine the application of market orientation strategies among rural micro and small businesses and to assess the impact on their performance. Additionally, this study aims to examine government policy implications on rural micro and small businesses' pursuit of market orientation strategies. To that end, the study poses the following key research questions (RQs):

1. What key market orientation strategies do rural micro and small businesses in Ghana pursue?
2. In view of government-backed macro-economic reforms in the form of small loans to rural micro and small businesses, harmonization of business tax and the institution of poverty alleviation policies in rural communities, to what extent have rural micro and small businesses in Ghana embraced market orientation?

3. In terms of profit, market share, and public policy, how successful are rural micro and small businesses in these areas when they employ market orientation strategies?

2   Literature Review

2.1   Market Orientation

A market-oriented firm is one which successfully applies the marketing concept (Kohli and Jaworski 1990; Caruana et al. 1999). The marketing concept refers to the case whereby the organizational success is determined through the determination and satisfaction of the needs, wants, and aspirations of target audiences. According to the concept, these must be pursued more effectively and efficiently than that of competitors and with the intention of achieving profitability and/or satisfying the organization's objectives. Marketing researchers have often derived their definitions from the conceptualizations of Kohli and Jaworski (1990) and Narver and Slater (1990).

Despite these discourses on market orientation, the concept of market orientation and its impact on firm performance in rural sub-Saharan African (i.e., Ghanaian) settings are still missing in the literature. An exception to the latter is Blankson et al.'s (2018) study probing marketing practices of rural micro and small businesses and government's poverty reduction policies and impact on performance. Still, market orientation is pivotal to rural micro and small businesses' aspirations in Ghana to reduce poverty (Boohene 2009). Our assertion is best captured in Slater and Narver's (1994: 54) exposition on the subject when they stated that "*being market oriented can never be negative*" and that market orientation should enhance performance.

2.2   Small Business Marketing

There are no standard definitions of small business (Mukhtar 1998) in that definitions vary from country to country and show lack of consistency. These variations depend largely on the size of the economy, the levels of development, and the size and type of business. Common factors used in defining small business are the annual inventory turnover (sales) and the number of employees. The European Union, for instance, defines small business as a company that has less than 250 workers (Loecher 2000). In Ghana, the official definition of small business refers to business activities capitalized at not more than GHC10,000.00 and with labor force of not more than nine persons (Masakure et al. 2009). This study adopts the official Ghanaian definition.

The call for greater research attention to be paid to micro and small business management and marketing practices in sub-Saharan Africa (e.g., Botswana, Ghana,

Kenya, Niger, Nigeria, South Africa) continues unabated (see Mambula 2002; Mensah et al. 2007; Otoo et al. 2012). In sub-Saharan Africa, like most regions of the world (developed and developing) (see for example, Loecher 2000; Li and Matlay 2006; Bhutta et al. 2008), micro and small business growth is a major pillar in governments' macro-economic development policies (International Finance Corporation 2000; Steer and Taussig 2003; Benzing and Chu 2009; Otoo et al. 2012).

However, one of the reasons hampering the path to achieving maximum potential in micro and small business is attributed to owner-managers' lack of managerial and marketing skills (Urban and Naidoo 2012). This assertion is clarified by Urban and Naidoo (2012: 147) who write that, *SMMEs in South Africa do not have the full range of skills and expertise to operate their production/operations systems efficiently, with a third of SMMEs recognizing that their competitiveness has suffered as a result of skill shortages.* Further, Masakure et al. (2009) write that differences in firm performance in Ghana are caused by firm-specific capabilities or advantages (including entrepreneurial ability, management and marketing skills, firm size, firm age, technology usage, and gender of owner-manager), the business sector, and the geographical location in which firms operate.

3 Research Methods

3.1 The Study Context

The rural micro and small business domain in Ghana serves as this study's context due to the expansion in recent years and attention from the Ghanaian government. Since 1983, Ghanaian governments have positioned Ghana as "the gateway to do business in the West African sub-region." Ghana is an emerging market in Africa with a lower middle-income economy. Within the broader context of sub-Saharan Africa as a viable domain suitable for academic study, the Ghanaian marketplace represents a challenging but potentially fruitful research domain. Small businesses comprise about 90% of all businesses in Ghana (Boohene 2009), and the majority of them are based in rural communities (Ghana Statistical Services 2000). The growing middle class and expatriate communities in urban areas (Bruner 1996; Zachary 2001; Blankson et al. 2017), growing rural population and comparatively poor infrastructure and low purchasing power, and socio-political challenges provide ample opportunities for academic research.

3.2 Government's Poverty Alleviation and Rural Development

With 23.4% of Ghanaians living in poverty in 2016, a reduction from 39.5% in 1999 and 28.5% in 2005 (World Bank 2020), successive government policies have concentrated on the acceleration of poverty reduction and national development with special focus on rural development. In addition, at $1.90 a day poverty head count ratio, Ghana recorded 12% and 13.3% poverty in 2012 and 2016, respectively. The GNI (Gross National Income) per capita (Atlas Method) of $1900 was recorded for 2017, while $2130 was recorded for 2018 (World Bank 2020). These improvements since 1991, when the Ghana Living Standards Survey (GLSS) assessed the poverty level at 51.7%, have a lot to do with the establishment of rural micro and small businesses (Blankson et al. 2018) and increased cocoa production (Breisinger et al. 2007).

Two main recent government policies geared toward poverty alleviation include community-based rural development and rural tourism under the auspices of Ghana Rural Enterprise Project. Specific goals of this policy include: participation and civic engagement aimed at empowerment, security and social inclusion, rural market construction, rural non-farm income generation, rural services, and infrastructure. The second rural development policy is the community rural development program (CBRDP) with an objective to strengthen the capacity of rural communities and to enhance their productive assets, rural infrastructure, and access to key support services from private and public sources (Darley 2012). Initiated in 1995 by the government under the auspices of the GRATIS Foundation and with the support of the International Monetary Fund for Agricultural Development (IFAD), the project seeks to reduce poverty and improve living conditions in rural areas through increased productivity for the rural poor (Nonor 2010). In 2004, the government of Ghana reinvigorated CBRDP with mandate to work on the Millennium Development Goals and to bridge the urban–rural development gap.

Overall, governmental rural development projects have been successful in building infrastructure such as dams, water bore holes, feeder roads, open market structures, slaughter houses, wind pumps, and irrigation facilities to the extent that many otherwise disillusioned rural residents can now engage in gainful micro and small business (Republic of Ghana 2005; Awaworyi and Danso 2010). State-driven social intervention can succeed with well-defined goals and international donor support. Darley (2012) suggests that the Ghanaian government should consider establishing carefully monitored export processing zones throughout the country to attract small businesses to export their products. Moreover, Awaworyi and Danso (2010) find that government-backed microfinance programs have not only attracted rural populations to micro and small businesses, but clients of the microfinance have improved their income levels as well as their standards of living compared to non-clients of microfinance.

4 Data Collection Methods

Following Blankson et al. (2018), an extensive pilot test in the form of in-depth face-to-face long interviews with six owner-managers preceded the main study (McCracken 1998). The pilot test enhanced our appreciation of the marketing practices of micro and small businesses in rural Ghana. Three interviews, each, took place at Atuabo, near Tarkwa, in the Western Region and at Asene-Aboabo in the

Eastern Region of Ghana. Malhotra (2004) believes that through exploratory study, researchers are able to easily probe respondents to uncover underlying motivations, beliefs, attitudes, and feelings. As stated by Stewart (2009: 381), *"what consumers tell us in a long, open-ended interview is often different from what we learn in a structured survey."*

In addition to the face-to-face interviews, participant observation techniques with a convenience sample of ten small businesses, in the Central, Eastern, and Western Regions of Ghana were undertaken in order to gain a deeper understanding of the study setting. The observation involved monitoring the activities of micro and small businesses including customer care/service, pricing tactics, relationships among staff members, marketing communications (including word-of-mouth promotions), and product/service quality over a period of 2 months (see also Penaloza 1995; Blankson et al. 2018). The observed businesses operated in the services domain (i.e., small retailers, small hotels, hair dressing and barber salons, small scale building construction, private elementary schools, and internet cafes) and the small-scale sawmilling (lumber) business. The participant observation involved the hiring of and working with two small-scale building contractors at Abontiakoon—near Tarkwa in the Western Region and at Akyem-Awisa—near Akyem-Oda in the Eastern Region and a car rental firm based at Kyebi in the Eastern Region. Supporting observation techniques in marketing research, Stewart (2009: 381) emphasizes that *"observation of behavior may reveal things about consumers that neither an interview nor survey reveals."*

Twenty owner-managers (see Appendix) out of the 38 invited accepted the invitation to participate in the main study. The first author arranged appointments for the interviews and met in person with the owner-managers. A combination of token compensation in the form of free lunch (i.e., take-away prepared lunch box) and non-alcoholic beverages and GHC10.00 [US$1.00 = GHC3.50] were offered to each of the owner-managers. Apart from key contacts known to the researchers, the researchers relied on snow-ball and foot-in-the-door data collection techniques to increase the number of interviewees. Interviews were conducted at the respondents' premises in non-contrived settings first, between December 2008 and January 2009, second, between May 2010 and August 2010, and third, between June 2012 and August 2012 (see also, Penaloza 1995; Blankson et al. 2018). It is important to mention that the interviews were undertaken during purposeful visits by the first author to extended family in Ghana and when faculty development leave (sabbatical leave) to Ghana (see also, Arnould 2001).

While the interviewer ensured that the areas under discussion were addressed, allowances were made for the discussion to develop naturally (Kirk and Miller 1986; Maxwell 2013). The interviews utilized open-ended questions to elicit stories surrounding day-to-day marketing deliberations and experiences of owner-managers in the context of their individual businesses. In addition to the discussion of marketing practices, owner-managers discussed reasons why they pursued the indicated marketing activities and whether they were successful or not successful in running their businesses. The owner-managers also discussed government's support in rural development and the impact on their firms' marketing activities. The open-ended and semi-structured questions were adopted from Blankson et al.'s (2006) study, originally adapted from Kohli and Jaworski (1990). Notes were taken and with permission, the interviews were audio-taped. The interviews lasted between 45 min and 1.5 h. All interviewees were promised anonymity.

5   Data Analysis

We employed a connected narrative approach (Mishler 1990; Nwankwo 2005) in presenting the results—in order to maintain richness of discovery-oriented context and share authorship with the respondents. More specifically, we transcribed and content-coded the data using content analysis to reveal the underlying themes (Kirk and Miller 1986; Feldman 1995; Wolcott 2001). The latter involved the identification of recurring thoughts or statements; ideas embedded in the practices that each respondent discussed in the conversation surrounding marketing practices and how profitable their activities have been. After several iterative analyses of the data, themes were assigned to categories reflecting Kohli and Jaworski's (1990) dimensions. The themes and respondents' verbatim statements were then discussed among the authors in line with inductive reasoning (see Wolcott 2001; Maxwell 2013).

Qualitative research methods such as the method adopted in this study is useful for informing public policy because it examines the implications of marketing activities at micro and small business owner-managers' lived experiences with their firms (Penaloza 1995; Stewart 2009). In view of the subjective nature of the study and following Kirk and Miller's (1986) and Nwankwo's (2005) suggestions, we assessed validity through research team checks and soliciting feedback from Ghanaian and American academic scholars with expertise in the context and study, respectively. Their inputs were incorporated in the final discussion and conclusions. The next section provides the results in the form of the themes and verbatim comments of owner-managers.

6   Results and Discussion

6.1   Customer Service/Care

Through the interview and observations, it appears customer care is a top priority, "[the] customer is the king" (Kofi); owner-managers acknowledge the importance of customer service in the business environment, "I think customer relationship [management] depends on [a good] personal relationship- the way you treat them…" (Emma). As each interviewee acknowledged, "customers are the reason for our business," (Dorothy), or the "prime" (Isaac). Additionally, owner-managers were familiar with the challenges of owning a micro or small business. "People are in a hurry…and…[there are] not enough customers these days" (Nana). Without strate- gically planning customer orientation, it appears that micro and small business own- ers in rural Ghana are cognizant of one of the dimensions of market orientation. In fact, observations confirm this dimension as an integral part of business ownership. Ghanaian rural micro and small business owners' customer focus is not surprising when considering their culture; customer care is simply a normal way of life for the friendliest people in Africa. The evidence gives credence to a market orientation stemming from organizational culture (Narver and Slater 1990).

"We have a fitting room and we usually ask customers to wear their dresses to see if they fit. In the end, we ask them whether they are happy with our product. If not, we try as much as possible to do any needed changes, alterations to get a perfect dress for the customer. Customers who are happy tell us about how they are happy about their dresses even without asking" (Akos). *"When some are not happy, we try to do alterations and to arrive at a final quality product. When I come across a dif- ficult customer, I go every length to please them by altering their dresses as they want and then deliver it to their homes at my own cost. Sometimes, I have to travel to the next town in order to deliver the dresses to the customer"* (Akos). I do all these to make sure I stay in profit and that my business flourishes.

6.2   Top Management

Owner-managers often take an informal approach toward relationships with employ- ees. "[The] relationship between staff is very cordial and happy," (Sam and Ante B); "…when there is the need for jokes, we joke- but when there is serious work, we work hard…" (Isaac). The words "commitment" and "motivation" came up fre- quently with regard to employee management. While some owner-managers bragged about paying their employee above average wages, others were relegated to the fact that "…in Ghana, you need a second/private job to sustain yourself so at times I think our staff do other jobs and hence may not be all that committed. Other than that, they are motivated" (Kwasi). Bonuses, "family-like" operations, rewards for hard work, loans, and holiday gifts motivate employees. One owner-manager admits "[the staff] are motivated but only when I motivate them. The work ethic is good but not like in Europe, specifically in Holland where I lived for fifteen years before returning home…." Very few businesses (only two) reported holding formal staff meetings. All others held meetings on a case-by-case basis. Despite this, most participants admitted to "sit[ting] down and talk[ing] about how things are faring" with employees. Without having large and formal operations, as those in developed nations, businesses get by through managing staff using ad hoc personnel manage- ment practices. This suggests that rural micro and small businesses in Ghana are also employee-oriented. Addressing issues as they arise provides for a market orien- tation, through organization-wide responsiveness.

My staff sometimes had some grudges among themselves. This started by some of the apprentices teasing their colleagues but it was tribal-based I think. It was based on the dresses some of them wore. I never tolerated tribal teasing between my staff. From that time, I decided that all apprentices should wear uniforms. This stopped the teasing problem. This brought a level playing field among the apprentices. This was well accepted by the apprentices eventually (Akos).

In terms of meeting, every morning, we have a prayer session, and the apprentices will discuss their problems. We all try to solve the problem amicably but I take final decision. We meet every day because we believe in God. In everything, God is first, and this is my motto both personal and my business. The prayers are usually for 30 minutes in a devotional Christian fashion. The Muslim apprentices go to a nearby mosque for similar 30 minutes prayers (Akos).

Although I do not receive any government assistance in my business, I have attended government-sponsored tutorials about "how to be successful in business" organized at the local community center (Baaba). At times, I attend talks given by government agricultural officers. Even though these talks are meant for rural cocoa farmers, they are good ways to know about various small loans offered by the rural banks and how to apply for them. I am yet to consider one of these small loans though, but for now, I am doing fine (Baaba).

6.3   Marketing Research

While no formal research is conducted in these small businesses, the owner-managers do solicit feedback from customers from time to time; this was true for all business types involved in this study. While opinions surrounding the quantity and skill of competitors differed among business types, all businesses understood "customers' needs are changing in terms of demand …" (Kwadwo). Customers play a large role in assessing market conditions and needs. While they do not employ sophisticated statistical and analytical software, small rural business owner-managers indirectly conduct market research in a qualitative capacity. Thus, even so, the statements substantiate a market orientation. Their desire to provide value and anticipate needs underlies the philosophy of market orientation, according to Gray and Hooley (2002).

6.4   Profitability/Objectives

The majority of owner-managers interviewed reported increasing profits and market share. The other businesses reported either "break[ing] even" or "static profits"; both types anticipated better returns in the coming years. Although the businesses had no formal business objectives, the owner-managers claim, comparatively, they are doing "good business." It appears some understood the 20/80 principle, "we concentrate on a few profitable customers" (Pat and James). While competition did not come up as a large factor, customers provided the marketing intelligence to owner-managers regarding competitive efforts. Again, customers play a large role in business operations and support. While profit goals exist, businesses center around providing for customers; "we are friendly with our customers and we operate like friends/family" (Sam and Ante B). Customer-centricity thus underpins a market orientation through "[give[ing] something to customers all the time," (Nana) based on what they need. By integrating a "service conscious" philosophy, the findings show that Ghanaian rural micro and small business owner-managers instill market orientation as part of a business culture. Competition is tough in Ghana. There is a lot of jealousy among my competitors because I am comparatively younger and I tend to get all the young customers who work at the local banks (Ama).

Compared to my competitors, I believe I am successful when it comes to business profitability and the number of customers. That is because I incorporate other business such as selling cloths, soft drinks, bread, ice cream in addition to my tailoring business (OB). The majority (18 out of 20) of the respondents were categorical in stating that they were doing well financially.

> I have good working capital and I am very happy because my children went to private schools. This is something I can never do without my business. I never had the opportunity to go to high school and to university but now my children have benefited, thanks to my business. So, for me I am very happy about my business. (Baaba)

Following Penaloza (1995), the following section presents a case in point of an informant's (i.e., interviewee) experience in setting up and running her small business in a rural town in Ghana. In line with Penaloza's stance, the description is intended to give readers a sense of basic marketing practices of rural Ghanaian micro and small business. Akos is 44 years of age and lives in a rural town in the Ashanti Region. She is a seamstress and fashion designer having started business in 1985. Akos said that she started business because she had a passion for sewing and so when her father could not afford to send her to secondary school, even though she had passed the "common entrance examination" to enter secondary school, she pressed her father to enroll her at a fashion design school in Kumasi. Following the completion of her 2-year training, she returned to her village to settle down and to set up her own business. With her savings accumulated from part-time work in Kumasi, she started with three female trainees. With time, she ended up with 20 girls in training. The core business is seamstress and dress making. She narrated her initial experiences this way: "*I decorated the shop with my certificate since I had just completed school. I did not have money, so I bought brown paper to sew dresses and then decorated my store. I also used my own dresses and cloths to decorate the shop. Relatives were my customers initially. Over time, customers who did not know me but were window-shopping became my customers. By the second year of operation, I was already making profit. This has continued till today. However, there are a few seasons that are naturally difficult for customers (especially the month after Christmas and the month before school re-opens) which affects my profits*." More importantly, she attributes business growth to the fact that she always makes customers very comfortable. "*I do not want them to go to my competitors…I enjoy good relationship with my customers*," Akos affirmed.

Akos simply put it that: "*it is important to build trust and above all, you have to love and respect your customers*." She said that these acts help her to boost her profits and customer base. She stated that her customer perceptions have improved because they appreciate the quality products and the special care she gives them. Akos described a case in point in her business when once a passenger on a bus spotted her shop and came to browse the dresses she displayed and the atmosphere in the shop. According to Akos, at first, the customer said that she was looking for a top seamstress to sew some dresses for two important occasions she was attending in a weeks' time—an outdooring and a wedding in Kumasi. The customer decided to try her service. *"I think she was on to a trial and error engagement with me...obviously, at first, she was not comfortable giving all the four cloths she had planned to sew... I told her that may be she could give me the styles she wanted and I will sew the dresses for her...because it was the first time she was using my service, she gave me one cloth to sew...when she collected her dress the following week, she was so impressed that she introduced her friends and work colleagues to me...since then we have remained friends and at the same time it is financially rewarding as well as good customer perception for my business."* She narrated with joy on her face.

7 Conclusion and Implications

This study is exploratory and basic, yet important for micro and small business marketing and entrepreneurial literature. Ghanaian policymakers instituted rural poverty alleviation policy as part of Ghana's structural adjustment program in 1983 and will benefit from the present study that, to a degree, reveals the impact of government's policy on rural poverty alleviation (Republic of Ghana 2005). To that end, the value of qualitative research in producing data that are useful for policy dialog is evident (White 1990; Arnould 2001) (see RQ 2). Through empirical research, this study has investigated market orientation within the small business domain in Ghana and in particular the rural micro and small business sector. While there have been important advances in the conceptualization of firm market orientation, these have mostly reflected large organizations' contexts and Western economies' perspectives. The present study presents a sub-Saharan African economy and micro and small business perspective—adding to the literature on marketing practices (i.e., market orientation) of micro and small businesses (see RQ 1). The study enhances a deeper understanding about market orientation of micro and small businesses in rural Ghana (see also Sashittal and Jassawalla 2001; Blankson et al. 2018) and reveal how these businesses go about achieving profitability and market share and enhance customer perception (RQ 3). To a degree, these findings contribute to the scant research activities in small businesses in rural Ghana.

The study confirms, overall, that the key factors underpinning market orientation are appreciated and customers are an important dimension for micro and small business survival (Carson and Gilmore 2000). The study finds that marketing activities appear unplanned and informal, yet still addressed appropriately for the market economy. In part, marketing practices are intuitively driven and based on a "common sense approach" and not the textbook approach (Stokes and Blackburn 1999; Kotler 2000) (RQ 1).

Further, this study contributes to the literature by confirming prior research conclusions that a micro and small business market orientation is embedded in adaptation, informality, and largely on the intuition and energy of the owner-manager
(Stokes 2002). To that end, this chapter concludes that the size of the business, i.e.,
micro, small, or large, does not moderate the importance attached to and the application of market orientation (RQ 1). The study paves the way to conduct additional
empirical research in the small business sector in developing African economies.

In terms of public policy contribution, three key players in the entrepreneurial
ecosystem are the government, business, and academic institutions. Government,
businesses, and educational institutions can team up and put forward a public–private partnership policy, paving the way for an enabling environment where micro
and small businesses and entrepreneurs can prosper, try new ideas, and put their
ideas to the service of their communities, countries, and the continent (see Darley
2002; World Economic Forum 2009). The government can support entrepreneurial
education by encouraging educational institutions to embrace entrepreneurship and
incorporate entrepreneurship into their curriculum. The government can set up policies and "locate the appropriate legal and fiscal frameworks to encourage entrepreneurship and to fill market gaps as necessary" (World Economic Forum 2009: 146;
Darley 2012). In addition, governments can create funding mechanisms to support
entrepreneurial activity (see for example, Adejimola and Olufunmilayo 2009;
Blankson et al. 2018).

8   Limitations and Future Research Directions

Despite reliance on extant literature and adherence to theoretical development, there
is an opportunity for further amplification of the suggestions put forward in this
chapter. We believe that research is required that explores, clarifies, and elucidates
the nature, context, and dynamics of how and along which dimensions market orientation is applied in the rural small business sector in developing African economies such as Ghana.

The research undertaken for this chapter is exploratory and could form the starting point of future robust explorations, both empirical and conceptual, into studies
delineating sub-Saharan African and specifically, Ghanaian micro and small business marketing practices and entrepreneurship behavior. The relationship between
Ghanaian and other African countries' idiosyncratic and nuanced culture and entrepreneurial behavior have received meager attention and necessitate empirical investigation. Another limitation of this study concerns the collection of data solely in the
southern part of Ghana (i.e., Ashanti, Central, Eastern, and Western Regions).
Future research would add robustness, allowing better generalization of the findings. Additionally, embarking upon a survey to measure market orientation to differentiate micro and small businesses among diverse market economies, or even
business types within a developing economy context, would support distinctions
observed and ameliorate methodological limitations of this qualitative study.

Research should endeavor to embark upon research from the northern regions of Ghana to enhance generalizability of our findings.

We acknowledge that because our data originate from convenience sample of owner-managers, future studies should explore the possibility of using probability samples. However, our sample represents a lot of the population who have knowledge about micro and small business management activities in rural Ghana and are conversant with government's assistance to small businesses in rural areas.

Appendix: Characteristics of Informants

Informant@	Owner-manager or manager	Gender	Nature of business	Location—town/village and region
Nana	Owner-manager	Female	Hair dressing and beauty salon	Akyem-Awisa, ER
Isaac	Owner-manager	Male	Internet cafe	Akyem-Oda, ER
Sam	Joint owner-manager	Male	Private elementary school	Akyem-Awisa, ER
Ante B	Joint owner-manager	Female	Private elementary school	Akyem-Awisa, ER
Kofi	Manager	Male	Petrol (gas) station and retail store	Akyem-Aboabo, ER
Dorothy	Owner-manager	Female	Kindergarten school	Akyem-Oda, ER
Emma	Owner-manager	Male	Retail store and distribution agent	Akyem-Awisa, ER
Pat	Manager	Female	Hotel	Akyem-Oda, ER
James	Manager	Male	Hotel	Akyem-Oda, ER
Nana	Owner-manager	Male	Car rental	Akyem-Oda, ER
OB	Owner-manager	Male	Tailoring—dress making	Akyem-Swedru, ER
Kwasi	Owner-manager	Male	Architecture	Akyem Oda, ER
Kwaku	Owner-manager	Male	Sawmill	Akyem-Oda, ER
Ama	Owner-manager	Female	Retail store	Dompoasi, AR
Akos	Owner-manager	Female	Fashion designer and seamstress	Jamasi, AR
Kwadwo	Manager	Male	Building construction (masonry)	Abontiakoon, WR
Doris	Owner-manager	Female	Retail store	Abontiakoon, WR
Araba	Owner-manager	Female	Seamstress and retail store	Nkamponasi, WR
Baaba	Owner-manager	Female	Warehouse and teak tree plantation	Tarkwa, WR
Paapa	Owner-manager	Male	Retail store	Agona-Nsaba, CR

Notes: *ER* Eastern Region, *AH* Ashanti Region, *WR* Western Region, *CR* Central Region; @ In order to protect the anonymity of respondents, first names or pseudonyms are used to describe interviewees

References

Adejimola, A. S., & Olufunmilayo, T. O. (2009). Spinning off an entrepreneurship culture among Nigerian university students: Prospects and challenges. *African Journal of Business Management, 3*(3), 80–88.

Arnould, E. J. (2001). Ethnography, export marketing policy, and economic development in Niger. *Journal of Public Policy & Marketing, 20*(2), 151–169.

Awaworyi, S. K., & Danso, J. K. (2010). *Poverty reduction in Ghana—The role of microfinance and socioeconomic education.* Unpublished Report, University of Ghana.

Benzing, C., & Chu, H. M. (2009). A comparison of the motivations of small business owners in Africa. *Journal of Small Business and Enterprise Development, 16*(1), 60–77.

Bhutta, M. K. S., Rana, A. I., & Asad, U. (2008). Owner characteristics and health of SMEs in Pakistan. *Journal of Small Business and Enterprise Development, 15*(1), 130–149.

Blankson, C., & Nukpezah, J. A. (2019). Market orientation and poverty reduction: A study of rural microentrepreneurs in Ghana. *Africa Journal of Management, 5*(4), 332–357.

Blankson, C., Motwani, J. G., & Levenburg, N. M. (2006). Understanding the patterns of market orientation among small businesses. *Marketing Intelligence & Planning, 24*(6), 572–590.

Blankson, C., Ketron, S., & Coffie, S. (2017). Positioning strategies by foreign retailers at the Accra mall in Ghana: A case study approach. *Journal of Managerial Issues, 24*(3), 294–314.

Blankson, C., Cowan, K., & Darley, W. K. (2018). Marketing practices of rural micro and small businesses in Ghana: The role of public policy. *Journal of Macromarketing, 38*(1), 29–56.

Boohene, R. (2009). The relationships among gender, strategic capabilities, and performance of small retail firms in Ghana. *Journal of African Business, 10*(1), 121–138.

Breisinger, C., Diao, X., & Kolavalli, S. (2007). *The role of cocoa in Ghana's growth and poverty reduction.* International Food Policy Research Institute (IFPRI)—Ghana Strategy Support Program.

Bruner, E. M. (1996). Tourism in Ghana: The representation of slavery and the return of the black diaspora. *American Anthropologist, 98,* 290–304.

Carson, D., & Gilmore, A. (2000). Marketing at the interface: Not "what" but "how". *Journal of Marketing Theory & Practice, 8*(2), 1–7.

Caruana, A., Pitt, L., & Berthon, P. (1999). Excellence-market orientation link: Some consequences for service firms. *Journal of Business Research, 44*(1), 5–15.

Darley, W. K. (2002). Enhancing sub-Saharan Africa's export performance: Challenges, opportunities, and implications. *Journal of African Business, 3*(2), 7–32.

Darley, W. K. (2012). Increasing sub-Saharan Africa's share of foreign direct investment: Public policy challenges, strategies, and implications. *Journal of African Business, 13*(1), 62–69.

Darley, W. K., & Smith, R. E. (1993). Advertising claim objectivity: Antecedents and effects. *Journal of Marketing, 57*(October), 100–113.

Feldman, M. S. (1995). *Strategies for interpreting qualitative data.* Thousand Oaks: Sage Publications.

Ghana Statistical Service. (2000). *Ghana living standards survey: Report of the fourth round (GLSS4), 1998/99.* Accra: Ghana Statistical Office.

Gray, B. J., & Hooley, G. J. (2002). Guest editorial: Market orientation and service firm performance—A research agenda. *European Journal of Marketing, 36*(9/10), 980–989.

International Finance Corporation. (2000). *Paths out of poverty: The role of private enterprise in developing countries.* Washington, DC: International Finance Corporation.

Kirk, J., & Miller, M. L. (1986). *Reliability and validity in qualitative research* (Vol. 1). Newbury Park: Sage Publications.

Kohli, A. K., & Jaworski, B. J. (1990). Market orientation: The construct, research propositions, and managerial implications. *Journal of Marketing, 54*(2), 1–18.

Kotler, P. (2000). *Marketing management* (the Millenium edition). Upper Saddle River: Prentice Hall.

Kuada, J., & Buatsi, S. N. (2005). Market orientation and management practices in Ghanaian firms: Revisiting the Jaworski and Kohli framework. *Journal of International Marketing, 13*(1), 58–88.

Li, J., & Matlay, H. (2006). Chinese entrepreneurship and small business development: An overview and research agenda. *Journal of Small Business and Enterprise Development, 13*(2), 248–262.

Loecher, U. (2000). Small and medium-sized enterprises: Delimitation and the European definition in the area of industrial business. *European Business Review, 12*(5), 261–264.

Malhotra, N. K. (2004). *Marketing research: An applied orientation.* New York: Pearson.

Mambula, C. (2002). Perceptions of SME growth constraints in Nigeria. *Journal of Small Business Management, 40*(1), 58–65.

Masakure, O., Henson, S., & Cranfield, J. (2009). Performance of microenterprises in Ghana: A resource-based view. *Journal of Small Business and Enterprise Development, 16*(3), 466–484.

Maxwell, J. A. (2013). *Qualitative research design: An interactive approach.* Sage applied social research methods series (3rd ed.). Los Angeles.

McCracken, G. (1998). *The long interview.* A Sage University paper. Qualitative research methods series (Vol. 13). Newbury Park, CA: Sage.

Mensah, J. V., Tribe, M., & Wess, J. (2007). The small-scale manufacturing sector in Ghana: A source of dynamism or of subsistence. *Journal of International Development, 19*(2), 253–273.

Mishler, E. G. (1990). Validation in inquiry-guided research: The role of exemplars in narrative studies. *Harvard Educational Review, 60*(4), 415–442.

Mukhtar, S. M. (1998). Business characteristics of male and female small and medium enterprises in the UK: Implications for gender based entrepreneurialism and business competence development. *British Journal of Management, 9*(1), 41–51.

Narver, J. C., & Slater, S. F. (1990). The effect of a market orientation on business profitability. *Journal of Marketing, 54*(4), 20–35.

Ndemo, B., & Weiss, T. (2017). Making sense of Africa's emerging digital transformation and its many futures. *Africa Journal of Management, 3*(3–4), 328–347.

Ng, I. C. L., & Wakenshaw, S. Y. L. (2017). The internet-of-things: Review and research directions. *International Journal of Research in Marketing, 34*, 3–21.

Nonor, D. (2010, July 28). *Review of Ghana's community-based rural development project.* Unpublished Paper, University of Ghana.

North, D., & Smallbone, D. (1996). Small business development in remote rural areas: The example of mature manufacturing firms in Northern England. *Journal of Rural Studies, 12*(2), 151–167.

Nwankwo, S. (2005). Characterization of Black African entrepreneurship in the UK: A pilot study. *Journal of Small Business and Enterprise Development, 12*(1), 120–136.

Otoo, M., Ibro, G., Fulton, J., & Lowenberg-DeBoer, J. (2012). Micro-entrepreneurship in Niger: Factors affecting the success of women street food vendors. *Journal of African Business, 13*(1), 16–28.

Penaloza, L. (1995). Immigrant consumers: Marketing and public policy considerations in the global economy. *Journal of Public Policy & Marketing, 14*(1), 83–94.

Republic of Ghana. (2005, November). *Growth and poverty reduction strategy (GPRS II) (2006–2009).* National Development Planning Commission.

Robson, P. J. A., Haugh, H. M., & Obeng, B. A. (2009). Entrepreneurship and innovation in Ghana: Enterprising Africa. *Small Business Economics, 32*(3), 331–350.

Sashittal, H. C., & Jassawalla, A. R. (2001). Marketing implementation in smaller organizations: Definitions, framework, and propositional inventory. *Journal of the Academy of Marketing Science, 29*(1), 50–69.

Slater, S. F., & Narver, J. C. (1994). Does competitive environment moderate the market orientation—Performance relationship? *Journal of Marketing, 58*(1), 46–55.

Steer, L., & Taussig, M. (2003, August). *A little engine that could...domestic private companies and Vietnam's pressing need for wage employment* (World Bank policy research working paper 2873). Washington, DC.

Stewart, D. W. (2009). The role of method: Some parting thoughts from a departing editor. *Journal of the Academy of Marketing Science, 37*, 381–383.

Stokes, D. (2002). Entrepreneurial marketing in the public sector: The lessons of head teachers as entrepreneurs. *Journal of Marketing Management, 18*(3–4), 397–414.

Stokes, D., & Blackburn, R. (1999). *Entrepreneurship: Building for the future*. Working Paper Series, Small Business Research Centre, Kingston University, UK.

Tagoe, N., Nyarko, E., & Anuwa-Amarh, E. (2005). Financial challenges facing urban SMEs under financial sector liberalization in Ghana. *Journal of Small Business Management, 43*(3), 331–343.

Urban, B., & Naidoo, R. (2012). Business sustainability: Empirical evidence on operational skills in SMEs in South Africa. *Journal of Small Business and Enterprise Development, 19*(1), 146–163.

White, L. G. (1990). Policy reforms in sub-Saharan Africa: Conditions for establishing a dialogue. *Studies in Comparative International Development, 25*(Summer), 24–42.

Wolcott, H. F. (2001). *Writing up qualitative research* (2nd ed.). Thousand Oaks: Sage Publications.

World Economic Forum. (2009, April). *Educating the next wave of entrepreneurs: Unlocking entrepreneurial capabilities to meet the global challenges of the 21st century* (p. 11). Switzerland: World Economic Forum.

Zachary, G. P. (2001, March 14). Tangled roots: For African-Americans in Ghana, the grass isn't always greener. *Wall Street Journal, CCXXXVII*(51), A1 & A10.

Web-Based Reference

The World Bank. (2020). *Poverty & equity data portal*. Retrieved May 13, 2020, from www.povertydata.worldbank.org/poverty/country/GHA

Attitudes to Globalization in the Public, Private and NGO Sectors

Aminu Mamman, Ken Kamoche, and Christopher J. Rees

1 Introduction

Over recent decades, the world has gone through tremendous economic, political and cultural change. This change is widely referred to as convergence of systems and structures as well as mindsets across societies and is recognized as globalization. Perhaps the most powerful dimension of globalization is the economic dimension, and nothing symbolizes the potency of globalization more than the rapid growth of the digital economy. Yet the digital economy is triggered and driven by digital technology although political decisions also play a significant role (Bukht and Heeks 2017). Therefore, any discussion of globalization or convergence of the world's systems and structures, and related human behaviour, must acknowledge the role of digital technology as an enabler. When it comes to the role of human behaviour, it has been widely reported that global crises occur as a result of human agency. Yet, the subject of how policymakers, business leaders and key actors in the economies of Africa interpret globalization and global economic crises has not attracted the attention it deserves, in spite of the spread of globalization which now involves a significant influx of Chinese investments into Africa (Kamoche and Siebers 2015). While some scholars have considered the impact of globalization (Berman and Machin 2000; Chuang 2000; Pissarides 1997; Scholte 2005; Woods 2000), few have examined how leaders of institutions and organizations in Africa interpret the phenomenon let alone how they react to it in their strategies and practices.

A. Mamman (✉) · C. J. Rees
Global Development Institute, University of Manchester, Manchester, UK
e-mail: aminu.mamman@manchester.ac.uk; chris.rees@manchester.ac.uk

K. Kamoche
Nottingham University Business School, Nottingham University, Nottingham, UK
e-mail: ken.kamoche@nu.ac.uk

Some researchers have investigated social actors' attitudes to wider issues including globalization (Mamman et al. 2006, 2009; Hay and Smith 2010; Smith and Hay 2008; Wated et al. 2008). For example, Hay and Smith (2010: 903) investigated how policymakers in Europe understand globalization and concluded that *'Above all, it suggests that Anglophone globalization discourse in Europe is principally structured in terms of a number of dimensions which relate to the acceptance or rejection of a series of core neoliberal premises'*. Wated et al. (2008: 107) on the other hand showed how attitudes and beliefs among workers and labour union members relate to privatization in Ecuador. The authors concluded that *'results underscored the importance of assessing beliefs associated with privatisation when implementing privatisation programs and highlighted the distinct role played by positive and negative beliefs'*. Thus, given the theoretical link between attitudes and behaviour, as well as research evidence which demonstrates such a link exists, an enhanced understanding of social actors' interpretation of globalization should help inform public policy on globalization as well as managerial strategies in the public, private and NGO sectors.

One discipline suited to investigate organizational-level reactions to globalizations is strategic management, hence the choice of managerial and organizational cognition (MOC) literature to study the subject matter (Hambrick 1982; Hambrick and Mason 1984). MOC literature not only provides insights into what informed managerial decisions but also helps to understand the organizational strategies and practices within the context of globalization. In order to explore these issues, we build on the economic, political and cultural perspectives to develop an instrument to explore attitudes to globalization. We used a sample of managers and professionals in the private, public and non-governmental organization (NGO) sectors in Kenya. Thus, the chapter has two main aims: (1) to explore the proposition that beliefs about and attitudes to globalization can influence attitudes to the role of government in the economy; (2) to draw research and practical implications for multinational corporations' (MNCs) strategies and strategic human resource management.

The chapter is organized as follows: First, we highlight the rationale for the study and discuss the theoretical arguments leading to the research questions. Second, we briefly present the economic, political, and cultural perspectives of globalization as the main constructs to investigate attitudes to globalization. Third, we present the methodology of the study. Finally, the analyses of the data, discussion of the findings and conclusions are presented.

2   Rationale for the Study and Research Questions

Global economic crises demand a greater attention on decision-making of social actors in the globalization era than is currently the case (Hay and Smith 2010). This is because the analyses of the recent economic crisis have been largely attributed to individual decisions in addition to systemic and structural inadequacies of the world's economic regulatory systems (Crotty 2009). Although other disciplines have highlighted a number of issues related to the impact of globalization on trade, poverty, transfer of knowledge, skills and technology (Berman and Machin 2000; Chuang 2000; Scholte 2005; Stiglitz 2006), more research is needed from the managerial cognition perspective to understand what informs social actors' interpretations of globalization and how such interpretations might affect decision-making. The neglect of this line of investigation has left many questions unanswered in the current literature on globalization. For example, there are legitimate questions regarding how social actors interpret and perceive the impact of globalization.

The managerial and organizational cognition literature indicates that organizational practices are influenced by organizational context as well as the orientations and values of organizational actors who decide or implement the practices (Kossek et al. 1994; Mamman 2002). It follows from this argument that the interpretation of the organizational environment provides a means of understanding social actors' dominant logic informing their strategic decisions and actions. Indeed, researchers have found that organizational practices are not wholly pre-determined by environmental forces but shaped by the interaction of institutional forces as well as choices and values of decision-makers (Kochan et al. 1994).

The concepts of managerial individual logic are apt for investigations of individual perspectives on globalizations. According to Prahalad and Bettis (1986), managerial dominant logic is a schema or mindset pertaining to how managers operate in a particular context. This logic is developed based on prior experience in the industry as well as demographic background. Therefore, attitudes to phenomena such as globalization as a dominant logic in the minds of social factors such as managers and professionals would vary according to economic sectors and demographic backgrounds. In fact, previous research on organizations has found that managerial beliefs and values towards organizational practices were related to personal work histories, organizational and environment characteristics (Priem 1994).

Following Wated et al. (2008), this chapter used a multi-factor approach to the study of attitudes to globalization. Rather than assuming that people would have either a positive or negative perspective on globalization, the chapter assumes that social actors' positive and negative perspectives on globalization are relatively independent. In other words, people can have positive views on certain aspects of globalization at the same time abhor certain aspects of its manifestations. This is because the two perspectives are not mutually exclusive. As Wated et al. (2008) pointed out in a study of attitudes to privatization '*the coexistence of pro- and anti-privatisation beliefs as relatively independent phenomena seems plausible because the fear of socially negative, short term effects and the desire for long-term economic prosperity are not mutually exclusive*'. Thus, like privatization, globalization is a two-pronged process and phenomenon that has negative consequences or impacts as well as positive impacts on individuals, specific groups and the society, if viewed from economic, political and cultural dimensions. The aim of this chapter is to explore this dichotomy. Hence the following question:

Question 1: In what ways might the meanings of globalization be categorized? And what might those categories look like?

Having demonstrated in the foregoing that mental models can influence social actors' behaviour, the theory of reasoned action provides explanations of the mechanism through which the relationship between mental models and behaviour is established. Reason action theorists argue that people's attitudes are shaped by their beliefs about an objective (Ajzen and Fishbein 1980). While belief is viewed as the representation of the consequences people associated with attitudinal object, attitude is viewed as people's evaluation about performing the behaviour (Wated et al. 2008; Cam 1999).

For example, the belief that globalization (meaning of globalization mental model) reduces the influences of nation states to control their destiny links the attitudinal object '*globalization*' to the consequence *reduces the influence of nation states*. Therefore, the first step to assess a person's attitude towards an object is to identify the sets of both positive and negative consequences thought to be related to the object (Wated et al. 2008: 109). Thus, our *attitudinal measure* of globalization is the perceived negative and positive impact of globalization while the *belief* is what globalization means to social actors. The equation can be completed by measuring the behaviour in terms of what social actors proceed to do as a result of beliefs and attitudes towards globalization. However, this is beyond the scope of this investigation. Instead we investigated what they would do by asking them to indicate what they would like government to do. Based on these theoretical analyses, we explore the following questions.

Question 2: Is there a significant relationship between the meaning of globalization (belief) and perceived impact of globalization (attitude)? For example, do negative beliefs relate to negative attitudes while positive beliefs relate to positive attitudes?

Question 3: Is there a significant relationship between attitude to globalization and preferences for government policies? For example, do social actors (e.g. managers) who view globalization from a negative perspective prefer government to enact policies to restrict the influence of market forces?

Studies on attitudes and beliefs suggest that demographic, personal experience and circumstances influence people's attitudes and beliefs about a particular phenomenon or issue. For example, Debardeleben (1999) reported a significant relationship between age, standard of living and expected future standard of living with support for privatization in Russia. Similarly, Wated et al. (2008) reported a strong relationship between attitude to privatization and gender, age, numbers of dependents and sector. In fact, given the uniqueness of the public sector organizations, researchers have found that employees in the public sector tend to have unique attitudes towards issues affecting them and the wider society. For example, Wheeler and Brady (1998) reported variation in ethical dispositions between public and private sector employees. Therefore, we explore the following question pertaining to the relationship between social actors' backgrounds and their general attitudes to globalization:

Question 4: Do attitudes to globalization vary with the backgrounds of the managers and professionals? For example, do NGO and public sector respondents see globalization from a negative point of view as opposed to respondents from the private sector?

3 Globalization

The economic dimension of globalization is by far the most dominant perspective in the globalization discourse. The economic perspective is represented by the liberalization of the national economies through privatization and deregulation, leading to economic and political integration and interdependence (Contractor 1990; Hirst and Thompson 1999). This is specifically evidenced by, *'widespread reduction or even abolition of regulatory trade barriers, foreign-exchange restrictions, capital controls, and visas'* (Scholte 2005: 16). For example, McGrew and Lewis (1992: 23) define globalization as, *'the multiplicity of linkages and interconnections between the states and societies which make up the present world system. It describes the process by which events, decisions, and activities in one part of the world come to have significant consequences for individuals and communities in quite distant parts of the globe.'*

Other commentators such as George Soros (2004: 1) view globalization as, *'the development of global financial markets, the growth of transnational corporations, and their increasing domination over national economies'*. In the same vein, the IMF (1997) refers to globalization as *'the growing interdependencies of countries worldwide through the increasing volume and variety of cross-border transactions in goods and services, and of international capital flows and also through the rapid and widespread diffusion of all kinds of technology'*. Woods (2000), on the other hand, views globalization as the transformation of global economic activity leading to market expansion. Those who view globalization as a philosophy argue that it has a hegemonic role in organizing and decoding the meaning of the world (Mattelart 2000). Indeed, Bello (2002: 1) views the role of global institutions such as the IMF, World Bank and WTO as the 'maintenance of the hegemony of the system of global capitalism and promotion of the primacy of the states and economic interests that mainly benefit from it'.

Those who take the political dimension of globalization see it as a representation of the dwindling role and power of governments as we know it (Fukuyama 1992; Ohmae 2000). For example, some describe globalization as a world without political boundaries where nation states are governed by global political order and in which political boundaries are dissolving (McGrew and Lewis 1992). In the new political world order, they argue, political power and political activity extend across traditional boundaries (Woods 2000). Hence, globalization is viewed as a representation of the growing convergence of political systems under the philosophy of political democracy (Scholte 2005). In essence, the political dimension of globalization involves the proliferation of international or governing regulatory organizations and international regimes to ensure maintenance of coherence across global political system (Randall and Theobald 1998: 239–240).

The culture perspective on globalization criticizes the growing erosion of traditional values aided by rapid development of information technology and transnational corporations (Arnett 2002). At its extreme, proponents of this school seem to suggest that globalization is another form of cultural imperialism. In Mattelart's (2000) view, the current globalization is similar to the imperialistic activities of the dominant political powers of the late nineteenth century. Mattelart referred to the imposition of standardization of Greenwich Time and the dividing up of the world into spheres of influence as examples of imperialistic activities of the past which are not dissimilar to what is happening now. If cultures are converging, what form or shape are they taking? Critics of the growing dominance of transnational companies and global institutions point to the concept of *McDonaldisation*, *Westernization* or *Americanization* of cultural artefacts and values (Drane 2000; Ritzer and Malone 2000; Ritzer and Stillman 2003). All the three concepts relate to the notion of cultural domination by the West. However, sometimes, globalization is viewed as the neutral transfer of organizational and processual systems of production and consumption from the West to other parts of the world (Ritzer and Stillman 2003). Ritzer and Stillman (2003: 50) contend that there is a *'connection between a global-modern institutional/technological context of increasing connectivity and emergent cultural styles, imaginations, sensibilities, practices and values'*. Chan and Scarritt (2002: 3) also point out: *'as inhabitants of this global village we increasingly share the same thoughts, values, and habits—a cultural convergence, if you will'*. This is why some proponents of the culture perspective view the phenomenon as leading to the decline of cultural identity (Arnett 2002; McBride and Wiseman 2000). While most scholars in the cultural perspective view globalization as convergence of values or leading to it (see Albrow 1990), others in the same school argue that globalization is the increasing polarization of cultures brought about by desire to reconnect to traditional values and beliefs due to the growing threat of globalization (Arnett 2002).

It can be argued that globalization cannot be neatly defined in terms of economic or socio-political perspectives. This is because the process and its impact are multi-dimensional and complex. Hence, it is perhaps easier to explain its ramifications than to define it. Indeed, Beeson (2000) pointed out that economic integration impacts both culture and political autonomy. The drivers of globalization are varied and interrelated and include technology, multinational companies and intergovernmental organizations (for example, IMF, UN, World Bank).

In addition to the debate on the meaning of globalization, there is also a debate on whether globalization has a positive impact, especially for developing countries. For example, some argue that globalization is impoverishing weaker nations (Buckman 2004), others point to the erosion of the influence of nation states (Fukuyama 1992; McBride and Wiseman 2000; Ohmae 2000; Soros 2004). Buckman (2004) points out that: *'in 1820 the difference between the per capita incomes of the world's richest and poorest countries was 3:1, by 1913 they estimate it had grown to 11:1, by 1950 35:1, by 1973 44:1 and by 1992 they say it had blown out to a horrendous 72:1'* (Buckman 2004: 69). Similarly, Stiglitz (2006: 20) argues that governments find it very difficult to control the activities of individuals and companies because of international agreements. As he puts it: *'a government that wants to ensure that banks lend a certain fraction of their portfolio to underserved areas or to ensure that accounting frameworks accurately reflect a company's true status, may find it unable to pass the appropriate laws, signing on to international trade agreement can prevent government from regulating the influx and outflow of hot, speculative money, even though capital market liberalization can lead to economic crises'.*

It is worth noting that others point to the real and potential economic benefits of globalization in terms of FDI and international trade (Hirst and Thompson 1999; Jesudason 1997; Stiglitz 2006). Other positive impacts of globalization include the diffusion of good business practices aided by multinational companies (Berman and Machin 2000; Chuang 2000) as well as better methods of communication and transportation (Edward and Rees 2006; Scholte 2005). Even at the domestic level, some businesses have experienced the benefits of globalization. For example, in the mid and late 1990s, globalization was the main driver for the Malaysian government to enact business-friendly policies for small- and medium-sized enterprises (Mamman 2004). As Jesudason (1997: 135) pointed out: *'The pressure of international competition had led to new initiatives in promoting domestic investment... The small and medium-sized enterprises (SME) sector, which is dominated by Chinese businesses, has been given more backing by the government since it recognized the importance of the sector as a source of inputs for large enterprises'.*

4 Methodology

Based on our literature review, we have identified possible components of the dominant logic of globalization that can be subjected to empirical investigation. These components can be expressed in terms of economic, political and cultural dimensions (see Albrow 1990; Beeson 2000; Bello 2002; Drane 2000; Fukuyama 1992; Hirst and Thompson 1999; Mattelart 2000; Ohmae 2000; Ritzer and Stillman 2003; Stiglitz 2006). Therefore, the chapter investigates the extent to which such a dominant logic exists in the minds of social actors (that is, managers, civil society actors and professionals) in the globalization space. Based on the literature review, we explored the respondents' perspectives on globalization (i.e. in terms of beliefs/ meaning and attitudes/perceived impact).

The data from which this study is based were generated from a sample of managers and professionals from the public, state-owned enterprises (SOEs), private and NGO sectors. In contexts in which there are inadequate records to allow systematic random sampling, researchers argue for the use of snow-balling and convenient sampling techniques (Saunders et al. 2012). We heeded this advice. Hence, several government departments, NGOs, SOEs and private organizations were initially targeted for survey. This generated a snow-balling effect for the data collection; 500

questionnaires were distributed, and 301 usable ones were returned. This produced a response rate of 60.2%. The majority (42.5%) are middle managers. The rest are professionals (40.2%), senior managers (11.0%), CEOs (3.7%) and business owners (2.7%). Most of the samples are derived from the private sector (44.2%). The rest are from government SOEs (24.6%) public service (20.6%) and NGO (10.6%) sectors. A significant number (41.9%) indicated that they have the opportunity to influence government policy either through policy formulation or implementation (e.g. through membership of pressure groups, lobby groups, business and trade associations, policymaking body and professional associations).

5   Analysis and Findings

Question 1   To explore the question as to whether the meaning and perception of the impact of globalization can be categorized, we carried out factor analysis. Factor analysis is an inductive approach which does not assume the existence of factor (s) in a set of responses. Specifically, principal component technique was chosen to discern the patterns in the beliefs and attitudes to globalization. This technique allowed us to determine the categories of responses to the large sets of questions in a simplified fashion. Thus, to determine the number of categories (factors) in the meaning of globalization and perception of the impact of globalization, a two-step process was used (Hay and Smith 2010). The analyses in Table 1 produced four factors which are subject to interpretation as would any factor generated through factor analysis (Pallant 2005).

As can be seen in Table 1, all the 13 items were loaded on the final categories produced by the principal component technique. Factor 1 accounted for 14.9% of the total variance; we interpreted this factor as *neutral meaning* of globalization. In other words, their responses are structured in terms of phenomenon that is inevitable. The factor can also be interpreted as perceiving globalization as an event beyond the influence of any people, state or institution. Factor 2 which accounts for 14.1% of the total variance is structured in terms of *convergence of systems and practices*. For example the spread of liberal values and democratic systems as well as the dwindling role of the state in the economy are clustered in this category. This finding mirrors Hay and Smith (2010) who found European policymakers view globalization as convergence of policies especially in the areas of taxation, monetary and educational policies.

Factor 3 accounted for 14% of the variance. The responses are structured in terms of *international trade*. Here, movements of financial capital, labour and goods are clustered in the same category. Thus, those who view globalization as a means of exporting goods also view it as a means of investing abroad and also as a means of finding job opportunities in Europe and America. This category is in line with the economic interpretation of globalization where economic liberalization is viewed as the key feature (Hirst and Thompson 1999; Scholte 2005; Woods 2000).

Table 1 Internal structure of the meaning of globalization

Factors	Component extracted			
	1	2	3	4
Neutral meaning				
Globalization means that the world is shrinking in time and space	0.747			
The growing influence of technology in our lives	0.698			
The Kenyan economy is part of the world economy	0.648			
Doing business is becoming more and more similar.	0.629			
Convergence of systems and practices				
The spread of western democratic system of governance		0.811		
The government is playing less and less role in the economy		0.759		
The whole world is adopting western liberal values and behaviour		0.674		
International trade				
Kenyans will find it easier to invest their money in Europe and America			0.777	
Kenyan workers will find it easier to find jobs in Europe and America			0.776	
Fair and equitable trade among countries			0.650	
Negative beliefs				
Everyone for himself in a free market globally				0.777
MNCs and global companies have more freedom to operate				0.709
Capitalism is the only economic system in the world				0.691
Eigenvalue	**2.675**	**2.338**	**1.238**	**1.123**
% of variance explained	**14.94**	**14.10**	**14.08**	**13.59**
Total variance explained	**56.72%**			

Finally, Factor 4 is structured in terms of *negative beliefs* about globalization. This factor accounts for 13.6% of the total variance. Here, items such as globalization means *everyone for himself*, hegemony of capitalism and freedom of MNCs to behave the way they like are clustered in the same category. This perspective reflects the political and cultural interpretation of globalization (Fukuyama 1992; Ohmae 2000; McGrew and Lewis 1992). Factor analysis thus confirmed the utility of the argument that beliefs about globalization, though not mutually exclusive, can be categorized into a set of meaningful factors that provide a way of understanding social actors' general attitudes towards the phenomenon.

Perceived Impact of Globalization As a further exploration of the mutual exclusivity of attitudes to globalization, we carried out factor analysis using *principal component analysis* technique (see Table 2).

The analysis produced four factors. In Factor 1, eight items were initially extracted. However, one item had low loading of 0.337 and was therefore dropped. The seven remaining items accounted for 14.60% of the total variance. Given that the seven items were structured along the lines of positive impact of globalization (e.g. boosting the economy through FDI; helping business practices), we interpreted the first factor as *positive impact of globalization*. The second factor was structured

Table 2 Internal structure of perceived impact of globalization

	Component			
	1	2	3	4
Positive impact				
Boost the economy of Kenya	0.750			
Improve the management and business practices	0.739			
IMF and World Bank are playing a positive role	0.616			
The benefits of globalization far outweigh its disadvantages	0.589			
Companies to have easy access to world markets	0.585			
Companies export to European and American markets	0.566			
Incentives for government to pursue beneficial economic policies	0.562			
Negative impact				
Does not allow Kenya to introduce its brand of economic system		0.762		
Does not allow Kenya to introduce its brand of political system		0.725		
Has weakened the government's ability to control its economy		0.622		
Has weakened government's ability to control its political boundaries		0.582		
Hinders government from formulating favourable economic policies		0.422		
Fairness of globalization				
World will be a fairer place if all countries share western values and beliefs			0.780	
World will be a fairer place if all countries embrace a western democratic political system			0.706	
World will be a fairer place if all countries embrace free market economy			0.686	
Benefits of globalization are shared evenly across the world			0.538	
Threat of globalization				
Privatization is beneficial to the organizations and the economy				
Has weakened government's ability to control its political boundaries				0.654
Globalization has made the Kenyan economy more vulnerable				0.559
Globalization is threatening the identity of Kenyans				0.506
Rich countries benefit more from globalization than poor countries				0.479
Eigenvalue	**3.767**	**3.182**	**1.984**	**1.265**
% of variance explained	**14.60**	**12.30**	**10.25**	**9.20**
Total variance explained	**46.56%**			

in terms of perceived *negative impact of globalization*. In this factor, six items were initially extracted, but only five met our cut-off point of the required loading of 0.40 or above. This factor accounted for 12.30% of the total variance. In the third factor, five items were extracted. However, one item had a loading of 0.366 and was therefore dropped. This accounted for 10.20% of the total variance. It was structured in terms of perceived *fairness of globalization*. Respondents who view the impact of globalization as the adoption of western political systems that would make the world a fairer place also view the adoption of the capitalist economic system as one that would make the world a fairer place. The fourth factor accounted for 9.20% of the total variance. This factor was structured in terms of perceived *threat of globalization*. In this factor, items such as 'threat to cultural values', 'vulnerability of the economy' and 'threat to identity' were clustered together.

In a nutshell, our analyses have confirmed the existence of categories of the meaning of globalization as well as its perceived impact. The analyses suggest that social actors' understanding of globalization in Kenya is structured coherently and consistently. However, as will be demonstrated later, there are slight differences across the sample regarding attitudes to globalization. Nevertheless, the analysis generates interesting insights into the extent that it appears to replicate studies in Europe which used public servants and politicians (Hay and Smith 2010) while our sample was made up of managers and professionals from the public, private and NGO sectors. This seems to suggest that the globalization discourse is 'globalized'. Similarly, its meanings and manifestations are shared more widely than perhaps experts and commentators might acknowledge or even realize.

Question 2 In this question, we explored the relationship between the meaning of globalization and its perceived impact. Our analyses have demonstrated that respondents who hold negative *meaning(belief)* of globalization are more likely to view globalization as having a negative impact ($r = 0.301$, $n = 302$, $p < 0.000$). Similarly, we found a significant relationship between *negative meaning(belief)* of globalization and perceived unfairness of globalization ($r = 0.129$, $n = 301$, $p < 0.025$). To confirm this result, we also found significant negative relationship between perceived negative impact of globalization and perceived positive impact of globalization ($r = -0.153$, $n = 301$, $p < 0.008$). Hence, those who see globalization as having negative impact are less likely to see its positive side in spite of the mutual exclusivity of the two constructs. The analyses also revealed a significant relationship between the perception of the impact of globalization as a *threat* and the *meaning(belief)* of globalization as *convergence* ($r = 0.273$, $n = 301$; $p < 0.000$). Similarly, there is a significant relationship between perception of the impact of globalization as a *threat* and the *meaning(belief)* of globalization as *negative* ($r = 0.214$, $n = 301$; $p < 0.000$). An interesting feature of our finding is that *convergence* appears to be viewed from a negative perspective by our respondents. This is not unexpected because previous studies of policymakers and politicians also suggest that convergence of economic policy is not viewed favourably by some people (Hay and Smith 2010). The analyses further revealed a significant relationship between the *meaning(belief)* of globalization as *convergence* and its perceived *negative impact* ($r = 0.339$, $n = 302$, $p < 0.000$). Based on the partial correlation analyses, our expectation is confirmed. It further supports the thesis that belief (represented by meaning) influences attitude (represented by perception of impact) (Wated et al. 2008). The results replicate Hay and Smith's (2010: 921) study which found that 'those who view the benefits of globalization in economic neo-liberal terms are less likely than their peers to see globalization as any kind of threat to political autonomy and national governance'.

Question 3 In this question, we explored the relationship between attitudes to globalization and the role of government in the economy. Partial correlation analysis revealed a significant relationship between perception of the impact of globalization and our respondents' views pertaining to the role of government in the economy and the wider society. For example, there is a significant relationship between the perceived negative impact of globalization and 'external' and 'internal' roles of government ($r = 0.274$, $n = 301$, $p < 0.000$; $r = 0.167$, $n = 301$, $p < 0.004$, respectively). Similarly, those who perceive globalization as a *threat* are more likely to see the need for government to regulate the economy ($r = 0.293$, $n = 301$, $p < 0.000$, $r = 0.277$, $n = 301$, $p < 0.000$).

Question 4 To explore variation in beliefs and attitudes regarding globalization, we carried out analysis of variance (ANOVA). This was aimed at determining whether respondents from government, state-owned enterprises (SOEs), NGOs and private sectors share a similar or different attitudes and beliefs about globalization. In general, the respondents shared a similar outlook except in three areas (globalization as *convergence;* perceived *threat* of globalization; *fairness* of globalization). Specifically, we found that NGO respondents were more likely to believe that globalization is the *convergence* of economic, political and cultural systems ($F = 4.018$; $p < 0.008$). Respondents from SOEs were more likely to view the impact of globalization from *fairness* ($F = 3.150$, $p < 0.025$) and *threat* ($F = 2.755$, $p < 0.043$) perspectives. This finding suggests that belief and attitudes to globalization can be influenced by social actors' contact with global forces. For example, NGOs are at the forefront of the fight against global forces, which entails seeking to limit the influence of MNCs and inter-government organizations such as the IMF. Also, state-owned enterprises that have been sheltered from competition by government policies have now been forced to compete in an open market due to liberalization of the local economies. Therefore, it is not counter-intuitive to see that respondents from these sectors differ from their counterparts in the public and private sectors. The similarities across the groups regarding attitudes to global phenomenon suggest that, regardless of the sector in which social actors operate, they are likely to share similar hopes and fears regarding globalization.

6   Conclusion and Discussion

The main goal of this study was to examine beliefs and attitudes pertaining to globalization and to draw implications in terms of research and practice. The result of this study provides interesting insights into the relationship between beliefs, attitudes and the potential behaviour of social actors within the context of globalization. Consistent with previous studies and theories, it seems plausible to explain and perhaps predict what social actors might do if they had the opportunity to influence organizational and government policy. This is because we found strong relationships between specific attitudes to globalization and preferences for particular roles of government in the economy. For example, we found that negative beliefs and attitudes are related to a preference for direct control of activities of multinational companies and domestic economic policies. To the extent that beliefs and attitudes influence behaviour, these findings have opened up potential avenues for explaining strategic behaviour and intent of decision-makers within organizations and within state policy-making structures.

These results have implications for MNEs operating in an environment where the local actors hold negative views of the key tenets of globalization. Therefore, from the point of view of firms' political strategy, MNEs might not only have to focus on influencing government policy, but also have to work hard to convince local actors, including pressure groups such as NGOs, of the merits of their contribution to the locality. In the past, MNEs' efforts were focused largely on policymakers in Africa. The recent democratic developments in many African countries have ensured the proliferation of NGOs that challenge the orthodoxy of the past where political office-holders can guarantee smooth-sailing for MNEs under the guise of economic development. Our findings are a call for MNEs to engage with these NGOs as well.

This study partially supports the argument that there are practical and theoretical rationales for the study of attitudes and meaning of globalization. Although our approach to the study of globalization might appear novel, we are following the footsteps of several researchers who adopt attitudinal approach to the study of organizational and macro-policy issues such as globalization, privatization, liberalization, economic ideology and preferences for globalization strategies (see Debardeleben 1999; Mamman et al. 2009; Smith and Hay 2008; Wated et al. 2008). From the theoretical point of view, we see our work as building on the studies and theorization about how beliefs (that is, *meaning*) influence attitudes (see Ajzen and Fishbein 1980; Wated et al. 2008). For example, beliefs about what globalization means can influence stakeholders' attitude (that is, *perception of impact*) to globalization. This finding is also supported by prior research which reported the relationship between belief, attitudes and subsequent behaviour (Bell et al. 2000; Cam 1999; Debardeleben 1999; Durant and Ledge 2001; Kravitz and Platania 1993; Wated et al. 2008). One important dimension of belief is the causal logic or causal reasoning which refers to the beliefs by social actors such as managers regarding whether and how environmental variables impact on strategy. Researchers argue that '*These cause-effect beliefs about the environment- strategy relationship frame specific strategic issues and affect how they are interpreted and what strategic actions are initiated*' (Nadkarni and Barr 2008: 1398).

Therefore, signals from the environment are not acted upon until decision-makers interpret the casual relationships with the organization (Huff 1990). Hence, as a way of understanding why or how decision makers and social actors react to global phenomenon, it would be helpful to first understand their interpretation of causal relationships between global phenomena and organizational strategy or national policy. Hence, understanding decision-makers' or social actors' beliefs about causal logic pertaining to globalization can shed light on their current or future decisions regarding the phenomenon. Also managerial cognition research indicates that managerial decision making is influenced by prior interpretation of the environment or phenomenon which leads to specific decisions or action (Reger and Palmer 1996). This result should help to discern how globalization is interpreted and shed light on the complexities associated with various literatures on globalization. In particular, the discourse on globalization appears to be compartmentalized along social science disciplines (for example, economics, politics, sociology and management). Such compartmentalization does not do justice to the phenomenon given that social actors' interpretation is given limited attention.

6.1   Theoretical Implications

The literature on information processing modes has implications for the investigation of decision makers' interpretations of globalization. For example, the automatic and controlled processing modes suggest that managers either make decisions about the environment in an unintentional, involuntary and effortless fashion (Johnson and Hasher 1987), or in a flexible, intentional, effortful and active way but are constrained by temporal, resource and motivational factors (Uleman 1989). The former fits the argument that policymakers and managers in developing countries do not have many options when dealing with global phenomena such as liberalization, democratization and international treaties (McBride and Wiseman 2000). Hirst and Thompson (1999: 263) point out that as a result of globalization *'there are certain areas in which the role of the State has changed radically and its capacities to control its people and domestic social processes have declined as a consequence'*. The latter argument (controlled processing mode) seems to suggest that there is room for decision-makers (for example, policymakers and managers) to analyse the global environment and react 'rationally' within certain constraints (for example, relative economic and political power and influence). However, further research and theorization indicate that controlled and automatic information processing modes are not mutually exclusive but rather can be put on a continuum (Reger and Palmer 1996). This suggests that decision-makers are pragmatic when faced with complex external environments.

However, other researchers argue that decision-makers possess either controlled or automatic information processing schema derived from learned experience which are stable until a radical and sudden change in the environment arises (Barr et al. 1992; Reger and Palmer 1996). Nonetheless, it was found that even under such radical change in the environment, most managers do not change their cognitive schemas when the need for such changes arises (Uleman 1989). This prompted Reger and Palmer (1996: 35) to argue that because cognitive schemas do not change immediately as the environment changes, 'rather than expecting present managers to learn mental models, firms can recruit new executives with schemas that are appropriate for the changed environment'. This view has been advocated by other researchers (Barr et al. 1992). Hence, it can be argued that decision-makers' interpretation of globalization is a representation of their cognitive schema of globalization (i.e. their global Orientation or mindset) which is likely to be stable over a period of time. This would be acquired through experience with global economic, political and socio-cultural issues in their daily decision-making and observation. Therefore, although some who view globalization from a positive or neutral point of view might change their schema and potential decisions, such changes would be constrained by the relative power and influence of the decision-makers as well as the stability of their global orientation. To the extent that they have power and influence to do so, those who have a favourable view of MNEs and global institutions such as the World Bank, IMF and WTO might change their views and enact policies contrary to the views they held.

Further Research In spite of the contribution of this chapter, further research is needed to determine how specific social actors such as policymakers and senior executives in domestic and international firms interpret and react to globalization strategically and operationally. Similarly, there is a need to understand how decision-makers in NGOs interpret and react to globalization. In particular, given that NGOs vary in terms of their mission, strategies and practices, it will be of academic and practical value to discern if intrinsic differences among NGOs lead to a particular behaviour in their civil society role.

Another useful line of enquiry to pursue is the investigation of cross industry and cross-national differences and similarities in the interpretation of globalization. This should help to unearth cultural, ideological and economic factors that might impact on such interpretations. This might also help to explain variations in national and organizational globalization strategies across nations and industries. Similarly, it is not beyond the realm of possibility that revelations from such investigations across employees can help to explain any variation in their motivations given that employees' level of motivation would relate to their commitment to organizational strategy, policies and practices. Also, although a number of researchers have written about trade union reaction to privatization and liberalization, we do not have an adequate theoretical framework that explains trade union reaction to the manifestations of globalization demonstrated through states' public policies such as privatization. We believe the managerial cognition literature adopted in this chapter provides potential framework for building 'collectivist level' theory that can enable the understanding of union reactions.

Finally, given that mental models are acquired through learned experiences, changes in leadership from 'old guard' to new generations at the national and organizational levels should usher in new policies and decisions. As far as the study of globalization is concerned, there has been no systematic empirical study to confirm or to refute this argument. This opens up another avenue for research on this topic.

Acknowledgement The authors are grateful to the British Academy for funding this project.

References

Ajzen, I., & Fishbein, M. (1980). *Understanding attitudes and predicting social behavior*. Englewood Cliffs, NJ: Prentice Hall.

Albrow, M. (1990). Introduction. In M. Albrow & E. King (Eds.), *Globalization, knowledge and society*. London: Sage.

Arnett, J. (2002). The psychology of globalization. *American Psychologist, 57*(10), 774–783.

Barr, P. S., Stimpert, J. L., & Huff, A. S. (1992). Cognitive change, strategic action and organizational renewal. *Strategic Management Journal, Summer Special Issue, 13*, 15–36.

Beeson, M. (2000). Mahathir and the markets: Globalization and the pursuit of economic autonomy. *Pacific Affairs, 73*(3), 335–351.

Bell, M. P., Harrison, D. A., & McLaughlin, M. E. (2000). Forming, changing, and acting on attitude toward affirmative action programs in employment: A theory-driven approach. *Journal of Applied Psychology, 85*, 784–798.

Bello, W. (2002). *Deglobalization: Ideas for a new world economy*. London: Zed Books.

Berman, E., & Machin, S. (2000). *Skilled-biased technology transfer: Evidence of factor-biased technological change in develop countries*. Boston University, Department of Economics.

Buckman, G. (2004). *Globalization: Tame it or scrap it?* London: Zed Books.

Bukht, R., & Heeks, R. (2017). *Defining, conceptualising and measuring the digital economy* (Development Informatics working paper, 68). University of Manchester.

Cam, S. (1999). Job security, unionization, wages and privatization: A case studying the Turkish cement industry. *The Sociological Review, 47*, 695–715.

Chan, S., & Scarritt, J. A. (2002). *Coping with globalization: Cross-national patterns in domestic governance and policy performance*. London: Frank Cass.

Chuang, Y. C. (2000). Human capital, exports, and economic growth: A causality analysis for Taiwan, 1952-1995. *Review of International Economics, 8*, 712–720.

Contractor, F. J. (1990). Ownership patterns of U.S. joint ventures abroad and the liberalization of foreign government regulations in the 1980s: Evidence from the benchmark surveys. *Journal of International Business Studies, 21*(1), 55–73.

Crotty, J. (2009). Structural causes of the global financial crisis: A critical assessment of the 'new financial architecture'. *Cambridge Journal of Economics, 33*(4), 563–580.

Debardeleben, J. (1999). Attitudes towards privatisation in Russia. *Europe-Asia Studies, 51*(3), 447–465.

Drane, J. (2000). *The McDonaldization of the church*. London: Darton, Longman and Todd.

Durant, R. F., & Legge, J. S. (2001). Politics, public opinion, and privatization: A test of competing theories in Great Britain. Public Organization Review, *1*(1), 75–95.

Edwards, T., & Rees, C. (2006). International HRM: Globalization, national Systems and Multinational Companies. London: Prentice Hall.

Fukuyama, F. (1992). *The end of history and the last man*. London: Hamish Hamilton.

Hay, C., & Smith, N. J. (2010). How policy makers (really) understand globalization: The internal architecture of Anglophone globalization discourse in Europe. *Public Administration, 88*(4), 903–927.

Hambrick, D. C. (1982). Environmental scanning and organizational strategy. Strategic management journal, *3*(2), 159–174.

Hambrick, D. C., & Mason, P. A. (1984). Upper echelons: The organization as a reflection of its top managers. Academy of management review, *9*(2), 193–206.

Hirst, P., & Thompson, P. (1999). *Globalization in question: The international economy and the possibility of governance*. Cambridge: Polity Press.

Huff, A. S. (1990). *Mapping strategic thought*. Chichester: Wiley.

IMF (1997, May). *World economic outlook: Globalization, opportunities and challenges*. Washington, DC.

Jesudason, J. V. (1997). Chinese business and ethnic equilibrium in Malaysia. *Development and Change, 28*, 119–141.

Johnson, M. K., & Hasher, L. (1987). Human learning and memory. *Annual Review of Psychology, 38*, 631–668.

Kamoche, K., & Siebers, Q. (2015). Chinese investments in Kenya: Toward a post-colonial critique. *International Journal of Human Resource Management, 26*(21), 2718–2743.

Kochan, T. A., Katz, H. C., & McKersie, R. B. (1994). *The transformation of American industrial relations*. Boston: Cornell University Press.

Kossek, E. E., Dass, P., & DeMarr, B. (1994). The dominant logic of employer-sponsored work and family initiatives: Human resource managers' institutional role. *Human Relations, 47*(9), 1121–1149.

Kravitz, D. A., & Platania, J. (1993). Attitudes and beliefs about affirmative action: Effects of target and of respondent sex and ethnicity. *Journal of applied psychology, 78*(6), 928.

Mamman, A. (2002). Managerial attitudes to what government should do and should not do: Evidence from Australia. *International Journal of Management, 19*(4), 551–560.

Mamman, A. (2004). Managerial views on government intervention in Malaysia: Implications for international business. *Competition and Change, 8*(2), 137–152.

Mamman, A., Akuratiyagamage, V., & Rees, C. (2006). Managerial perceptions of the role of human resource function in Sri-Lanka: A comparative study of local, foreign-owned and joint-venture companies. *International Journal of Human Resource Management, 17*(10), 1–12.

Mamman, A., Baydoun, N., & Asumah, B. (2009). Transferability of management innovation to Africa: A study of two multinational companies' performance management system in Nigeria. *Global Business Review, 10*(1), 1–31.

Mattelart, A. (2000). Networking the world, 1794–2000. U of Minnesota Press.

McBride, S., & Wiseman, J. (2000). *Globalization and its discontents*. London: Macmillan.

McGrew, A., & Lewis, P. G. (1992). *Global politics*. Cambridge: Polity Press.

Nadkarni, S., & Barr, P. S. (2008). Environmental context, managerial cognition, and strategic action: An integrated view. *Strategy Management Journal, 29*, 1395–1427.

Ohmae, K. (2000). The end of the nation state. In J. Beynon & D. Dunkerley (Eds.), *Globalization: The reader* (pp. 238–241). London: Athlone Press.

Pallant, J. (2005). *SPSS survival manual*. Maidenhead: Open University Press.

Prahalad, C. K., & Bettis, R. A. (1986). The dominant logic: A new linkage between diversity and performance. *Strategic Management Journal, 7*(6), 485–501.

Pissarides, C. A. (1997). Learning by trading and the returns to human capital in developing countries. The World Bank Economic Review, *11*(1), 17–32.

Priem, R. L. (1994). Executive judgment, organizational congruence, and firm performance. *Organization Science, 5*(3), 421–437.

Randall, V., & Theobald, R. (1998). *Political change and underdevelopment: A critical introduction to third world politics*. Durham: London University Press.

Reger, R. K., & Palmer, T. B. (1996). Managerial categorization of competitors: Using old maps to navigate new environments. *Organization Science, 7*, 22–39.

Ritzer, G., & Malone, E. (2000). Globalization theory: Lessons from the exportation of McDonaldization and the new means of consumption. *American Studies, 41*(2), 97–109.

Ritzer, G., & Stillman, T. (2003). Assessing McDonaldization, Americanization and globalization. In U. Beck, N. Sznaider, & R. Winter (Eds.), *Global America? The cultural consequences of globalization* (pp. 30–48). London: Blackwell.

Saunders, M. N. K., Lewis, P., & Thornhill, A. (2012). *Research methods for business students* (6th ed.). Harlow, England: Pearson Education.

Scholte, J. A. (2005). *Globalization: A critical introduction*. London: Macmillan.

Smith, N. J. A., & Hay, C. (2008). Mapping the political discourse of globalization and European integration in the U.K and Ireland empirically. *European Journal of Political Research, 47*(3), 359–384.

Soros, G. (2004). *George Soros on globalization*. New Delhi: Viva Books.

Stiglitz, J. E. (2006). *Making globalization work*. New York: Norton.

Uleman, J. S. (1989). A framework for thinking intentionally about unintended thoughts. In J. S. Uleman & J. A. Bargh (Eds.), *Unintended thought* (pp. 425–449). New York: Guilford.

Wated, G, Sanchez, J & Gómez, C (2008). A Two-Factor Assessment of the Beliefs That Influence Attitudes towards privatisation. Group and Organization Management, *33*(1), 107–136.

Wheeler, G. F., & Brady, F. N. (1998). Do public-sector and private-sector personnel have different ethical dispositions? A study of two sites. *Journal of Public Administration Research and Theory, 8*(1), 93–115.

Woods, N. (2000). *The political economy of globalization.* New York: St Martins Press.

Lightning Source UK Ltd.
Milton Keynes UK
UKHW052015010722
405275UK00004B/12

9 783030 705404